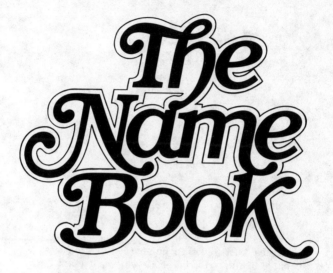

The Name Book

Dorothea Austin

BETHANY HOUSE PUBLISHERS
MINNEAPOLIS, MINNESOTA 55438
A Division of Bethany Fellowship, Inc.

Dorothea Austin worked under the direction of a
capable Minneapolis-based development team in
collecting and preparing the material found in
this book.

The Name Book
Dorothea Austin

Library of Congress Catalog Card Number 81-71282

ISBN 0-87123-412-2

Published by Bethany House Publishers
6820 Auto Club Road, Minneapolis, Minnesota 55438

Printed in the United States of America

Preface

Your name is a very important aspect of your personality, and this book has been compiled so that you may recognize the character-building value in understanding its meaning.

The Scriptures tell us that "a good name is rather to be chosen than great riches." Names are more than a means of identification. The name *Eve,* for example, means "mother of all living" and was given to the first woman in order to represent the fulfillment of God's plan for her. Abram's name was changed to *Abraham,* "for a father of many nations have I made thee." Jacob's name became *Israel,* "for as a prince hast thou power with God, and with man thou hast prevailed."

Our Western culture does not give the same importance to the meaning of names as has been given in the past, but the challenge still remains to make our names *good*—to live up to our full potential as God's creation.

Each name carries its own message, its own gift. Whether you are choosing a name for a baby or finding the meaning of your own, may this birthright be a special inspiration as you discover the heritage, significance and spiritual application inherent in a name.

A

AARON, Arron

Cultural Origin: Hebrew
Inherent Meaning: *LIGHT BRINGER*
Spiritual Connotation: *RADIATING GOD'S LIGHT*
Supporting Scripture: *Isaiah 60:1*
> *Arise, shine; for thy light is come, and the glory of the Lord is risen upon thee.*

ABBEY, see Abby

ABBOT, Abbott

Cultural Origin: Hebrew
Inherent Meaning: *SPIRITUAL LEADER*
Spiritual Connotation: *WALKS IN TRUTH*
Supporting Scripture: *1 Corinthians 2:13*
> *Which things also we speak, not in the words which man's wisdom teacheth, but which the Holy Ghost teacheth; comparing spiritual things with spiritual.*

ABBY, Abbey

Cultural Origin: Anglo-Saxon
Inherent Meaning: *SWEET REFUGE: PROTECTOR*
Spiritual Connotation: *RESOLUTE IN GOD*
Supporting Scripture: *Psalm 91:2*
> *I will say of the Lord, He is my refuge and my fortress: my God; in him will I trust.*

ABEL

Cultural Origin: Hebrew
Inherent Meaning: *BREATH*
Spiritual Connotation: *GUIDED OF GOD*
Supporting Scripture: *Psalm 92:4*
> *For thou, Lord, hast made me glad through thy work: I will triumph in the works of thy hands.*

ABELARD

Cultural Origin: Teutonic
Inherent Meaning: *NOBLE, RESOLUTE*
Spiritual Connotation: *ABIDING IN GOD*
Supporting Scripture: *Isaiah 42:6*
> *I the Lord have called thee in righteousness, and will hold thine hand, and will keep thee...*

ABIGAIL

Cultural Origin: Hebrew
Inherent Meaning: *JOY, UNDERSTANDING*
Spiritual Connotation: *DIRECTED OF GOD*
Supporting Scripture: *Isaiah 11:2,3*
> *And the spirit of the Lord shall rest upon him, the spirit of wisdom and understanding...and he shall not judge after the sight of his eyes, neither reprove after the hearing of his ears.*

ABNER

Cultural Origin: Hebrew
Inherent Meaning: *ENLIGHTENER*
Spiritual Connotation: *FATHER OF ENLIGHTENMENT*
Supporting Scripture: *Matthew 25:34*
> *...Come, ye blessed of my Father, inherit the kingdom prepared for you from the foundation of the world.*

ABRAHAM

Cultural Origin: Hebrew
Inherent Meaning: *SOURCE, FOUNDER*
Spiritual Connotation: *BRINGER OF FAITH TO THE MULTITUDES*
Supporting Scripture: *1 Corinthians 2:5*
That your faith should not stand in the wisdom of men, but in the power of God.

ACE

Cultural Origin: Latin
Inherent Meaning: *UNITY*
Spiritual Connotation: *ONE WITH THE FATHER*
Supporting Scripture: *Psalm 36:9*
For with thee is the fountain of life: in thy light shall we see light.

ADA, Adah

Cultural Origin: Anglo-Saxon
Inherent Meaning: *PROSPEROUS, HAPPY*
Spiritual Connotation: *JUBILANT SPIRIT*
Supporting Scripture: *Revelation 19:6*
. . . Alleluia: for the Lord God omnipotent reigneth.

ADAIR

Cultural Origin: Gaelic
Inherent Meaning: *STEADFASTNESS*
Spiritual Connotation: *ESTABLISHED IN TRUTH*
Supporting Scripture: *Ephesians 5:2*
And walk in love, as Christ also hath loved us.

ADALIA

Cultural Origin: Teutonic
Inherent Meaning: *NOBLE ONE*
Spiritual Connotation: *GUIDED OF GOD*
Supporting Scripture: *Joshua 1:9*
> *Have not I commanded thee? Be strong and of a good courage; be not afraid, neither be thou dismayed: for the Lord thy God is with thee whithersoever thou goest.*

ADAM

Cultural Origin: Hebrew
Inherent Meaning: *FORMED OF EARTH*
Spiritual Connotation: *IN GOD'S IMAGE*
Supporting Scripture: *Ezekiel 36:26*
> *A new heart also will I give you, and a new spirit will I put within you.*

ADDIE, see Adelaide

ADDISON

Cultural Origin: Anglo-Saxon
Inherent Meaning: *WORTHY OF TRUST*
Spiritual Connotation: *GOD'S HELPER*
Supporting Scripture: *Ezekiel 36:27*
> *And I will put my spirit within you, and cause you to walk in my statutes, and ye shall keep my judgments, and do them.*

ADELAIDE, Adelaid, Addie

Cultural Origin: Teutonic
Inherent Meaning: *JOYFUL*
Spiritual Connotation: *GIFT OF A SPIRIT OF JOY*
Supporting Scripture: *Proverbs 8:14*
> *Counsel is mine, and sound wisdom: I am understanding;*
> *I have strength.*

ADELINE

Cultural Origin: Teutonic
Inherent Meaning: *NOBLE, WORTHY*
Spiritual Connotation: *UNDER GOD'S GUIDANCE*
Supporting Scripture: *Psalm 19:14*
> *Let the words of my mouth, and the meditation of my*
> *heart, be acceptable in thy sight, O Lord, my strength and*
> *my redeemer.*

ADLAI

Cultural Origin: Hebrew
Inherent Meaning: *WITNESS*
Spiritual Connotation: *LIVING GOD'S WORD*
Supporting Scripture: *1 Corinthians 15:58*
> *Be ye stedfast, unmoveable, always abounding in the*
> *work of the Lord, forasmuch as ye know that your labour*
> *is not in vain in the Lord.*

ADLAR

Cultural Origin: Teutonic
Inherent Meaning: *SWIFT OF MIND*
Spiritual Connotation: *CARRYING GOD'S WORD*
Supporting Scripture: *Psalm 91:11*
> *For he shall give his angels charge over thee, to keep thee*
> *in all thy ways.*

ADOLPH, Adolf, Adolpho

Cultural Origin: Teutonic
Inherent Meaning: *NOBLE*
Spiritual Connotation: *EXALTING GOD*
Supporting Scripture: *Psalm 139:14*
> *I will praise thee; for I am fearfully and wonderfully made: marvelous are thy works; and that my soul knoweth right well.*

ADORA, Adoree

Cultural Origin: Latin
Inherent Meaning: *BELOVED*
Spiritual Connotation: *GIFT OF GOD*
Supporting Scripture: *Isaiah 58:14*
> *Then shalt thou delight thyself in the Lord; and I will cause thee to ride upon the high places of the earth...*

ADRIA

Cultural Origin: Latin
Inherent Meaning: *LOVE OF LIFE*
Spiritual Connotation: *FILLED WITH LIFE*
Supporting Scripture: *Psalm 119:35*
> *Make me to go in the path of thy commandments; for therein do I delight.*

ADRIAN

Cultural Origin: Greek
Inherent Meaning: *BRAVE*
Spiritual Connotation: *WARRIOR FOR THE RIGHT*
Supporting Scripture: *Psalm 16:8*
> *I have set the Lord always before me: because he is at my right hand, I shall not be moved.*

ADRIENNE, Adriene

Cultural Origin: Greek
Inherent Meaning: *CONFIDENT SPIRIT*
Spiritual Connotation: *FAITH IN GOD*
Supporting Scripture: *Mark 9:23*
If thou canst believe, all things are possible to him that believeth.

AGATHA

Cultural Origin: Greek
Inherent Meaning: *GOOD, BENEVOLENT*
Spiritual Connotation: *WAY SHOWER*
Supporting Scripture: *Matthew 5:16*
Let your light so shine before men, that they may see your good works, and glorify your Father which is in heaven.

AGNES

Cultural Origin: Greek
Inherent Meaning: *PURE ONE*
Spiritual Connotation: *GOD INSPIRED*
Supporting Scripture: *Proverbs 8:14*
Counsel is mine, and sound wisdom: I am understanding; I have strength.

AILEEN, Ailene

Cultural Origin: Anglo-Saxon
Inherent Meaning: *LIGHT BEARER*
Spiritual Connotation: *MESSENGER OF TRUTH AND KNOWLEDGE*
Supporting Scripture: *1 John 5:4*
For whatsoever is born of God overcometh the world: and this is the victory that overcometh the world, even our faith.

AIMEE, Amy

Cultural Origin: Latin
Inherent Meaning: *BELOVED*
Spiritual Connotation: *SERENITY IN SPIRIT*
Supporting Scripture: *Matthew 6:31-33*
> *Therefore take no thought. . . .But seek ye first the*
> *kingdom of God, and his righteousness; and all these*
> *things shall be added unto you.*

AINSLEY

Cultural Origin: Anglo-Saxon
Inherent Meaning: *INSPIRED*
Spiritual Connotation: *BRINGER OF THE WORD OF LIFE*
Supporting Scripture: *Philippians 2:16*
> *Holding forth the word of life; that I may rejoice in the*
> *day of Christ, that I have not run in vain, neither*
> *laboured in vain.*

ALAN, Allen, Allan

Cultural Origin: Gaelic
Inherent Meaning: *HARMONIOUS ONE*
Spiritual Connotation: *AT ONE WITH CREATION*
Supporting Scripture: *2 Corinthinas 13:11*
> *Be perfect, be of good comfort, be of one mind, live in*
> *peace; and the God of love and peace shall be with you.*

ALANNA, Alana

Cultural Origin: Gaelic
Inherent Meaning: *BRIGHT, BEAUTIFUL*
Spiritual Connotation: *UNIVERSAL HARMONY*
Supporting Scripture: *John 13:35*
  By this shall all men know that ye are my disciples, if ye have love one to another.

ALASTAIR, Alister, Allyster, Alistair

Cultural Origin: Gaelic
Inherent Meaning: *DEFENDER*
Spiritual Connotation: *COURAGE OF SPIRIT*
Supporting Scripture: *Psalm 27:14*
  Wait on the Lord: be of good courage, and he shall strengthen thine heart: wait, I say, on the Lord.

ALBEN, Alban

Cultural Origin: Latin
Inherent Meaning: *FAIR, STEADFAST*
Spiritual Connotation: *SECURE IN GOD'S LOVE*
Supporting Scripture: *Isaiah 41:13*
  For I the Lord thy God will hold thy right hand, saying unto thee, Fear not; I will help thee.

ALBERT, Al

Cultural Origin: Anglo-Saxon
Inherent Meaning: *BRILLIANT, NOBLE*
Spiritual Connotation: *ILLUMINATED ONE*
Supporting Scripture: *Proverbs 16:20*
  He that handleth a matter wisely shall find good: and whoso trusteth in the Lord, happy is he.

ALBERTINE, Alberta, Allie, Berta

Cultural Origin: Anglo-Saxon
Inherent Meaning: *BRILLIANT, NOBLE*
Spiritual Connotation: *ILLUMINATED ONE*
Supporting Scripture: *Psalm 45:2*
> *Thou art fairer than the children of men: grace is poured into thy lips: therefore God hath blessed thee forever.*

ALDA

Cultural Origin: Teutonic
Inherent Meaning: *WISE, PROSPEROUS*
Spiritual Connotation: *UNDER GOD'S DIRECTION*
Supporting Scripture: *Joshua 1:8*
> *This book of the law shall not depart out of thy mouth. . . for then thou shalt make thy way prosperous, and then thou shalt have good success.*

ALDEN, Aldwin

Cultural Origin: Anglo-Saxon
Inherent Meaning: *WISE PROTECTOR*
Spiritual Connotation: *GOD GUIDED*
Supporting Scripture: *Job 22:28*
> *Thou shalt also decree a thing, and it shall be established unto thee: and the light shall shine upon thy ways.*

ALDIS, Aldous

Cultural Origin: Teutonic
Inherent Meaning: *HABITATION OF JUSTICE*
Spiritual Connotation: *ONE WHO LIVES RIGHTEOUSLY*
Supporting Scripture: *Psalm 143:10*
> *Teach me to do thy will; for thou art my God: thy spirit is good; lead me into the land of uprightness.*

ALDRICH, Audric

Cultural Origin: Teutonic
Inherent Meaning: *WISE RULER*
Spiritual Connotation: *GOD DIRECTS*
Supporting Scripture: *Ephesians 4:23,24*
> *And be renewed in the spirit of your mind...which after God is created in righteousness and true holiness.*

ALETHA, Alethea, Aleta

Cultural Origin: Greek
Inherent Meaning: *TRUTHFUL ONE*
Spiritual Connotation: *WISDOM AND UNDERSTANDING*
Supporting Scripture: *Isaiah 55:12*
> *For ye shall go out with joy...the mountains and the hills shall break forth before you into singing, and all the trees of the field shall clap their hands.*

ALEXANDER, Alessandro, Alexis, Alec

Cultural Origin: Greek
Inherent Meaning: *HELPER AND DEFENDER OF MANKIND*
Spiritual Connotation: *BRAVE PROTECTOR*
Supporting Scripture: *Psalm 5:11*
> *But let all those that put their trust in thee rejoice: let them ever shout for joy, because thou defendest them: let them also that love thy name be joyful in thee.*

ALEXANDRA, Alexis, Alexia

Cultural Origin: Greek
Inherent Meaning: *HELPER AND DEFENDER OF*
MANKIND
Spiritual Connotation: *QUICKENED BY SPIRIT*
Supporting Scripture: *1 John 4:16*
And we have known and believed the love that God hath
to us. God is love; and he that dwelleth in love dwelleth in
God, and God in him.

ALFRED

Cultural Origin: Anglo-Saxon
Inherent Meaning: *BENEVOLENT RULER*
Spiritual Connotation: *GOOD COUNSELOR*
Supporting Scripture: *Proverbs 3:5*
Trust in the Lord with all thine heart; and lean not unto
thine own understanding.

ALFREDA, Elfrida, Elva

Cultural Origin: Anglo-Saxon
Inherent Meaning: *WISDOM AND DIPLOMACY*
Spiritual Connotation: *PEACE*
Supporting Scripture: *Colossians 3:14,15*
And above all these things put on charity, which is the
bond of perfectness. And let the peace of God rule in your
hearts...

ALICE, Alicia, Allie

Cultural Origin: Greek
Inherent Meaning: *ONE OF INTEGRITY*
Spiritual Connotation: *TRUTHFUL*
Supporting Scripture: *2 Timothy 1:7*
For God hath not given us the spirit of fear; but of power,
and of love, and of a sound mind.

ALINE

Cultural Origin: Gaelic
Inherent Meaning: *NOBLE*
Spiritual Connotation: *HONORABLE*
Supporting Scripture: *John 11:22*
  *But I know, that even now, whatsoever thou wilt ask of
  God, God will give it thee.*

ALLISON, Alison, Allyson

Cultural Origin: Gaelic
Inherent Meaning: *TRUTHFUL ONE*
Spiritual Connotation: *HOLY ONE*
Supporting Scripture: *Ezekiel 36:27*
  *And I will put my spirit within you, and cause you to walk
  in my statutes, and ye shall keep my judgments, and do
  them.*

ALISTAIR, see Alastair

ALLARD

Cultural Origin: Anglo-Saxon
Inherent Meaning: *BRAVE*
Spiritual Connotation: *DEDICATED*
Supporting Scripture: *Psalm 50:15*
  *And call upon me in the day of trouble: I will deliver thee,
  and thou shalt glorify me.*

ALLEGRA

Cultural Origin: Latin
Inherent Meaning: *LIVELY, CHEERFUL*
Spiritual Connotation: *EAGER TO LIVE*
Supporting Scripture: *Psalm 37:4*
  *Delight thyself also in the Lord; and he shall give thee the
  desires of thine heart.*

ALLEN, see Alan

ALMA

Cultural Origin: Latin
Inherent Meaning: *LOVING AND KIND*
Spiritual Connotation: *A SPARK OF GOD'S CELESTIAL LIGHT*
Supporting Scripture: *Psalm 32:8*
   I will instruct thee and teach thee in the way which thou shalt go: I will guide thee with mine eye.

ALMIRA

Cultural Origin: Arabic
Inherent Meaning: *TRUTHFUL*
Spiritual Connotation: *FULFILLMENT OF THE WORD*
Supporting Scripture: *Psalm 25:10*
   All the paths of the Lord are mercy and truth unto such as keep his covenant and his testimonies.

ALMO

Cultural Origin: Anglo-Saxon
Inherent Meaning: *NOBLE*
Spiritual Connotation: *BLESSED OF GOD*
Supporting Scripture: *Ecclesiastes 7:19*
   Wisdom strengtheneth the wise more than ten mighty men which are in the city.

ALONZO

Cultural Origin: Teutonic
Inherent Meaning: *HELPER OF MANY*
Spiritual Connotation: *NOBLE*
Supporting Scripture: *John 14:12*
> *Verily, verily, I say unto you, He that believeth on me, the works that I do shall he do also; and greater works than these shall he do . . .*

ALOYSIUS

Cultural Origin: Latin
Inherent Meaning: *NOBLE, FAMOUS WARRIOR*
Spiritual Connotation: *GRACE*
Supporting Scripture: *Proverbs 1:23*
> *I will pour out my spirit unto you, I will make known my words unto you.*

ALPHONSO

Cultural Origin: Teutonic
Inherent Meaning: *NOBLE*
Spiritual Connotation: *PROTECTOR*
Supporting Scripture: *Jeremiah 33:3*
> *Call unto me, and I will answer thee, and shew thee great and mighty things, which thou knowest not.*

ALTA

Cultural Origin: Latin
Inherent Meaning: *LOFTY ONE*
Spiritual Connotation: *GREAT IN SPIRIT*
Supporting Scripture: *John 14:27*
> *Peace I leave with you, my peace I give unto you: not as the world giveth, give I unto you. Let not your heart be troubled, neither let it be afraid.*

ALTHEA

Cultural Origin: Greek
Inherent Meaning: *HEALER*
Spiritual Connotation: *LOVE MAKES ALL
THINGS RIGHT*
Supporting Scripture: *Ephesians 5:2*
*And walk in love, as Christ also hath loved us, and hath
given himself for us an offering and a sacrifice to God for
a sweet-smelling savour.*

ALVA

Cultural Origin: Latin
Inherent Meaning: *FRIEND OF ALL*
Spiritual Connotation: *CHERISHED ONE*
Supporting Scripture: *Job 33:4*
*The Spirit of God hath made me, and the breath of the
Almighty hath given me life.*

ALVIN

Cultural Origin: Teutonic
Inherent Meaning: *FRIEND OF ALL*
Spiritual Connotation: *BELOVED OF ALL*
Supporting Scripture: *Psalm 25:10*
*All the paths of the Lord are mercy and truth unto such as
keep his covenant and his testimonies.*

ALVINA

Cultural Origin: Teutonic
Inherent Meaning: *NOBLE FRIEND*
Spiritual Connotation: *BRIGHT AND JOYOUS*
Supporting Scripture: *Proverbs 17:22*
A merry heart doeth good like a medicine.

ALVIS, Elvis

Cultural Origin: Teutonic
Inherent Meaning: *CONQUEROR*
Spiritual Connotation: *BELOVED OF ALL*
Supporting Scripture: *Psalm 37:6*
> *And he shall bring forth thy righteousness as the light,*
> *and thy judgment as the noonday.*

ALYSSA

Cultural Origin: Greek
Inherent Meaning: *SINCERITY*
Spiritual Connotation: *WISDOM*
Supporting Scripture: *John 15:16*
> *. . . But I have chosen you, and ordained you, that ye*
> *should go and bring forth fruit, and that your fruit should*
> *remain: that whatsoever ye shall ask of the Father in my*
> *name, he may give it you.*

AMABEL, Amabelle

Cultural Origin: Latin
Inherent Meaning: *LOVABLE ONE*
Spiritual Connotation: *FILLED WITH GRACE*
Supporting Scripture: *1 John 3:18*
> *Let us not love in word, neither in tongue; but in deed and*
> *in truth.*

AMANDA

Cultural Origin: Latin
Inherent Meaning: *WORTHY OF LOVE*
Spiritual Connotation: *VIRTUOUS IN THOUGHT*
                                    AND DEED
Supporting Scripture: *Isaiah 52:7*
> *How beautiful upon the mountains are the feet of him*
> *that bringeth good tidings. . .*

AMARIS

Cultural Origin: Hebrew
Inherent Meaning: *PROMISE OF GOD*
Spiritual Connotation: *PROMISE FULFILLED*
Supporting Scripture: *Isaiah 45:2*
> *I will go before thee, and make the crooked places straight: I will break in pieces the gates of brass, and cut in sunder the bars of iron.*

AMBER

Cultural Origin: Latin
Inherent Meaning: *LIKE A JEWEL*
Spiritual Connotation: *CHERISHED ONE*
Supporting Scripture: *Psalm 143:8*
> *Cause me to hear thy lovingkindness in the morning; for in thee do I trust: cause me to know the way wherein I should walk; for I lift up my soul unto thee.*

AMBROSE

Cultural Origin: Greek
Inherent Meaning: *TRUSTWORTHY*
Spiritual Connotation: *DIVINE, IMMORTAL ONE*
Supporting Scripture: *Philippians 4:13*
> *I can do all things through Christ which strengtheneth me.*

AMELIA, Emelia

Cultural Origin: Teutonic
Inherent Meaning: *INDUSTRIOUS ONE*
Spiritual Connotation: *BLESSED*
Supporting Scripture: *Zephaniah 3:17*
> *The Lord thy God in the midst of thee is mighty; he will save, he will rejoice over thee with joy...*

AMERY, Emery

Cultural Origin: Teutonic
Inherent Meaning: *DIVINE*
Spiritual Connotation: *WAY SHOWER*
Supporting Scripture: *Job 32:8*
> *But there is a spirit in man: and the inspiration of the Almighty giveth them understanding.*

AMOS

Cultural Origin: Hebrew
Inherent Meaning: *COURAGEOUS*
Spiritual Connotation: *COMPASSIONATE SPIRIT*
Supporting Scripture: *John 14:16,17*
> *And I will pray the Father, and he shall give you another Comforter. . . even the Spirit of truth. . .*

AMY, see Aimee

ANASTASIA

Cultural Origin: Greek
Inherent Meaning: *RENEWAL OF SPIRIT*
Spiritual Connotation: *AWAKENING IN SPIRIT*
Supporting Scripture: *Proverbs 24:3,4*
> *Through wisdom is an house builded; and by understanding it is established: And by knowledge shall the chambers be filled with all precious and pleasant riches.*

ANDREA

Cultural Origin: Latin
Inherent Meaning: *BELOVED ONE*
Spiritual Connotation: *FILLED WITH GRACE*
Supporting Scripture: *Psalm 119:105*
> *Thy word is a lamp unto my feet, and a light unto my path.*

ANDREW, Andre

Cultural Origin: Greek
Inherent Meaning: *BRAVE*
Spiritual Connotation: *ENDURING*
Supporting Scripture: *Psalm 27:1*
> *The Lord is my light and my salvation; whom shall I fear?*
> *the Lord is the strength of my life; of whom shall I be*
> *afraid?*

ANGELA, Angeline

Cultural Origin: Teutonic
Inherent Meaning: *ANGEL OR MESSENGER*
Spiritual Connotation: *BRINGER OF GLAD TIDINGS*
Supporting Scripture: *Isaiah 30:29*
> *Ye shall have a song, as in the night when a holy solemni-*
> *ty is kept; and gladness of heart, as when one goeth with a*
> *pipe to come into the mountain of the Lord, to the mighty*
> *One of Israel.*

ANGELO

Cultural Origin: Latin
Inherent Meaning: *ANGEL OR MESSENGER*
Spiritual Connotation: *BRINGER OF GLAD TIDINGS*
Supporting Scripture: *Romans 15:13*
> *Now the God of hope fill you with all joy and peace in*
> *believing, that ye may abound in hope, through the power*
> *of the Holy Ghost.*

ANGUS

Cultural Origin: Gaelic
Inherent Meaning: *UNIQUE STRENGTH*
Spiritual Connotation: *CREATIVE SPIRIT*
Supporting Scripture: *Isaiah 64:5*
> *Thou meetest him that rejoiceth and worketh*
> *righteousness, those that remember thee in thy ways. . .*

ANITA

Cultural Origin: Latin
Inherent Meaning: *GRACIOUS ONE*
Spiritual Connotation: *LOVINGKINDNESS*
Supporting Scripture: *Proverbs 16:24*
Pleasant words are as an honeycomb, sweet to the soul, and health to the bones.

ANNABELL, Annabelle

Cultural Origin: Hebrew
Inherent Meaning: *GRACEFUL, BEAUTIFUL*
Spiritual Connotation: *BELOVED ONE*
Supporting Scripture: *Psalm 89:1*
I will sing of the mercies of the Lord forever: with my mouth will I make known thy faithfulness to all generations.

ANN, Anne, Anna, Ana, Annette

Cultural Origin: Hebrew
Inherent Meaning: *GRACEFUL ONE*
Spiritual Connotation: *DEVOTION BUILT THROUGH FAITHFULNESS*
Supporting Scripture: *Psalm 111:10*
The fear of the Lord is the beginning of wisdom: a good understanding have all they that do his commandments: his praise endureth for ever.

ANSEL

Cultural Origin: Teutonic
Inherent Meaning: *NOBLE*
Spiritual Connotation: *BEARER OF TRUTH*
Supporting Scripture: *Jeremiah 33:6*
Behold, I will bring it health and cure, and I will cure them, and will reveal unto them the abundance of peace and truth.

ANSLEY, Ainsley

Cultural Origin: Celtic
Inherent Meaning: *BOLD*
Spiritual Connotation: *AWE-INSPIRING*
Supporting Scripture: *Psalm 108:4*
> *For thy mercy is great above the heavens: and thy truth reacheth unto the clouds.*

ANTHONY, Tony, Toni

Cultural Origin: Latin
Inherent Meaning: *PRICELESS ONE*
Spiritual Connotation: *VALUED COUNSELOR*
Supporting Scripture: *Psalm 122:7-9*
> *Peace be within thy walls, and prosperity within thy palaces...Because of the house of the Lord our God I will seek thy good.*

ANTON

Cultural Origin: Unknown
Inherent Meaning: *WISE RULER*
Spiritual Connotation: *COMPASSIONATE ONE*
Supporting Scripture: *Proverbs 25:11*
> *A word fitly spoken is like apples of gold in pictures of silver.*

ANTONIA, Antoinette, Toni, Tonia

Cultural Origin: Latin
Inherent Meaning: *INESTIMABLE, PRICELESS ONE*
Spiritual Connotation: *JEWEL OF KINDNESS*
Supporting Scripture: *Matthew 5:16*
> *Let your light so shine before men, that they may see your good works, and glorify your Father which is in heaven.*

ANTONIO

Cultural Origin: Latin
Inherent Meaning: *INESTIMABLE, PRICELESS ONE*
Spiritual Connotation: *COMPASSIONATE*
Supporting Scripture: *Isaiah 54:14*

In righteousness shalt thou be established: thou shalt be far from oppression; for thou shalt not fear...

APRIL, Apryl

Cultural Origin: Latin
Inherent Meaning: *NEW IN FAITH*
Spiritual Connotation: *AWAKENED SOUL*
Supporting Scripture: *Ezekiel 37:14*

And shall put my spirit in you, and ye shall live, and I shall place you in your own land: then shall ye know that I the Lord have spoken it, and performed it...

ARCHER

Cultural Origin: Teutonic
Inherent Meaning: *DEFENDER*
Spiritual Connotation: *STEADFAST, BALANCED*
Supporting Scripture: *Isaiah 40:31*

But they that wait upon the Lord shall renew their strength; they shall mount up with wings as eagles; they shall run, and not be weary; and they shall walk, and not faint.

ARCHIBALD

Cultural Origin: Anglo-Saxon
Inherent Meaning: *VALIANT ONE*
Spiritual Connotation: *COURAGEOUS SPIRIT*
Supporting Scripture: *2 Samuel 22:31*

As for God, his way is perfect; the word of the Lord is tried: he is a buckler to all them that trust in him.

ARDATH, Ardeth, Ardith

Cultural Origin: Hebrew
Inherent Meaning: *FAITHFUL ONE*
Spiritual Connotation: *FULFILLMENT*
Supporting Scripture: *Psalm 28:7*
> *The Lord is my strength and my shield; my heart trusted in him, and I am helped...*

ARDELLE

Cultural Origin: Latin
Inherent Meaning: *ARDENT SPIRIT*
Spiritual Connotation: *ENTHUSIASTIC FOR LIFE*
Supporting Scripture: *Psalm 67:5,6*
> *Let the people praise thee, O God; let all the people praise thee. Then shall the earth yield her increase; and God, even our own God, shall bless us.*

ARIANA

Cultural Origin: Latin
Inherent Meaning: *HOLY ONE*
Spiritual Connotation: *PURE IN HEART*
Supporting Scripture: *Proverbs 1:23*
> *Behold, I will pour out my spirit unto you, I will make known my words unto you.*

ARLEN, Arlin

Cultural Origin: Gaelic
Inherent Meaning: *TRUTHFUL ONE*
Spiritual Connotation: *PRAISING AND BLESSING*
Supporting Scripture: *Psalm 34:1*
> *I will bless the Lord at all times: his praise shall continually be in my mouth.*

ARLENE, Arline, Arleen, Arlis

Cultural Origin: Gaelic
Inherent Meaning: *A PLEDGE*
Spiritual Connotation: *TRUTHFUL ONE*
Supporting Scripture: *Philippians 4:7*
> *And the peace of God, which passeth all understanding, shall keep your hearts and minds through Christ Jesus.*

ARLEY, Arleigh

Cultural Origin: Teutonic
Inherent Meaning: *PEACEFUL ONE*
Spiritual Connotation: *A PLEDGE FOR PEACE*
Supporting Scripture: *Romans 8:28*
> *And we know that all things work together for good to them that love God, to them who are the called according to his purpose.*

ARLIS, see Arlene

ARNELLE, Arnel

Cultural Origin: Teutonic
Inherent Meaning: *CLEAR-SIGHTED*
Spiritual Connotation: *GRACIOUS LEADER*
Supporting Scripture: *Psalm 36:9*
> *For with thee is the fountain of life: in thy light shall we see light.*

ARNOLD

Cultural Origin: Unknown
Inherent Meaning: *STRONG AS AN EAGLE*
Spiritual Connotation: *BRAVE, STRONG*
Supporting Scripture: *Psalm 103:1,5*
> *Bless the Lord, O my soul: and all that is within me, bless his holy name... Who satisfieth my mouth with good things; so that thy youth is renewed like the eagle's.*

ARRON, see Aaron

ARTHUR

Cultural Origin: Teutonic
Inherent Meaning: *BOLD, BRAVE*
Spiritual Connotation: *GRACIOUS RULER*
Supporting Scripture: *Proverbs 3:13*
> *Happy is the man that findeth wisdom, and the man that getteth understanding.*

ASA

Cultural Origin: Hebrew
Inherent Meaning: *HEALER*
Spiritual Connotation: *HEALER OF MIND AND BODY*
Supporting Scripture: *Jeremiah 33:6*
> *Behold, I will bring it health and cure, and I will cure them, and will reveal unto them the abundance of peace and truth.*

ASHER

Cultural Origin: Hebrew
Inherent Meaning: *JOYOUS ONE*
Spiritual Connotation: *FILLED WITH LAUGHTER*
Supporting Scripture: *Psalm 16:11*
> *Thou wilt shew me the path of life: in thy presence is fulness of joy; at thy right hand there are pleasures for evermore.*

ASHLEY

Cultural Origin: Anglo-Saxon
Inherent Meaning: *PEACEFUL*
Spiritual Connotation: *CONCORD, HARMONY*
Supporting Scripture: *Isaiah 30:15*
> *. . . in quietness and in confidence shall be your strength. . .*

ASTHER

Cultural Origin: Anglo-Saxon
Inherent Meaning: *A FLOWER*
Spiritual Connotation: *GOD'S GIFT*
Supporting Scripture: *Isaiah 58:8*
> *Then shall thy light break forth as the morning, and thine health shall spring forth speedily: and thy righteousness shall go before thee. . .*

ASTRID

Cultural Origin: Teutonic
Inherent Meaning: *DIVINE STRENGTH*
Spiritual Connotation: *STRENGTH OF GOD*
Supporting Scripture: *Psalm 42:8*
> *Yet the Lord will command his lovingkindness in the daytime, and in the night his song shall be with me, and my prayer unto the God of my life.*

ATHALIA

Cultural Origin: Greek
Inherent Meaning: *GOD IS EXALTED*
Spiritual Connotation: *HONOR AND POWER*
Supporting Scripture: *Colossians 3:14,15*
> *And above all these things put on charity, which is the
> bond of perfectness. And let the peace of God rule in your
> hearts...*

ATHERTON

Cultural Origin: Anglo-Saxon
Inherent Meaning: *FREE SOUL*
Spiritual Connotation: *ABUNDANT LIFE*
Supporting Scripture: *Proverbs 2:10,11*
> *When wisdom entereth into thine heart, and knowledge is
> pleasant unto thy soul; discretion shall preserve thee,
> understanding shall keep thee.*

AUBREY

Cultural Origin: Anglo-Saxon
Inherent Meaning: *ROYAL RULER*
Spiritual Connotation: *COMPASSIONATE ONE*
Supporting Scripture: *Proverbs 12:18*
> *...but the tongue of the wise is health.*

AUDREY

Cultural Origin: Anglo-Saxon
Inherent Meaning: *NOBLE STRENGTH*
Spiritual Connotation: *STRENGTH TO OVERCOME
                        DIFFICULTIES*
Supporting Scripture: *Proverbs 24:3,4*
> *Through wisdom is an house builded; and by understand-
> ing it is established: and by knowledge shall the
> chambers be filled with precious and pleasant riches.*

AUGUST, Augustine, Augustus

Cultural Origin: Latin
Inherent Meaning: *MAJESTIC DIGNITY*
Spiritual Connotation: *EXALTED ONE*
Supporting Scripture: *Deuteronomy 26:11*
  *And thou shalt rejoice in every good thing which the Lord
  thy God hath given unto thee...*

AUGUSTA

Cultural Origin: Latin
Inherent Meaning: *MAJESTIC ONE*
Spiritual Connotation: *NOBLE, QUEENLY*
Supporting Scripture: *Psalm 28:7*
  *The Lord is my strength and my shield; my heart trusted
  in him, and I am helped: therefore my heart greatly re-
  joiceth; and with my song will I praise him.*

AUSTIN

Cultural Origin: Latin
Inherent Meaning: *RENOWNED, ROYAL*
Spiritual Connotation: *WORTHY OF TRUST*
Supporting Scripture: *Isaiah 58:11*
  *And the Lord shall guide thee continually... and thou
  shalt be like a watered garden, and like a spring of water,
  whose waters fail not.*

AVA

Cultural Origin: Latin
Inherent Meaning: *FILLED WITH GRACE*
Spiritual Connotation: *ONE WHOSE HEART IS
                        FILLED WITH SONG*
Supporting Scripture: *Psalm 106:1*
> *Praise ye the Lord. O give thanks unto the Lord; for he is
> good: for his mercy endureth for ever.*

AVERY

Cultural Origin: Anglo-Saxon
Inherent Meaning: *WISE RULER*
Spiritual Connotation: *WISE COUNSELOR*
Supporting Scripture: *Proverbs 20:5*
> *Counsel in the heart of man is like deep water; but a man
> of understanding will draw it out.*

AVIS

Cultural Origin: Latin
Inherent Meaning: *A REFUGE*
Spiritual Connotation: *COMFORTER*
Supporting Scripture: *Galatians 5:1*
> *Stand fast therefore in the liberty wherewith Christ hath
> made us free. . .*

B

BAILEY

Cultural Origin: Latin
Inherent Meaning: *STEWARDSHIP*
Spiritual Connotation: *PROTECTOR*
Supporting Scripture: *1 Peter 4:10*
> As every man hath received the gift, even so minister the same one to another, as good stewards of the manifold grace of God.

BAIRD

Cultural Origin: Gaelic
Inherent Meaning: *RESPONSIVENESS*
Spiritual Connotation: *SONG OF HARMONY*
Supporting Scripture: *Psalm 81:1*
> Sing aloud unto God our strength: make a joyful noise unto the God of Jacob.

BALDWIN

Cultural Origin: Teutonic
Inherent Meaning: *COURAGEOUS ONE*
Spiritual Connotation: *FORCEFUL PROTECTOR*
Supporting Scripture: *1 Chronicles 28:20*
> ...fear not, nor be dismayed: for the Lord God, even my God, will be with thee...

BARBARA

Cultural Origin: Latin
Inherent Meaning: *STRANGER IN THE LAND*
Spiritual Connotation: *BEAUTIFUL, COURAGEOUS*
Supporting Scripture: *Acts 17:26-28*
> *And hath made of one blood all nations of men for to dwell on all the face of the earth. . . . For in him we live, and move, and have our being; as certain also of our own poets have said, For we are also his offspring.*

BARCLAY

Cultural Origin: Teutonic
Inherent Meaning: *MAKE NEW AGAIN*
Spiritual Connotation: *RENEWED IN SPIRIT*
Supporting Scripture: *John 6:63*
> *It is the spirit that quickeneth . . . the words that I speak unto you, they are spirit, and they are life.*

BARNABAS, Barnaby, Barney

Cultural Origin: Greek from Hebrew
Inherent Meaning: *PRAISE AND PROPHECY*
Spiritual Connotation: *CONSECRATED TO GOD*
Supporting Scripture: *Psalm 143:8,10*
> *Cause me to hear thy lovingkindness in the morning; for in thee do I trust: cause me to know the way wherein I should walk; for I lift up my soul unto thee.*

BARNARD, Bernard

Cultural Origin: Teutonic
Inherent Meaning: *BRAVE, NOBLE*
Spiritual Connotation: *VICTORIOUS SPIRIT*
Supporting Scripture: *Isaiah 30:21*
> *And thine ears shall hear a word behind thee, saying, This is the way, walk ye in it, when ye turn to the right hand, and when ye turn to the left.*

BARRY, Barrie

Cultural Origin: Gaelic
Inherent Meaning: *BOLD, STRONG*
Spiritual Connotation: *OF ONE MIND*
Supporting Scripture: *2 Corinthians 3:17*
　　*Now the Lord is that Spirit: and where the Spirit of the
　　Lord is, there is liberty.*

BARTHOLOMEW, Bart

Cultural Origin: Gaelic
Inherent Meaning: *FACULTY OF IMAGINATION*
Spiritual Connotation: *DISCERNING ONE*
Supporting Scripture: *Colossians 1:12*
　　*Giving thanks unto the Father, which hath made us meet
　　to be partakers of the inheritance of the saints in light.*

BARTRAM, Bertram

Cultural Origin: Anglo-Saxon
Inherent Meaning: *HEROIC*
Spiritual Connotation: *GLORIOUS WARRIOR*
Supporting Scripture: *Proverbs 30:5*
　　*Every word of God is pure: he is a shield unto them that
　　put their trust in him.*

BASIL

Cultural Origin: Latin
Inherent Meaning: *KINGLY*
Spiritual Connotation: *MAGNIFICENT ONE*
Supporting Scripture: *1 Chronicles 29:12*
　　*Both riches and honour come of thee, and thou reignest
　　over all; and in thine hand is power and might; and in
　　thine hand it is to make great, and to give strength unto
　　all.*

BAXTER

Cultural Origin: Celtic
Inherent Meaning: *PROVIDER, SUPPLIER*
Spiritual Connotation: *INDUSTRIOUS*
Supporting Scripture: *Psalm 37:3,4*
> *Trust in the Lord, and do good; so shalt thou dwell in the
> land, and verily thou shalt be fed. Delight thyself also in
> the Lord; and he shall give thee the desires of thine heart.*

BEATRICE, Beata

Cultural Origin: Latin
Inherent Meaning: *JOYFUL ONE*
Spiritual Connotation: *BRINGER OF JOY*
Supporting Scripture: *Psalm 32:11*
> *Be glad in the Lord, and rejoice, ye righteous: and shout
> for joy, all ye that are upright in heart.*

BEARFORT

Cultural Origin: Latin
Inherent Meaning: *NOBLE SPIRIT*
Spiritual Connotation: *ESTEEMED ONE*
Supporting Scripture: *Matthew 5:16*
> *Let your light so shine before men, that they may see your
> good works, and glorify your Father which is in heaven.*

BELINDA

Cultural Origin: Latin
Inherent Meaning: *PRECIOUS ONE*
Spiritual Connotation: *BEAUTY OF SOUL*
Supporting Scripture: *Ephesians 4:7*
> *But unto every one of us is given grace according to the
> measure of the gift of Christ.*

BELLE, Bell, Belva

Cultural Origin: Latin
Inherent Meaning: *BEAUTIFUL ONE*
Spiritual Connotation: *BLESSED ONE*
Supporting Scripture: *Psalm 104:33,34*
> *I will sing unto the Lord as long as I live: I will sing praise to my God while I have my being. . . . I will be glad in the Lord.*

BENEDICT

Cultural Origin: Latin
Inherent Meaning: *BLESSED ONE*
Spiritual Connotation: *FOLLOWER OF CHRIST*
Supporting Scripture: *Joshua 1:9*
> *Be strong and of a good courage; be not afraid, neither be thou dismayed: for the Lord thy God is with thee whithersoever thou goest.*

BENITA, Bonita, Bonnie

Cultural Origin: Latin
Inherent Meaning: *BLESSED ONE*
Spiritual Connotation: *PURE IN HEART*
Supporting Scripture: *Psalm 119:2*
> *Blessed are they that keep his testimonies, and that seek him with the whole heart.*

BENJAMIN, Ben

Cultural Origin: Hebrew
Inherent Meaning: *MIGHTY IN SPIRIT*
Spiritual Connotation: *ACTIVE, ACCOMPLISHING FAITH*
Supporting Scripture: *Psalm 31:1*
> *In thee, O Lord, do I put my trust; let me never be ashamed: deliver me in thy righteousness.*

BENNET, Bennett, Benny

Cultural Origin: Latin
Inherent Meaning: *BLESSED ONE*
Spiritual Connotation: *WALKS WITH GOD*
Supporting Scripture: *Romans 8:14*
   *For as many as are led by the Spirit of God, they are the
   sons of God.*

BENSON

Cultural Origin: Hebrew
Inherent Meaning: *HONORABLE, FAITHFUL*
Spiritual Connotation: *HONORING GOD*
Supporting Scripture: *Psalm 127:1*
   *Except the Lord build the house, they labour in vain that
   build it: except the Lord keep the city, the watchman
   waketh but in vain.*

BENTLEY

Cultural Origin: Anglo-Saxon
Inherent Meaning: *RESTFUL SPIRIT*
Spiritual Connotation: *PEACEFUL*
Supporting Scripture: *Psalm 121:8*
   *The Lord shall preserve thy going out and thy coming in
   from this time forth, and even for evermore.*

BERNADETTE, Bernadine, Bernardina

Cultural Origin: Latin
Inherent Meaning: *COURAGEOUS SPIRIT*
Spiritual Connotation: *VALIANT ONE*
Supporting Scripture: *1 Corinthians 15:57*
   *But thanks be to God, which giveth us the victory through
   our Lord Jesus Christ.*

BERNICE

Cultural Origin: Greek
Inherent Meaning: *HARBINGER OF VICTORY*
Spiritual Connotation: *VICTORIOUS ONE*
Supporting Scripture: *Mark 9:23*
>*If thou canst believe, all things are possible to him that believeth.*

BERTHA

Cultural Origin: Teutonic
Inherent Meaning: *GLORIOUS ONE*
Spiritual Connotation: *BRIGHT ONE*
Supporting Scripture: *Psalm 37:6*
>*And he shall bring forth thy righteousness as the light, and thy judgment as the noonday.*

BERTRAM

Cultural Origin: Anglo-Saxon
Inherent Meaning: *BRILLIANT ONE*
Spiritual Connotation: *MAGNIFICENT ONE*
Supporting Scripture: *Isaiah 62:3*
>*Thou shalt also be a crown of glory in the hand of the Lord, and a royal diadem in the hand of thy God.*

BERYL

Cultural Origin: Greek
Inherent Meaning: *AN EMBLEM OF GOOD FORTUNE*
Spiritual Connotation: *BRIGHT ONE*
Supporting Scripture: *Psalm 119:149*
>*Hear my voice according unto thy lovingkindness: O Lord, quicken me according to thy judgment.*

BESSIE, Betina, Betty

Cultural Origin: Latin
Inherent Meaning: *OATH OF GOD*
Spiritual Connotation: *LOYAL ONE*
Supporting Scripture: *Isaiah 30:29*
> *Ye shall have a song, as in the night when a holy solemnity is kept; and gladness of heart, as when one goeth with a pipe to come into the mountain of the Lord...*

BETH, Bethel

Cultural Origin: Hebrew
Inherent Meaning: *HOUSE OF GOD*
Spiritual Connotation: *HEART WISE*
Supporting Scripture: *Isaiah 48:17*
> *...I am the Lord thy God which teacheth thee to profit, which leadeth thee by the way that thou shouldest go.*

BETTY, see Bessie

BEULAH

Cultural Origin: Hebrew
Inherent Meaning: *DIVINE CONSCIOUSNESS*
Spiritual Connotation: *ONE WITH GOD*
Supporting Scripture: *1 John 3:2*
> *Beloved, now are we the sons of God, and it doth not yet appear what we shall be: but we know that, when he shall appear, we shall be like him...*

BEVAN, Bevin

Cultural Origin: Celtic
Inherent Meaning: *NOBLE YOUTHFUL ONE*
Spiritual Connotation: *A BRAVE HEART*
Supporting Scripture: *1 John 1:7*
> *But if we walk in the light, as he is in the light, we have fellowship one with another...*

BEVERLY, Beverley

Cultural Origin: Anglo-Saxon
Inherent Meaning: *PEACE AND HARMONY*
Spiritual Connotation: *ENLIGHTENED ONE*
Supporting Scripture: *James 1:17*
> *Every good gift and every perfect gift is from above, and cometh down from the Father of lights, with whom is no variableness, neither shadow of turning.*

BIANCA

Cultural Origin: Latin
Inherent Meaning: *FAIR ONE*
Spiritual Connotation: *INNER BEAUTY*
Supporting Scripture: *Job 5:8,9*
> *I would seek unto God, and unto God would I commit my cause: which doeth great things and unsearchable; marvellous things without number.*

BILL, see William

BIRNEY

Cultural Origin: Anglo-Saxon
Inherent Meaning: *ONE OF INTEGRITY*
Spiritual Connotation: *INDUSTRIOUS*
Supporting Scripture: *Romans 8:28*
> *And we know that all things work together for good to them that love God, to them who are the called according to his purpose.*

BLAINE

Cultural Origin: Gaelic
Inherent Meaning: *STEADFAST SPIRIT*
Spiritual Connotation: *WORTHY OF TRUST*
Supporting Scripture: *Isaiah 42:16*
> *. . . I will make darkness light before them, and crooked things straight. These things I will do unto them, and not forsake them.*

BLAIR

Cultural Origin: Gaelic
Inherent Meaning: *WORKER IN THE FIELD*
Spiritual Connotation: *DILIGENT ONE*
Supporting Scripture: *Ephesians 6:7,8*
> *With good will doing service, as to the Lord. . .knowing that whatsoever good thing any man doeth, the same shall he receive of the Lord, whether he be bond or free.*

BLAKE

Cultural Origin: Anglo-Saxon
Inherent Meaning: *HARMONIZER*
Spiritual Connotation: *ONE WHO BRINGS INTO AGREE-MENT*
Supporting Scripture: *Ephesians 2:4-6*
> *But God, who is rich in mercy, for his great love wherewith he loved us. . .hath raised us up together, and made us sit together in heavenly places in Christ Jesus.*

BLANCHE, Blanch

Cultural Origin: Latin
Inherent Meaning: *PURE ONE*
Spiritual Connotation: *GRACIOUS SPIRIT*
Supporting Scripture: *Psalm 49:3*
> *My mouth shall speak of wisdom; and the meditation of my heart shall be of understanding.*

BLYTHE

Cultural Origin: Anglo-Saxon
Inherent Meaning: *JOYFUL*
Spiritual Connotation: *CHEERFUL ONE*
Supporting Scripture: *Jude 1:2*
> *Mercy unto you, and peace, and love, be multiplied.*

BOGART

Cultural Origin: Teutonic
Inherent Meaning: *GREAT STRENGTH*
Spiritual Connotation: *RESOURCEFUL*
Supporting Scripture: *Isaiah 41:13*
> *For I the Lord thy God will hold thy right hand, saying unto thee, Fear not; I will help thee.*

BONITA, see Benita

BONNIE, see Benita

BORIS

Cultural Origin: Slavic
Inherent Meaning: *LOYAL*
Spiritual Connotation: *FAITHFUL ONE*
Supporting Scripture: *Psalm 36:7*
> *How excellent is thy lovingkindness, O God! therefore the children of men put their trust under the shadow of thy wings.*

BOYD

Cultural Origin: Gaelic
Inherent Meaning: *FAIR ONE*
Spiritual Connotation: *QUIET SPIRIT*
Supporting Scripture: *Proverbs 15:33*
The fear of the Lord is the instruction of wisdom; and before honour is humility.

BRADLEY, Brad

Cultural Origin: Anglo-Saxon
Inherent Meaning: *A MERRY HEART*
Spiritual Connotation: *JOYFUL ONE*
Supporting Scripture: *Proverbs 15:13*
A merry heart maketh a cheerful countenance.

BRADY

Cultural Origin: Gaelic
Inherent Meaning: *SPIRITED ONE*
Spiritual Connotation: *VICTORIOUS HEART*
Supporting Scripture: *Galatians 5:22,23*
The fruit of the Spirit is love, joy, peace, longsuffering, gentleness, goodness, faith, meekness, temperance: against such there is no law.

BRAINARD

Cultural Origin: Anglo-Saxon
Inherent Meaning: *FEARLESS*
Spiritual Connotation: *HUMILITY OF SPIRIT*
Supporting Scripture: *Hosea 14:9*
Who is wise, and he shall understand these things? prudent, and he shall know them? for the ways of the Lord are right, and the just shall walk in them . . .

BRENDA

Cultural Origin: Gaelic
Inherent Meaning: *BEAUTIFUL*
Spiritual Connotation: *NOBLE SPIRIT*
Supporting Scripture: *Psalm 70:4*
> *Let all those that seek thee rejoice and be glad in thee: and let such as love thy salvation say continually, Let God be magnified.*

BRENNA, Brena

Cultural Origin: Gaelic
Inherent Meaning: *LOVELY ONE*
Spiritual Connotation: *FAITHFUL FRIEND*
Supporting Scripture: *Philippians 2:13*
> *For it is God which worketh in you both to will and to do of his good pleasure.*

BRENT, Brant

Cultural Origin: Anglo-Saxon
Inherent Meaning: *PROUD ONE*
Spiritual Connotation: *ONE OF HONOR*
Supporting Scripture: *2 Timothy 1:6*
> *Wherefore I put thee in remembrance that thou stir up the gift of God, which is in thee by the putting on of my hands.*

BRETT

Cultural Origin: Celtic
Inherent Meaning: *GIFTED*
Spiritual Connotation: *BLESSED OF GOD*
Supporting Scripture: *Proverbs 18:16*
> *A man's gift maketh room for him, and bringeth him before great men.*

BRIAN

Cultural Origin: Celtic
Inherent Meaning: *VIRTUE AND HONOR*
Spiritual Connotation: *VICTORIOUS SPIRIT*
Supporting Scripture: *Isaiah 48:17*
> *. . . I am the Lord thy God which teacheth thee to profit, which leadeth thee by the way that thou shouldest go.*

BRICE, Bryce

Cultural Origin: Celtic
Inherent Meaning: *QUICKLY RESPONSIVE*
Spiritual Connotation: *COMPASSIONATE ONE*
Supporting Scripture: *Ecclesiastes 9:1*
> *For all this I considered in my heart even to declare all this, that the righteous, and the wise, and their works, are in the hand of God.*

BRIDGET, Bridgette

Cultural Origin: Gaelic
Inherent Meaning: *STRENGTH*
Spiritual Connotation: *ENDURING SPIRIT*
Supporting Scripture: *Psalm 27:1*
> *The Lord is my light and my salvation; whom shall I fear? the Lord is the strength of my life; of whom shall I be afraid?*

BROOK, Brooke, Brooks

Cultural Origin: Anglo-Saxon
Inherent Meaning: *PEACEFUL*
Spiritual Connotation: *REFRESHING SPIRIT*
Supporting Scripture: *Zechariah 2:10*
> *Sing and rejoice. . .for, lo, I come, and I will dwell in the midst of thee, saith the Lord.*

BRUCE

Cultural Origin: Latin
Inherent Meaning: *DWELLER AT THE THICKET*
Spiritual Connotation: *DIGNITY OF CHARACTER*
Supporting Scripture: *Ephesians 2:10*
For we are his workmanship, created in Christ Jesus unto good works, which God hath before ordained that we should walk in them.

BRUNO

Cultural Origin: Latin
Inherent Meaning: *FREE*
Spiritual Connotation: *IN GOD'S GRACE*
Supporting Scripture: *Philippians 4:19*
But my God shall supply all your need according to his riches in glory by Christ Jesus.

BRYAN, Bryant

Cultural Origin: Celtic
Inherent Meaning: *VIRTUE AND HONOR*
Spiritual Connotation: *STRONG IN THE LORD*
Supporting Scripture: *Deuteronomy 33:27*
The eternal God is thy refuge, and underneath are the everlasting arms.

BURGESS

Cultural Origin: Celtic
Inherent Meaning: *STEADFAST*
Spiritual Connotation: *DILIGENT, TRUSTWORTHY*
Supporting Scripture: *1 John 2:10*
He that loveth his brother abideth in the light, and there is none occasion of stumbling in him.

BURKE

Cultural Origin: Latin
Inherent Meaning: *DWELLER IN THE FORTRESS*
Spiritual Connotation: *CARING ONE*
Supporting Scripture: *Deuteronomy 31:6*
> *Be strong and of a good courage, fear not, nor be afraid of them; for the Lord thy God, he it is that doth go with thee; he will not fail thee, nor forsake thee.*

BURL, Byrle

Cultural Origin: Anglo-Saxon
Inherent Meaning: *ONE WHO SERVES*
Spiritual Connotation: *EXCELLENT VIRTUE*
Supporting Scripture: *Psalm 139:9,10*
> *If I take the wings of the morning, and dwell in the uttermost parts of the sea; even there shall thy hand lead me, and thy right hand shall hold me.*

BURTON

Cultural Origin: Anglo-Saxon
Inherent Meaning: *BOROUGH TOWN*
Spiritual Connotation: *WORTHY PROVIDER*
Supporting Scripture: *Psalm 23:1,2*
> *The Lord is my shepherd; I shall not want. He maketh me to lie down in green pastures. . .*

BYRAM

Cultural Origin: Anglo-Saxon
Inherent Meaning: *DWELLER IN THE FIELDS*
Spiritual Connotation: *FREEDOM*
Supporting Scripture: *Deuteronomy 33:12*
> *. . . The beloved of the Lord shall dwell in safety by him; and the Lord shall cover him all the day long, and he shall dwell between his shoulders.*

BYRON

Cultural Origin: Latin
Inherent Meaning: *MAGNANIMOUS NATURE*
Spiritual Connotation: *GENEROUS, FORGIVING SPIRIT*
Supporting Scripture: *James 1:17*

Every good gift and every perfect gift is from above, and cometh down from the Father of lights, with whom is no variableness, neither shadow of turning.

C

CACEY, Casey

Cultural Origin: Gaelic
Inherent Meaning: *VALOROUS, BRAVE, WATCHFUL*
Spiritual Connotation: *NOBLE LEADERSHIP*
Supporting Scripture: *1 John 5:4*
> *For whatsoever is born of God overcometh the world: and this is the victory that overcometh the world, even our faith.*

CAESAR

Cultural Origin: Latin
Inherent Meaning: *SHARP, KEEN*
Spiritual Connotation: *FEARLESS*
Supporting Scripture: *Matthew 7:12*
> *Therefore all things whatsoever ye would that men should do to you, do ye even so to them: for this is the law and the prophets.*

CALEB

Cultural Origin: Latin
Inherent Meaning: *FEARLESS, IMPETUOUS*
Spiritual Connotation: *GREAT SPIRITUAL POTENTIAL*
Supporting Scripture: *Isaiah 9:7*
> *Of the increase of his government and peace there shall be no end. . . .The zeal of the Lord of hosts will perform this.*

CALHOUN

Cultural Origin: Celtic
Inherent Meaning: *STRONG*
Spiritual Connotation: *GREAT IN SPIRIT*
Supporting Scripture: *Psalm 8:6*
> *Thou madest him to have dominion over the works of thy hands; thou hast put all things under his feet.*

CALVERT

Cultural Origin: Anglo-Saxon
Inherent Meaning: *ONE WHO LOVES ALL CREATURES*
Spiritual Connotation: *DIVINELY AWAKENED*
Supporting Scripture: *Psalm 9:2*
> *I will be glad and rejoice in thee: I will sing praise to thy name, O thou most High.*

CALVIN

Cultural Origin: Latin
Inherent Meaning: *FAVORED ONE*
Spiritual Connotation: *BLESSED ONE*
Supporting Scripture: *Proverbs 22:20,21*
> *Have not I written to thee excellent things in counsels and knowledge, that I might make thee know the certainty of the words of truth; that thou mightest answer the words of truth to them that send unto thee?*

CAMDEN

Cultural Origin: Anglo-Saxon
Inherent Meaning: *FROM THE WINDING VALLEY*
Spiritual Connotation: *DIVINE SPARK*
Supporting Scripture: *John 8:32*
> *And ye shall know the truth, and the truth shall make you free.*

CAMERON

Cultural Origin: Gaelic
Inherent Meaning: *INDIVIDUALITY*
Spiritual Connotation: *SPIRITUAL POTENTIAL*
Supporting Scripture: *Psalm 36:9*
> *For with thee is the fountain of life: in thy light shall we see light.*

CAMILLE, Camilla, Mille

Cultural Origin: Latin
Inherent Meaning: *DEVOTED ONE*
Spiritual Connotation: *DEDICATED*
Supporting Scripture: *1 John 4:7,8*
> *Beloved, let us love one another: for love is of God; and every one that loveth is born of God, and knoweth God. He that loveth not knoweth not God; for God is love.*

CANDACE, Candice, Candy

Cultural Origin: Greek
Inherent Meaning: *UNBLEMISHED, GLITTERING*
Spiritual Connotation: *BRIGHT, SHINING ONE*
Supporting Scripture: *Isaiah 62:3*
> *Thou shalt also be a crown of glory in the hand of the Lord, and a royal diadem in the hand of thy God.*

CANUTE, Knut, Knute

Cultural Origin: Old Norse
Inherent Meaning: *STEADFAST, RESOLUTE*
Spiritual Connotation: *TRUSTWORTHY*
Supporting Scripture: *2 Timothy 2:22*
> *...follow righteousness, faith, charity, peace, with them that call on the Lord out of a pure heart.*

CARA

Cultural Origin: Latin
Inherent Meaning: *DEAR, BELOVED*
Spiritual Connotation: *LOYAL HEART*
Supporting Scripture: *Matthew 25:34*
> *...Come, ye blessed of my Father, inherit the kingdom prepared for you from the foundation of the world.*

CARISSA

Cultural Origin: Latin
Inherent Meaning: *INGENIOUS*
Spiritual Connotation: *CREATIVE INDUSTRY*
Supporting Scripture: *Hebrews 13:20,21*
   Now the God of peace. . .make you perfect in every good work to do his will. . .

CARITA

Cultural Origin: Latin
Inherent Meaning: *BELOVED*
Spiritual Connotation: *DIVINELY BLESSED*
Supporting Scripture: *Isaiah 42:6*
   I the Lord have called thee in righteousness, and will hold thine hand, and will keep thee. . .

CARL, Karl

Cultural Origin: Teutonic
Inherent Meaning: *TILLER OF THE SOIL*
Spiritual Connotation: *STRONG IN SPIRIT*
Supporting Scripture: *Isaiah 40:31*
   But they that wait upon the Lord shall renew their strength; they shall mount up with wings as eagles; they shall run, and not be weary; and they shall walk, and not faint.

CARLA

Cultural Origin: Latin
Inherent Meaning: *ENDEARING ONE*
Spiritual Connotation: *FULL OF GRACE*
Supporting Scripture: *Isaiah 61:10*
   I will greatly rejoice in the Lord, my soul shall be joyful in my God. . .he hath covered me with the robe of righteousness. . .

CARLIN

Cultural Origin: Gaelic
Inherent Meaning: *CHAMPION*
Spiritual Connotation: *VICTORIOUS SPIRIT*
Supporting Scripture: *Isaiah 42:6*
> *I the Lord have called thee in righteousness, and will hold thine hand, and will keep thee.*

CARLISLE

Cultural Origin: Anglo-Saxon
Inherent Meaning: *BRAVE AND STRONG*
Spiritual Connotation: *DEFENDER OF TRUTH*
Supporting Scripture: *Proverbs 4:7*
> *Wisdom is the principal thing; therefore get wisdom: and with all thy getting get understanding.*

CARLOS

Cultural Origin: Latin
Inherent Meaning: *NOBLE SPIRIT*
Spiritual Connotation: *SPIRITUAL DISCERNMENT*
Supporting Scripture: *Matthew 25:34*
> *. . . Come, ye blessed of my Father, inherit the kingdom prepared for you from the foundation of the world.*

CARLOTTA

Cultural Origin: Teutonic
Inherent Meaning: *WOMANLY ONE*
Spiritual Connotation: *GODLY HEROINE*
Supporting Scripture: *Isaiah 26:3*
> *Thou wilt keep him in perfect peace, whose mind is stayed on thee: because he trusteth in thee.*

CARLTON, Carleton

Cultural Origin: Anglo-Saxon
Inherent Meaning: *GATHERING PLACE FOR FARMERS*
Spiritual Connotation: *INDUSTRIOUS*
Supporting Scripture: *Ezekiel 34:27*
> *And the tree of the field shall yield her fruit, and the earth shall yield her increase, and they shall be safe in their land...*

CARMEN

Cultural Origin: Latin
Inherent Meaning: *VOICE LIKE SOFT MUSIC*
Spiritual Connotation: *JOYFUL ONE*
Supporting Scripture: *Psalm 149:1*
> *Praise ye the Lord. Sing unto the Lord a new song, and his praise in the congregation of saints.*

CARMICHAEL

Cultural Origin: Latin
Inherent Meaning: *ABUNDANT POWER*
Spiritual Connotation: *PROSPEROUS*
Supporting Scripture: *Philippians 4:13*
> *I can do all things through Christ which strengtheneth me.*

CAROL, Carole

Cultural Origin: Latin
Inherent Meaning: *PERCEPTIVE*
Spiritual Connotation: *DISCERNING SPIRIT*
Supporting Scripture: *John 15:11*
> *These things have I spoken unto you, that my joy might remain in you, and that your joy might be full.*

CAROLINE, Carolyn, Carrie

Cultural Origin: Latin
Inherent Meaning: *NOBLE, WOMANLY*
Spiritual Connotation: *DIVINE CONSCIOUSNESS*
Supporting Scripture: *Psalm 150:4-6*
> *Praise him with timbrel and dance: praise him with stringed instruments and organs. . . .Let every thing that hath breath praise the Lord.*

CARRICK

Cultural Origin: Gaelic
Inherent Meaning: *DWELLER SURROUNDED BY SEA*
Spiritual Connotation: *SPIRITUAL UNDERSTANDING*
Supporting Scripture: *Jeremiah 31:33*
> *But this shall be the covenant that I will make. . . .I will put my law in their inward parts, and write it in their hearts; and will be their God, and they shall be my people.*

CARRIE, see Caroline (fem.), Cary (masc.)

CARROL

Cultural Origin: Gaelic
Inherent Meaning: *CHAMPION*
Spiritual Connotation: *PROTECTOR, DEFENDER*
Supporting Scripture: *Psalm 119:27*
> *Make me to understand the way of thy precepts: so shall I talk of thy wondrous works.*

CARSON

Cultural Origin: Anglo-Saxon
Inherent Meaning: *DILIGENT ONE*
Spiritual Connotation: *LOYAL, FAITHFUL*
Supporting Scripture: *John 15:16*
> *Ye have not chosen me, but I have chosen you, and ordained you, that ye should go and bring forth fruit, and that your fruit should remain: that whatsoever ye shall ask of the Father in my name, he may give it you.*

CARTER

Cultural Origin: Gaelic
Inherent Meaning: *HUMBLE SERVANT*
Spiritual Connotation: *SPIRITUAL DIMENSION*
Supporting Scripture: *Revelation 3:8*
> *. . . behold, I have set before thee an open door, and no man can shut it. . .*

CARY, Carrie

Cultural Origin: Latin
Inherent Meaning: *BELOVED ONE*
Spiritual Connotation: *DIVINE SPARK*
Supporting Scripture: *Luke 6:38*
> *Give, and it shall be given unto you; good measure, pressed down, and shaken together, and running over. . .*

CASEY, see Cacey

CASPER

Cultural Origin: Persian
Inherent Meaning: *TREASURE-MASTER*
Spiritual Connotation: *WATCHFUL ONE*
Supporting Scripture: *Jeremiah 31:16*
> *. . . thy work shall be rewarded, saith the Lord.*

CASSANDRA, Cassie, Sandy

Cultural Origin: Greek
Inherent Meaning: *FULL OF WISDOM*
Spiritual Connotation: *HELPER TO ALL*
Supporting Scripture: *Hebrews 13:1,2*
> *Let brotherly love continue. Be not forgetful to entertain strangers: for thereby some have entertained angels unawares.*

CATHERINE, Cathie, Cathy

Cultural Origin: Greek
Inherent Meaning: *PURE ONE*
Spiritual Connotation: *ESTEEMED ONE*
Supporting Scripture: *Psalm 119:15,16*
> *I will meditate in thy precepts, and have respect unto thy ways. I will delight myself in thy statutes: I will not forget thy word.*

CAVANAUGH

Cultural Origin: Celtic
Inherent Meaning: *COMELY, CARING*
Spiritual Connotation: *A MERRY HEART*
Supporting Scripture: *Ecclesiastes 3:1-4*
> *To every thing there is a season, and a time to every purpose under the heaven. . .a time to weep, and a time to laugh; a time to mourn, and a time to dance. . .*

CECIL, Cecile

Cultural Origin: Latin
Inherent Meaning: *INSIGHTFUL*
Spiritual Connotation: *HUMBLE IN SPIRIT*
Supporting Scripture: *Ephesians 5:8*
> *For ye were sometimes darkness, but now are ye light in the Lord: walk as children of light.*

CECILIA, Celia, Cece

Cultural Origin: Latin
Inherent Meaning: *INSIGHTFUL*
Spiritual Connotation: *HUMBLE IN SPIRIT*
Supporting Scripture: *1 Corinthians 2:14*
> *But the natural man receiveth not the things of the Spirit of God: for they are foolishness unto him: neither can he know them, because they are spiritually discerned.*

CEDRIC

Cultural Origin: Anglo-Saxon
Inherent Meaning: *BATTLE CHIEFTAIN*
Spiritual Connotation: *COURAGEOUS DEFENDER*
Supporting Scripture: *Galatians 6:4*
> *But let every man prove his own work, and then shall he have rejoicing in himself. . .*

CELESTE, Celestine

Cultural Origin: Latin
Inherent Meaning: *HEAVENLY*
Spiritual Connotation: *BLESSED ONE*
Supporting Scripture: *Ephesians 1:3*
> *Blessed be the God and Father of our Lord Jesus Christ, who hath blessed us with all spiritual blessings. . .*

CELINA

Cultural Origin: Latin
Inherent Meaning: *FULL OF WISDOM*
Spiritual Connotation: *VICTORIOUS HEART*
Supporting Scripture: *1 John 5:4*
> *For whatsoever is born of God overcometh the world: and this is the victory that overcometh the world, even our faith.*

CHADWICK, Chad

Cultural Origin: Anglo-Saxon
Inherent Meaning: *GOD'S WARRIOR*
Spiritual Connotation: *BRAVE, NOBLE*
Supporting Scripture: *Revelation 22:1,2*
> *And he shewed me a pure river of water of life, clear as crystal. . .and on either side of the river, was there the tree of life. . .*

CHALMERS

Cultural Origin: Celtic
Inherent Meaning: *PROSPEROUS PROTECTOR*
Spiritual Connotation: *NOBLE, JUST*
Supporting Scripture: *Isaiah 55:11*

So shall my word be that goeth forth out of my mouth: it shall not return unto me void, but it shall accomplish that which I please, and it shall prosper in the thing whereto I sent it.

CHANDLER

Cultural Origin: Anglo-Saxon
Inherent Meaning: *CANDLE-MAKER*
Spiritual Connotation: *LIGHT BEARER*
Supporting Scripture: *John 8:12*

. . . he that followeth me shall not walk in darkness, but shall have the light of life.

CHARITY

Cultural Origin: Latin
Inherent Meaning: *BENEVOLENT*
Spiritual Connotation: *CHARITABLE, COMPASSIONATE*
Supporting Scripture: *Psalm 23:6*

Surely goodness and mercy shall follow me all the days of my life: and I will dwell in the house of the Lord for ever.

CHARLEEN, Charlene

Cultural Origin: Teutonic
Inherent Meaning: *STRONG, VALIANT*
Spiritual Connotation: *COURAGEOUS HEART*
Supporting Scripture: *1 Chronicles 28:20*

. . . the Lord God, even my God, will be with thee; he will not fail thee, nor forsake thee, until thou hast finished all the work . . .

CHARLES

Cultural Origin: Teutonic
Inherent Meaning: *STRONG, MANLY*
Spiritual Connotation: *VALIANT ONE*
Supporting Scripture: *Joshua 1:9*
> *. . . Be strong and of a good courage; be not afraid,*
> *neither be thou dismayed: for the Lord thy God is with*
> *thee whithersoever thou goest.*

CHARLOTTE, Sheryl, Sherre, Sherry, Sheri

Cultural Origin: Latin
Inherent Meaning: *WOMANLY, NOBLE*
Spiritual Connotation: *SPIRITUAL UNDERSTANDING*
Supporting Scripture: *Zephaniah 3:17*
> *The Lord thy God in the midst of thee is mighty; he will*
> *save, he will rejoice over thee with joy. . .*

CHARMAIN

Cultural Origin: Latin
Inherent Meaning: *HAPPY SINGER*
Spiritual Connotation: *JOYFUL ONE*
Supporting Scripture: *Jeremiah 15:16*
> *Thy words were found, and I did eat them; and thy word*
> *was unto me the joy and rejoicing of mine heart: for I am*
> *called by thy name, O Lord God of hosts.*

CHAUNCEY

Cultural Origin: Anglo-Saxon
Inherent Meaning: *CHANCELLOR*
Spiritual Connotation: *WORTHY OF TRUST*
Supporting Scripture: *Romans 8:16*
> *The Spirit itself beareth witness with our spirit, that we*
> *are the children of God.*

CHERISE

Cultural Origin: Latin
Inherent Meaning: *CHERISHED ONE*
Spiritual Connotation: *BELOVED, BLESSING*
Supporting Scripture: *Psalm 62:5*
> *My soul, wait thou only upon God; for my expectation is from him.*

CHERYL, Cheri, Cher

Cultural Origin: Latin
Inherent Meaning: *FILLED WITH GRACE AND BEAUTY*
Spiritual Connotation: *BELOVED ONE*
Supporting Scripture: *Zephaniah 3:17*
> *The Lord thy God in the midst of thee is mighty; he will save, he will rejoice over thee with joy. . .*

CHESTER

Cultural Origin: Anglo-Saxon
Inherent Meaning: *COURAGEOUS DEFENDER*
Spiritual Connotation: *VALIANT SPIRIT*
Supporting Scripture: *Psalm 31:3*
> *For thou art my rock and my fortress; therefore for thy name's sake lead me, and guide me.*

CHLOE

Cultural Origin: Greek
Inherent Meaning: *VIBRANT*
Spiritual Connotation: *FILLED WITH LIFE*
Supporting Scripture: *Psalm 105:4*
> *Seek the Lord, and his strength: seek his face evermore.*

CHRISTIAN

Cultural Origin: Greek
Inherent Meaning: *BELIEVER IN CHRIST*
Spiritual Connotation: *WORSHIP IN SPIRIT AND IN*
TRUTH
Supporting Scripture: *Psalm 86:12*
I will praise thee, O Lord my God, with all my heart: and
I will glorify thy name for evermore.

CHRISTINA, Christine, Crissy, Tina

Cultural Origin: Latin
Inherent Meaning: *DEVOTED FOLLOWER OF CHRIST*
Spiritual Connotation: *CHRIST AWARENESS*
Supporting Scripture: *2 Corinthians 4:6*
For God, who commanded the light to shine out of
darkness, hath shined in our hearts, to give the light of the
knowledge of the glory of God.

CHRISTOPHER, Chris

Cultural Origin: Greek
Inherent Meaning: *VIGILANT IN CHRIST*
Spiritual Connotation: *WATCHFUL ONE*
Supporting Scripture: *Isaiah 42:9*
Behold, the former things are come to pass, and new
things do I declare: before they spring forth I tell you of
them.

CLAIRE, see Clara

CLARA, Claire, Clarette, Clarinda, Clarita

Cultural Origin: *Latin*
Inherent Meaning: *BRILLIANT, ILLUSTRIOUS*
Spiritual Connotation: *SHINING CHRIST LIGHT*
Supporting Scripture: *Psalm 36:9*
> *For with thee is the fountain of life: in thy light shall we see light.*

CLARENCE

Cultural Origin: *Latin*
Inherent Meaning: *FAMOUS ONE*
Spiritual Connotation: *FULL OF HONOR*
Supporting Scripture: *Philippians 4:8*
> *Finally, brethren, whatsoever things are true, whatsoever things are honest, whatsoever things are just, whatsoever things are pure, whatsoever things are lovely, whatsoever things are of good report; if there be any virtue, and if there be any praise, think on these things.*

CLARICE, Clarissa

Cultural Origin: *Latin*
Inherent Meaning: *BRILLIANT ONE*
Spiritual Connotation: *WISE DISCERNER*
Supporting Scripture: *Hosea 14:9*
> *. . .for the ways of the Lord are right, and the just shall walk in them.*

CLARK

Cultural Origin: *Latin*
Inherent Meaning: *LEARNED ONE*
Spiritual Connotation: *ENLIGHTENED SPIRIT*
Supporting Scripture: *James 3:17*
> *But the wisdom that is from above is first pure, then peaceable, gentle, and easy to be entreated, full of mercy and good fruits, without partiality, and without hypocrisy.*

CLAUDE, Claudio, Claudius

Cultural Origin: Latin
Inherent Meaning: *OVERCOMER*
Spiritual Connotation: *STRONG IN VICTORY*
Supporting Scripture: *Isaiah 40:29*
> *He giveth power to the faint; and to them that have no might he increaseth strength.*

CLAUDIA, Claudette

Cultural Origin: Latin
Inherent Meaning: *OVERCOMER*
Spiritual Connotation: *STRONG IN VICTORY*
Supporting Scripture: *1 Peter 5:7*
> *Casting all your care upon him; for he careth for you.*

CLAY

Cultural Origin: Anglo-Saxon
Inherent Meaning: *MALLEABLE EARTH*
Spiritual Connotation: *ONE OF GREAT ADAPTABILITY*
Supporting Scripture: *2 Corinthians 4:7*
> *But we have this treasure in earthen vessels, that the excellency of the power may be of God, and not of us.*

CLAYBORNE

Cultural Origin: Anglo-Saxon
Inherent Meaning: *FROM THE CLAY BROOK*
Spiritual Connotation: *MOLDED UNDER GOD'S DIRECTION*
Supporting Scripture: *Jeremiah 18:6*
> *. . . Behold, as the clay is in the potter's hand, so are ye in mine hand. . .*

CLAYTON

Cultural Origin: Anglo-Saxon
Inherent Meaning: *FROM THE CLAY ESTATE*
Spiritual Connotation: *MOLDED UNDER GOD'S DIRECTION*
Supporting Scripture: *Isaiah 64:8*
> *. . .we are the clay, and thou our potter; and we all are the work of thy hand.*

CLEMENT

Cultural Origin: Latin
Inherent Meaning: *GENTLE, KIND*
Spiritual Connotation: *BENEVOLENT ONE*
Supporting Scripture: *Leviticus 19:34*
> *But the stranger that dwelleth with you shall be unto you as one born among you, and thou shalt love him as thyself. . .*

CLEMENTINE, Clementia

Cultural Origin: Latin
Inherent Meaning: *CALM, MERCIFUL*
Spiritual Connotation: *CHARITABLE*
Supporting Scripture: *John 13:34*
> *A new commandment I give unto you, That ye love one another; as I have loved you, that ye also love one another.*

CLEO

Cultural Origin: Greek
Inherent Meaning: *ONE OF EMINENCE*
Spiritual Connotation: *UNDERSTANDING SPIRIT*
Supporting Scripture: *Psalm 36:9*
> *For with thee is the fountain of life: in thy light shall we see light.*

CLEVE, see Clive

CLIFFORD, Cliff

Cultural Origin: Anglo-Saxon
Inherent Meaning: *FROM THE HEIGHTS*
Spiritual Connotation: *VIGILANT SPIRIT*
Supporting Scripture: *Psalm 18:32,33*
> *It is God that girdeth me with strength, and maketh my way perfect. He maketh my feet like hinds' feet, and setteth me upon my high places.*

CLIFTON

Cultural Origin: Anglo-Saxon
Inherent Meaning: *FROM THE CLIFF ESTATE*
Spiritual Connotation: *PROSPEROUS ONE*
Supporting Scripture: *Psalm 91:11*
> *For he shall give his angels charge over thee, to keep thee in all thy ways.*

CLINTON, Clint

Cultural Origin: Anglo-Saxon
Inherent Meaning: *FROM THE HEADLAND ESTATE*
Spiritual Connotation: *HONORABLE, JUST*
Supporting Scripture: *Malachi 3:10*
> *. . . And prove me now herewith, saith the Lord of hosts, if I will not open you the windows of heaven, and pour you out a blessing, that there shall not be room enough to receive it.*

CLIVE

Cultural Origin: Anglo-Saxon
Inherent Meaning: *UPON THE CLIFF*
Spiritual Connotation: *STRONG, ENDURING*
Supporting Scripture: *Jeremiah 33:11*
> *. . . Praise the Lord of hosts: for the Lord is good; for his mercy endureth for ever. . .*

CLOTILDA

Cultural Origin: Teutonic
Inherent Meaning: *FAMOUS BATTLE MAID*
Spiritual Connotation: *CONQUERING SPIRIT*
Supporting Scripture: *Isaiah 26:3*
> *Thou wilt keep him in perfect peace, whose mind is stayed on thee: because he trusteth in thee.*

CLYDE

Cultural Origin: Celtic
Inherent Meaning: *WARM, LOVING SPIRIT*
Spiritual Connotation: *TEACHABLE SPIRIT*
Supporting Scripture: *Luke 12:32*
> *Fear not. . . for it is your Father's good pleasure to give you the kingdom.*

CLYTIE

Cultural Origin: Greek
Inherent Meaning: *SPLENDID, BEAUTIFUL ONE*
Spiritual Connotation: *GRACIOUS GIFT*
Supporting Scripture: *Psalm 118:28*
> *Thou art my God, and I will praise thee: thou art my God, I will exalt thee.*

COLBERT

Cultural Origin: Anglo-Saxon
Inherent Meaning: *BRILLIANT SEAFARER*
Spiritual Connotation: *ANCHORED IN GOD*
Supporting Scripture: *Psalm 46:1*
> *God is our refuge and strength, a very present help in trouble.*

COLBY

Cultural Origin: Anglo-Saxon
Inherent Meaning: *MAN OF HONOR*
Spiritual Connotation: *TRUSTWORTHY*
Supporting Scripture: *1 Peter 5:7*
> *Casting all your care upon him; for he careth for you.*

COLE, see Nicholas

COLETTE

Cultural Origin: Greek-French
Inherent Meaning: *VICTORIOUS ONE*
Spiritual Connotation: *LOYAL AND BRAVE*
Supporting Scripture: *Galatians 5:22*
> *But the fruit of the Spirit is love, joy, peace, longsuffering, gentleness, goodness, faith. . . against such there is no law.*

COLIN, Colan

Cultural Origin: Gaelic
Inherent Meaning: *VICTORIOUS ONE*
Spiritual Connotation: *STEADFAST IN TRUTH*
Supporting Scripture: *1 Corinthians 2:9*
> *. . . Eye hath not seen, nor ear heard, neither have entered into the heart of man, the things which God hath prepared for them that love him.*

COLLEEN, Collene

Cultural Origin: Gaelic
Inherent Meaning: *MAIDEN*
Spiritual Connotation: *EXCELLENT VIRTUE*
Supporting Scripture: *Psalm 107:9*
For he satisfieth the longing soul, and filleth the hungry soul with goodness.

COLLIER

Cultural Origin: Anglo-Saxon
Inherent Meaning: *MERCHANT*
Spiritual Connotation: *PRICELESS ONE*
Supporting Scripture: *2 Samuel 22:33*
God is my strength and power: and he maketh my way perfect.

COLTER

Cultural Origin: Anglo-Saxon
Inherent Meaning: *LOVER OF ANIMALS*
Spiritual Connotation: *INDUSTRIOUS*
Supporting Scripture: *Romans 13:10*
Love worketh no ill to his neighbour: therefore love is the fulfilling of the law.

COLTON

Cultural Origin: Anglo-Saxon
Inherent Meaning: *FROM THE ESTATE*
Spiritual Connotation: *RESOURCEFUL ONE*
Supporting Scripture: *Romans 5:5*
And hope maketh not ashamed; because the love of God is shed abroad in our hearts by the Holy Ghost which is given unto us.

CONAN

Cultural Origin: Celtic
Inherent Meaning: *INTELLIGENCE, WISDOM*
Spiritual Connotation: *SPIRITUAL DISCERNMENT*
Supporting Scripture: *Exodus 31:3*
> *And I have filled him with the spirit of God, in wisdom, and in understanding, and in knowledge, and in all manner of workmanship.*

CONLAN

Cultural Origin: Gaelic
Inherent Meaning: *HERO*
Spiritual Connotation: *ESTEEMED ONE*
Supporting Scripture: *Proverbs 2:6*
> *For the Lord giveth wisdom: out of his mouth cometh knowledge and understanding.*

CONRAD

Cultural Origin: Teutonic
Inherent Meaning: *BOLD COUNSELOR*
Spiritual Connotation: *DISCERNER OF EXCELLENCE*
Supporting Scripture: *Colossians 3:15,16*
> *And let the peace of God rule in your hearts. . . . Let the word of Christ dwell in you richly in all wisdom. . .*

CONROY

Cultural Origin: Gaelic
Inherent Meaning: *WISE ONE*
Spiritual Connotation: *STRONG LEADER*
Supporting Scripture: *Ecclesiastes 2:26*
> *For God giveth to a man that is good in his sight wisdom, and knowledge, and joy.*

CONSTANCE, Connie

Cultural Origin: Latin
Inherent Meaning: *STEADFAST, FIRM*
Spiritual Connotation: *CONSECRATED*
Supporting Scripture: *Romans 8:16*
   *The Spirit itself beareth witness with our spirit, that we
   are the children of God.*

CONSUELA

Cultural Origin: Latin
Inherent Meaning: *WONDERFUL FRIEND*
Spiritual Connotation: *COMPASSIONATE*
Supporting Scripture: *Proverbs 27:9*
   *Ointment and perfume rejoice the heart: so doth the
   sweetness of a man's friend by hearty counsel.*

CORA, Corrie

Cultural Origin: Greek
Inherent Meaning: *THE MAIDEN*
Spiritual Connotation: *VICTORIOUS HEART*
Supporting Scripture: *1 John 4:16*
   *And we have known and believed the love that God hath
   to us. God is love; and he that dwelleth in love dwelleth in
   God, and God in him.*

CORDELL

Cultural Origin: Latin
Inherent Meaning: *CRAFTSMAN, INDUSTRIOUS*
Spiritual Connotation: *CREATIVE SPIRIT*
Supporting Scripture: *1 Chronicles 29:12*
   *. . . and in thine hand is power and might; and in thine
   hand it is to make great, and to give strength unto all.*

CORDELIA, Cordie, Delia, Della

Cultural Origin: Celtic
Inherent Meaning: *JEWEL OF THE SEA*
Spiritual Connotation: *PRECIOUS ONE*
Supporting Scripture: *Psalm 139:17*
> *How precious also are thy thoughts unto me, O God! how great is the sum of them!*

CORETTA

Cultural Origin: Latin
Inherent Meaning: *SEEKER OF TRUTH*
Spiritual Connotation: *DEVOTED ONE*
Supporting Scripture: *Psalm 25:5*
> *Lead me in thy truth, and teach me: for thou art the God of my salvation; on thee do I wait all the day.*

COREY, Cory

Cultural Origin: Gaelic
Inherent Meaning: *DWELLER BY THE WATERS*
Spiritual Connotation: *PROSPEROUS ONE*
Supporting Scripture: *Psalm 1:3*
> *And he shall be like a tree planted by the rivers of water, that bringeth forth his fruit in his season; his leaf also shall not wither; and whatsoever he doeth shall prosper.*

CORINNE, Corrine, Corine

Cultural Origin: Greek
Inherent Meaning: *FAIR MAIDEN*
Spiritual Connotation: *PERCEPTIVE ONE*
Supporting Scripture: *Job 22:28*
> *Thou shalt also decree a thing, and it shall be established unto thee: and the light shall shine upon thy ways.*

CORISSA

Cultural Origin: Latin-Greek
Inherent Meaning: *MOST MAIDENLY*
Spiritual Connotation: *DEDICATED SPIRIT*
Supporting Scripture: *Psalm 145:3*
> *Great is the Lord, and greatly to be praised; and his greatness is unsearchable.*

CORLISS

Cultural Origin: Anglo-Saxon
Inherent Meaning: *CHEERFUL, GOOD-HEARTED*
Spiritual Connotation: *HARMONIOUS SPIRIT*
Supporting Scripture: *2 Corinthians 3:18*
> *But we all, with open face beholding as in a glass the glory of the Lord, are changed into the same image from glory to glory, even as by the Spirit of the Lord.*

CORNELIA

Cultural Origin: Latin
Inherent Meaning: *WOMANLY, NOBLE*
Spiritual Connotation: *LOYAL*
Supporting Scripture: *Matthew 5:16*
> *Let your light so shine before men, that they may see your good works, and glorify your Father which is in heaven.*

CORNELIUS

Cultural Origin: Latin
Inherent Meaning: *MANLY, STRONG*
Spiritual Connotation: *NOBLE IN STRENGTH*
Supporting Scripture: *2 Peter 3:13*
> *Nevertheless we, according to his promise, look for new heavens and a new earth, wherein dwelleth righteousness.*

CORWIN

Cultural Origin: Latin
Inherent Meaning: *FRIEND OF THE HEART*
Spiritual Connotation: *SUPPORTING SPIRIT*
Supporting Scripture: *2 Corinthians 4:6*
For God, who commanded the light to shine out of darkness, hath shined in our hearts, to give the light of the knowledge of the glory of God in the face of Jesus Christ.

COSETTE

Cultural Origin: Latin-French
Inherent Meaning: *VICTORIOUS ONE*
Spiritual Connotation: *CONFIDENT SPIRIT*
Supporting Scripture: *Isaiah 42:16*
. . . I will make darkness light before them, and crooked things straight. These things will I do unto them, and not forsake them.

COURTLAND

Cultural Origin: Anglo-Saxon
Inherent Meaning: *DWELLER AT THE FARMSTEAD*
Spiritual Connotation: *DWELLER IN TRUTH*
Supporting Scripture: *Psalm 19:14*
Let the words of my mouth, and the meditation of my heart, be acceptable in thy sight, O Lord, my strength, and my redeemer.

COURTNEY

Cultural Origin: Latin
Inherent Meaning: *DWELLER IN THE COURT LAND*
Spiritual Connotation: *SURROUNDED BY GOD'S LOVE*
Supporting Scripture: *1 John 4:16*
. . . God is love; and he that dwelleth in love dwelleth in God, and God in him.

COWAN

Cultural Origin: Gaelic
Inherent Meaning: *DWELLER ON THE HILLSIDE*
Spiritual Connotation: *GENEROUS SPIRIT*
Supporting Scripture: *Luke 6:38*
> *Give, and it shall be given unto you; good measure,*
> *pressed down, and shaken together, and running over, shall*
> *men give into your bosom. For with the same measure*
> *that ye mete withal it shall be measured to you again.*

COYLE

Cultural Origin: Gaelic
Inherent Meaning: *COURAGEOUS FOLLOWER*
Spiritual Connotation: *GOD'S WARRIOR*
Supporting Scripture: *1 Timothy 6:12*
> *Fight the good fight of faith, lay hold on eternal life,*
> *whereunto thou art also called...*

CRAIG

Cultural Origin: Gaelic
Inherent Meaning: *DWELLER ON THE CRAG*
Spiritual Connotation: *STRONG, ENDURING SPIRIT*
Supporting Scripture: *Matthew 7:24*
> *Therefore whosoever heareth these sayings of mine, and*
> *doeth them, I will liken him unto a wise man, which built*
> *his house upon a rock.*

CRANDELL

Cultural Origin: Anglo-Saxon
Inherent Meaning: *VALLEY DWELLER*
Spiritual Connotation: *SPIRITUALLY AWAKENED*
Supporting Scripture: *2 Corinthians 3:17*
> *Now the Lord is that Spirit: and where the Spirit of the*
> *Lord is, there is liberty.*

CREIGHTON

Cultural Origin: Anglo-Saxon
Inherent Meaning: *DWELLER AT THE CREEK*
Spiritual Connotation: *HUMBLE SPIRIT*
Supporting Scripture: *3 John 2*
  Beloved, I wish above all things that thou mayest prosper and be in health, even as thy soul prospereth.

CRYSTAL

Cultural Origin: Latin
Inherent Meaning: *CLEAR, SPARKLING*
Spiritual Connotation: *PURE ONE*
Supporting Scripture: *Psalm 119:73*
  Thy hands have made me and fashioned me: give me understanding, that I may learn thy commandments.

CULLEN, Cullin

Cultural Origin: Gaelic
Inherent Meaning: *PLEASING, GOOD TO LOOK UPON*
Spiritual Connotation: *DIVINE SPARK*
Supporting Scripture: *Romans 13:10*
  Love worketh no ill to his neighbour: therefore love is the fulfilling of the law.

CURTIS

Cultural Origin: Latin-French
Inherent Meaning: *COURTEOUS ONE*
Spiritual Connotation: *JUST, HONORABLE*
Supporting Scripture: *Zechariah 7:9*
  Thus speaketh the Lord of hosts, saying, Execute true judgment, and shew mercy and compassions every man to his brother.

CUTHBERT

Cultural Origin: Anglo-Saxon
Inherent Meaning: *FAMOUS, BRILLIANT*
Spiritual Connotation: *ESTEEMED ONE*
Supporting Scripture: *Hebrews 10:16*
This is the covenant that I will make with them after those days, saith the Lord, I will put my laws into their hearts, and in their minds will I write them.

CYNTHIA, Cindy

Cultural Origin: Greek
Inherent Meaning: *THE MOON*
Spiritual Connotation: *CELESTIAL LIGHT*
Supporting Scripture: *Psalm 27:1*
The Lord is my light and my salvation; whom shall I fear?

CYRIL, Cyrille, Cyrill

Cultural Origin: Greek
Inherent Meaning: *LORDLY ONE*
Spiritual Connotation: *GREAT SPIRITUAL POTENTIAL*
Supporting Scripture: *Malachi 3:10*
. . . prove me now herewith, saith the Lord of hosts, if I will not open you the windows of heaven, and pour you out a blessing, that there shall not be room enough to receive it.

CYRUS

Cultural Origin: Persian
Inherent Meaning: *THE SUN*
Spiritual Connotation: *SPIRITUAL ENLIGHTENMENT*
Supporting Scripture: *Zechariah 7:9*
Thus speaketh the Lord of hosts . . . Execute true judgment, and shew mercy and compassions every man to his brother.

D

DACEY

Cultural Origin: Gaelic
Inherent Meaning: *HONORED ONE*
Spiritual Connotation: *DIGNITY OF CHARACTER*
Supporting Scripture: *Hebrews 2:7*
Thou madest him a little lower than the angels; thou crownedst him with glory and honour, and didst set him over the works of thy hands.

DACIA

Cultural Origin: Greek
Inherent Meaning: *HONORED ONE*
Spiritual Connotation: *DIVINE PERSPECTIVE*
Supporting Scripture: *Isaiah 65:17*
For, behold, I create new heavens and a new earth: and the former shall not be remembered, nor come into mind.

DAGAN

Cultural Origin: Hebrew
Inherent Meaning: *REASONING FACULTY*
Spiritual Connotation: *ABUNDANT INCREASE*
Supporting Scripture: *Ecclesiastes 7:19*
Wisdom strengtheneth the wise more than ten mighty men which are in the city.

DAGMAR

Cultural Origin: Teutonic
Inherent Meaning: *GLORIOUS DAY*
Spiritual Connotation: *UNDERSTANDING SPIRIT*
Supporting Scripture: *Romans 8:2*
For the law of the Spirit of life in Christ Jesus hath made me free from the law of sin and death.

DAISY

Cultural Origin: Anglo-Saxon
Inherent Meaning: *QUICKENED SPIRIT*
Spiritual Connotation: *SPIRITUAL CHAMPION*
Supporting Scripture: *Ephesians 1:4*
   According as he hath chosen us in him before the founda-
   tion of the world, that we should be holy and without
   blame before him in love.

DALBERT, Delbert

Cultural Origin: Anglo-Saxon
Inherent Meaning: *PROUD, BRILLIANT ONE*
Spiritual Connotation: *ABUNDANT LIFE*
Supporting Scripture: *Deuteronomy 5:33*
   Ye shall walk in all the ways which the Lord your God
   hath commanded you, that ye may live, and that it may be
   well with you.

DALE

Cultural Origin: Anglo-Saxon
Inherent Meaning: *DWELLER IN THE VALLEY*
Spiritual Connotation: *PEACEFUL ONE*
Supporting Scripture: *Psalm 85:11,12*
   Truth shall spring out of the earth; and righteousness shall
   look down from heaven. Yea, the Lord shall give that
   which is good; and our land shall yield her increase.

DALLAS

Cultural Origin: Gaelic
Inherent Meaning: *GENTLE*
Spiritual Connotation: *TENDERHEARTED*
Supporting Scripture: *Deuteronomy 15:10*
   . . . the Lord thy God shall bless thee in all thy works, and
   in all that thou puttest thine hand unto.

DALTON

Cultural Origin: Anglo-Saxon
Inherent Meaning: *CALM, SERENE*
Spiritual Connotation: *FILLED WITH PEACE*
Supporting Scripture: *Luke 6:45*
> *A good man out of the good treasure of his heart bringeth forth that which is good...*

DALY

Cultural Origin: Gaelic
Inherent Meaning: *COUNSELOR*
Spiritual Connotation: *BRINGER OF LIGHT*
Supporting Scripture: *Isaiah 52:7*
> *How beautiful upon the mountains are the feet of him that bringeth good tidings, that publisheth peace; that bringeth good tidings of good...*

DAMITA

Cultural Origin: Latin
Inherent Meaning: *NOBLE LADY*
Spiritual Connotation: *GRACIOUS SPIRIT*
Supporting Scripture: *Psalm 97:11*
> *Light is sown for the righteous, and gladness for the upright in heart.*

DAMON, Damian

Cultural Origin: Greek
Inherent Meaning: *CONSTANT ONE*
Spiritual Connotation: *WALKS WITH GOD*
Supporting Scripture: *Zechariah 8:16*
> *These are the things that ye shall do; Speak ye every man the truth to his neighbour; execute the judgment of truth and peace...*

DANA, Danna

Cultural Origin: Scandinavian
Inherent Meaning: *MAN FROM DENMARK*
Spiritual Connotation: *BRINGER OF PEACE*
Supporting Scripture: *Deuteronomy 16:20*
> *That which is altogether just shalt thou follow, that thou
> mayest live, and inherit the land which the Lord thy God
> giveth thee.*

DANIEL, Dan

Cultural Origin: Hebrew
Inherent Meaning: *SPIRITUAL JUDGMENT*
Spiritual Connotation: *INTEGRITY, SPIRITUAL
                                    DISCERNMENT*
Supporting Scripture: *Psalm 119:142*
> *Thy righteousness is an everlasting righteousness, and thy
> law is the truth.*

DANIELLE, Daniela

Cultural Origin: Hebrew
Inherent Meaning: *SPIRITUAL JUDGMENT*
Spiritual Connotation: *SPIRITUAL DISCERNMENT*
Supporting Scripture: *Psalm 119:112*
> *I have inclined mine heart to perform thy statutes alway,
> even unto the end.*

DAPHNE

Cultural Origin: Greek
Inherent Meaning: *HONOR, FAME*
Spiritual Connotation: *VICTORIOUS ONE*
Supporting Scripture: *1 Kings 3:12*
> *. . . lo, I have given thee a wise and an understanding
> heart; so that there was none like thee before thee, neither
> after thee shall anyone arise like unto thee.*

DARA

Cultural Origin: Hebrew
Inherent Meaning: *PEARL OF WISDOM*
Spiritual Connotation: *BEARER OF TRUE*
                    SPIRITUAL UNDERSTANDING
Supporting Scripture: *Matthew 25:40*
> *. . . Verily I say unto you, Inasmuch as ye have done it un-
> to one of the least of these my brethren, ye have done it
> unto me.*

DARBY

Cultural Origin: Gaelic
Inherent Meaning: *FREEDOM*
Spiritual Connotation: *FREE SPIRIT*
Supporting Scripture: *Exodus 31:3*
> *And I have filled him with the spirit of God, in wisdom,
> and in understanding, and in knowledge, and in all man-
> ner of workmanship.*

DARCIE

Cultural Origin: Latin
Inherent Meaning: *BRAVE, STRONG*
Spiritual Connotation: *ESTABLISHED IN PEACE*
Supporting Scripture: *Psalm 5:11*
> *But let all those that put their trust in thee rejoice: let
> them ever shout for joy, because thou defendest them: let
> them also that love thy name be joyful in thee.*

DARCY

Cultural Origin: Latin
Inherent Meaning: *STRONG, ENDURING*
Spiritual Connotation: *WISE DISCERNER*
Supporting Scripture: *Psalm 25:10*
> *All the paths of the Lord are mercy and truth unto such as
> keep his covenant and his testimonies.*

DARIA

Cultural Origin: Greek
Inherent Meaning: *WEALTHY, QUEENLY*
Spiritual Connotation: *GRACIOUS SPIRIT*
Supporting Scripture: *Psalm 9:1*
> *I will praise thee, O Lord, with my whole heart; I will shew forth all thy marvellous works.*

DARRIN, see Darren

DARIUS

Cultural Origin: Greek
Inherent Meaning: *PROSPEROUS ONE*
Spiritual Connotation: *DWELLING IN SPIRIT*
Supporting Scripture: *Isaiah 42:6*
> *I the Lord have called thee in righteousness, and will hold thine hand, and will keep thee...*

DARLENE, Darleen, Darla

Cultural Origin: Latin
Inherent Meaning: *BELOVED ONE*
Spiritual Connotation: *BLESSED ONE*
Supporting Scripture: *Proverbs 4:23*
> *Keep thy heart with all diligence; for out of it are the issues of life.*

DARRELL, Daryl

Cultural Origin: Anglo-Saxon
Inherent Meaning: *BELOVED ONE*
Spiritual Connotation: *BLESSED ONE*
Supporting Scripture: *Psalm 18:32*
> *It is God that girdeth me with strength, and maketh my way perfect.*

DARREN, Daren, Darin

Cultural Origin: Gaelic
Inherent Meaning: *GREAT ONE*
Spiritual Connotation: *ESTEEMED ONE*
Supporting Scripture: *2 Corinthians 9:8*
> *God is able to make all grace abound toward you; that ye, always having all sufficiency in all things, may abound to every good work.*

DARRICK, Derrick, Derek

Cultural Origin: Teutonic
Inherent Meaning: *RULER*
Spiritual Connotation: *IN DIVINE ORDER*
Supporting Scripture: *Ecclesiastes 2:26*
> *. . . God giveth to a man that is good in his sight wisdom, and knowledge, and joy. . .*

DAVID

Cultural Origin: Hebrew
Inherent Meaning: *CHRIST LOVE*
Spiritual Connotation: *FOLLOWING THE SPIRIT
OF CHRIST*
Supporting Scripture: *1 John 4:16*
> *. . . God is love; and he that dwelleth in love dwelleth in God, and God in him.*

DAVIDA

Cultural Origin: Hebrew
Inherent Meaning: *CHRIST LOVE*
Spiritual Connotation: *DIVINE LOVE MANIFESTED*
Supporting Scripture: *Ephesians 3:17-19*
> *. . .ye, being rooted and grounded in love. . .might be filled with all the fulness of God.*

DAVINA

Cultural Origin: Scandinavian
Inherent Meaning: *BRIGHTNESS*
Spiritual Connotation: *ENLIGHTENED ONE*
Supporting Scripture: *Zechariah 4:6*
> *... Not by might, nor by power, but by my spirit, saith the Lord of hosts.*

DAVIS

Cultural Origin: Anglo-Saxon
Inherent Meaning: *HONORABLE ONE*
Spiritual Connotation: *BELOVED ONE*
Supporting Scripture: *1 John 4:8*
> *He that loveth not knoweth not God; for God is love.*

DAWN

Cultural Origin: Anglo-Saxon
Inherent Meaning: *BEGINNING ANEW*
Spiritual Connotation: *JOY AND PRAISE*
Supporting Scripture: *Psalm 113:2,3*
> *Blessed be the name of the Lord from this time forth and for evermore. From the rising of the sun unto the going down of the same the Lord's name is to be praised.*

DEAN

Cultural Origin: Anglo-Saxon
Inherent Meaning: *ABUNDANT SUPPLIER*
Spiritual Connotation: *PROSPEROUS ONE*
Supporting Scripture: *Matthew 12:35*
> *A good man out of the good treasure of the heart bringeth forth good things...*

DEANNA, Deana

Cultural Origin: Latin
Inherent Meaning: *DIVINE ONE*
Spiritual Connotation: *BRIGHTNESS OF THE NEW DAY*
Supporting Scripture: *Psalm 143:8*
> *Cause me to hear thy lovingkindness in the morning; for in thee do I trust: cause me to know the way wherein I should walk; for I lift up my soul unto thee.*

DEBORAH, Debora, Debra, Debby

Cultural Origin: Hebrew
Inherent Meaning: *LEADERSHIP*
Spiritual Connotation: *SPIRITUAL DISCRIMINATION*
Supporting Scripture: *Isaiah 65:17*
> *For, behold, I create new heavens and a new earth: and the former shall not be remembered, nor come into mind.*

DEIRDRE Deidre

Cultural Origin: Gaelic
Inherent Meaning: *WANDERER, SEEKER*
Spiritual Connotation: *SEEKER OF TRUTH AND RIGHTEOUSNESS*
Supporting Scripture: *Psalm 119:35*
> *Make me to go in the path of thy commandments; for therein do I delight.*

DELBERT, Dalbert

Cultural Origin: Anglo-Saxon
Inherent Meaning: *NEW DAY BRIGHT*
Spiritual Connotation: *MESSENGER OF LIGHT*
Supporting Scripture: *1 John 3:11*
> *For this is the message that ye heard from the beginning, that we should love one another.*

DELICIA, Delia

Cultural Origin: Latin
Inherent Meaning: *DELIGHTFUL ONE*
Spiritual Connotation: *JOYOUS SPIRIT*
Supporting Scripture: *Psalm 16:11*
> . . . in thy presence is fulness of joy; at thy right hand
> there are pleasures for evermore.

DELLA

Cultural Origin: Teutonic
Inherent Meaning: *NOBLE MAIDEN*
Spiritual Connotation: *EXCELLENT VIRTUE*
Supporting Scripture: *1 Corinthians 13:13*
> And now abideth faith, hope, charity [love], these three;
> but the greatest of these is charity.

DELORES, Dolores, Dee

Cultural Origin: Latin
Inherent Meaning: *SYMPATHY FOR THE SORROWING*
Spiritual Connotation: *COMPASSIONATE ONE*
Supporting Scripture: *Psalm 121:1*
> I will lift up mine eyes unto the hills, from whence cometh
> my help.

DELPHINE

Cultural Origin: Greek
Inherent Meaning: *FILLED WITH GRACE*
Spiritual Connotation: *ANCHORED IN SPIRIT*
Supporting Scripture: *Colossians 3:3*
> . . . your life is hid with Christ in God.

DEMETRIA

Cultural Origin: Greek
Inherent Meaning: *ABUNDANT, PLENTIFUL*
Spiritual Connotation: *FRUITFUL*
Supporting Scripture: *John 10:10*
> *. . . I am come that they might have life, and that they might have it more abundantly.*

DEMETRIUS

Cultural Origin: Greek
Inherent Meaning: *ABUNDANT, PLENTIFUL*
Spiritual Connotation: *FRUITFUL INCREASE*
Supporting Scripture: *Luke 11:10*
> *For every one that asketh receiveth; and he that seeketh findeth; and to him that knocketh it shall be opened.*

DEMPSEY

Cultural Origin: Gaelic
Inherent Meaning: *PROUD ONE*
Spiritual Connotation: *HIGHLY HONORABLE*
Supporting Scripture: *Galatians 5:1*
> *Stand fast therefore in the liberty wherewith Christ hath made us free. . .*

DENA

Cultural Origin: Anglo-Saxon
Inherent Meaning: *FROM THE VALLEY*
Spiritual Connotation: *PEACEFUL, HAPPY ONE*
Supporting Scripture: *Isaiah 2:5*
> *. . . come ye, and let us walk in the light of the Lord.*

DENISE, Denice, Deni

Cultural Origin: Latin
Inherent Meaning: *FAVORED ONE*
Spiritual Connotation: *HAPPY SPIRIT*
Supporting Scripture: *Isaiah 65:17*
> *For, behold, I create new heavens and a new earth: and the former shall not be remembered, nor come into mind.*

DENNIS, Denis, Denny

Cultural Origin: Greek
Inherent Meaning: *HANDSOME, HAPPY MAN*
Spiritual Connotation: *A GLAD HEART*
Supporting Scripture: *Isaiah 55:11*
> *So shall my word be that goeth forth out of my mouth: it shall not return unto me void, but it shall accomplish that which I please, and it shall prosper in the thing whereto I sent it.*

DENTON

Cultural Origin: Anglo-Saxon
Inherent Meaning: *FROM THE VALLEY ESTATE*
Spiritual Connotation: *TRUSTING SPIRIT*
Supporting Scripture: *Romans 8:28*
> *And we know that all things work together for good to them that love God, to them who are the called according to his purpose.*

DEREK, Derrick, see Darrick

DERWARD, Durward

Cultural Origin: Anglo-Saxon
Inherent Meaning: *GUARDIAN*
Spiritual Connotation: *DIVINE SPARK*
Supporting Scripture: *Psalm 37:3*
   Trust in the Lord, and do good; so shalt thou dwell in the land, and verily thou shalt be fed.

DERWIN

Cultural Origin: Anglo-Saxon
Inherent Meaning: *BELOVED FRIEND*
Spiritual Connotation: *COMPANION, SUPPORTER*
Supporting Scripture: *Proverbs 16:1*
   The preparations of the heart in man, and the answer of the tongue, is from the Lord.

DESIREE, Desirae

Cultural Origin: Latin
Inherent Meaning: *SEARCHED FOR*
Spiritual Connotation: *FAIR, GRACIOUS ONE*
Supporting Scripture: *Isaiah 55:12*
   For ye shall go out with joy, and be led forth with peace...

DESMONA

Cultural Origin: Greek
Inherent Meaning: *SEEKER IN TRUTH*
Spiritual Connotation: *CARING ONE*
Supporting Scripture: *Ezekiel 18:31, 32*
   ...and make you a new heart and a new spirit...saith the Lord God: wherefore turn yourselves, and live ye.

DESMOND

Cultural Origin: Gaelic
Inherent Meaning: *YOUTHFUL ONE*
Spiritual Connotation: *REFRESHING ONE*
Supporting Scripture: *Ecclesiastes 3:17*
> *. . .for there is a time there for every purpose and for every work.*

DEVA

Cultural Origin: Sanskrit
Inherent Meaning: *BLESSED ONE*
Spiritual Connotation: *GRACIOUS, DIVINE*
Supporting Scripture: *Psalm 8:1*
> *O Lord our Lord, how excellent is thy name in all the earth!*

DEVIN

Cultural Origin: Gaelic
Inherent Meaning: *POET, SAVANT*
Spiritual Connotation: *SEEKER OF WISDOM*
Supporting Scripture: *Hebrews 13:16*
> *But to do good and to communicate forget not: for with such sacrifices God is well pleased.*

DEWEY

Cultural Origin: Gaelic
Inherent Meaning: *BELOVED ONE*
Spiritual Connotation: *ONE OF GOOD JUDGMENT*
Supporting Scripture: *3 John 2*
> *Beloved, I wish above all things that thou mayest prosper and be in health, even as thy soul prospereth.*

DEXTER

Cultural Origin: Latin
Inherent Meaning: *SKILLED IN WORKMANSHIP*
Spiritual Connotation: *INDUSTRIOUS ONE*
Supporting Scripture: *John 3:35*
   The Father loveth the Son, and hath given all things into his hand.

DIANA, Dyana, Dianne

Cultural Origin: Latin
Inherent Meaning: *DIVINE ONE*
Spiritual Connotation: *GLORIOUS ONE*
Supporting Scripture: *Psalm 40:5*
   Many, O Lord my God, are thy wonderful works which thou hast done, and thy thoughts to which are to us-ward: they cannot be reckoned up . . . they are more than can be numbered.

DILLON

Cultural Origin: Gaelic
Inherent Meaning: *FAITHFUL ONE*
Spiritual Connotation: *STEADFAST IN CHRIST*
Supporting Scripture: *1 John 3:18*
   . . . let us not love in word, neither in tongue; but in deed and in truth.

DINAH

Cultural Origin: Hebrew
Inherent Meaning: *INTUITIVE JUDGMENT*
Spiritual Connotation: *SPIRITUAL DISCERNMENT*
Supporting Scripture: *1 John 4:16*
   . . . God is love; and he that dwelleth in love dwelleth in God, and God in him.

DIRK

Cultural Origin: Teutonic
Inherent Meaning: *RULER OF PEOPLE*
Spiritual Connotation: *PERCEPTIVE LEADERSHIP*
Supporting Scripture: *Psalm 91:2*
> *I will say of the Lord, He is my refuge and my fortress:*
> *my God; in him will I trust.*

DIXIE

Cultural Origin: Latin
Inherent Meaning: *A BLESSING*
Spiritual Connotation: *BLESSED ONE*
Supporting Scripture: *2 Corinthians 4:15*
> *For all things are for your sakes, that the abundant grace*
> *might through the thanksgiving of many redound to the*
> *glory of God.*

DIXON

Cultural Origin: Anglo-Saxon
Inherent Meaning: *YOUTHFUL ONE*
Spiritual Connotation: *RESOLUTE COURAGE*
Supporting Scripture: *Psalm 92:4*
> *For thou, Lord, hast made me glad through thy work: I*
> *will triumph in the works of thy hands.*

DOLAN

Cultural Origin: Gaelic
Inherent Meaning: *ADVENTURER*
Spiritual Connotation: *FULL OF LIFE*
Supporting Scripture: *Psalm 145:10*
> *All thy works shall praise thee, O Lord; and thy saints*
> *shall bless thee.*

DOLORES, see Deloras

DOMINIC

Cultural Origin: Latin
Inherent Meaning: *BORN ON SUNDAY*
Spiritual Connotation: *VICTORIOUS SPIRIT*
Supporting Scripture: *Psalm 119:105*
> *Thy word is a lamp unto my feet, and a light unto my path.*

DOMINIQUE, Dominica

Cultural Origin: Latin
Inherent Meaning: *BELONGING TO GOD*
Spiritual Connotation: *CONSECRATED ONE*
Supporting Scripture: *Isaiah 58:11*
> *And the Lord shall guide thee continually . . . and thou shalt be like a watered garden, and like a spring of water, whose waters fail not.*

DONALD, Don

Cultural Origin: Celtic
Inherent Meaning: *WORLD-MIGHTY*
Spiritual Connotation: *COURAGEOUS HEART*
Supporting Scripture: *James 2:22*
> *Seest thou how faith wrought with his works, and by works was faith made perfect?*

DONALDA

Cultural Origin: Gaelic
Inherent Meaning: *WORLD RULER*
Spiritual Connotation: *COURAGEOUS SPIRIT*
Supporting Scripture: *Philippians 4:19*
> *But my God shall supply all your need according to his riches in glory by Christ Jesus.*

DONATA

Cultural Origin: Latin
Inherent Meaning: *GIFT OF GOD*
Spiritual Connotation: *BELOVED ONE*
Supporting Scripture: *Psalm 25:5*
> *Lead me in thy truth, and teach me: for thou art the God of my salvation; on thee do I wait all the day.*

DONATO

Cultural Origin: Latin
Inherent Meaning: *MAN OF GOD*
Spiritual Connotation: *DEVOTED HEART*
Supporting Scripture: *Proverbs 16:24*
> *Pleasant words are as an honeycomb, sweet to the soul, and health to the bones.*

DONNA

Cultural Origin: Latin
Inherent Meaning: *CULTURED, REFINED*
Spiritual Connotation: *GRACIOUS, HONORABLE*
Supporting Scripture: *Matthew 4:4*
> *. . . It is written, Man shall not live by bread alone, but by every word that proceedeth out of the mouth of God.*

DONOVAN

Cultural Origin: Gaelic
Inherent Meaning: *DELIGHTFUL ONE*
Spiritual Connotation: *REFRESHING SPIRIT*
Supporting Scripture: *Colossians 3:10*
> *And have put on the new man, which is renewed in knowledge after the image of him that created him.*

DORA

Cultural Origin: Greek
Inherent Meaning: *FAVORED ONE*
Spiritual Connotation: *GIFT OF GOD*
Supporting Scripture: *Isaiah 33:6*
> *And wisdom and knowledge shall be the stability of thy times, and strength of salvation: the fear of the Lord is his treasure.*

DORCAS

Cultural Origin: Greek
Inherent Meaning: *FILLED WITH GRACE*
Spiritual Connotation: *SOURCE OF JOY*
Supporting Scripture: *Psalm 37:18*
> *The Lord knoweth the days of the upright: and their inheritance shall be for ever.*

DORE, Doreen

Cultural Origin: Latin
Inherent Meaning: *GOLDEN ONE*
Spiritual Connotation: *PEERLESS SPIRIT*
Supporting Scripture: *Psalm 100:4,5*
> *Enter into his gates with thanksgiving, and into his courts with praise: be thankful unto him, and bless his name. For the Lord is good; his mercy is everlasting; and his truth endureth to all generations.*

DORIAN

Cultural Origin: Greek
Inherent Meaning: *GIFT*
Spiritual Connotation: *GOD'S GRACIOUS GIFT*
Supporting Scripture: *1 John 3:2*
> *Beloved, now are we the sons of God, and it doth not yet appear what we shall be: but we know that, when he shall appear, we shall be like him...*

DORINDA

Cultural Origin: Greek
Inherent Meaning: *BEAUTIFUL GIFT*
Spiritual Connotation: *GOD'S GRACIOUS GIFT*
Supporting Scripture: *Psalm 19:7*
> *The law of the Lord is perfect, converting the soul: the testimony of the Lord is sure, making wise the simple.*

DORIS, Dorice, Doria, Dorris

Cultural Origin: Greek
Inherent Meaning: *BOUNTIFUL*
Spiritual Connotation: *LOVING, GENEROUS*
Supporting Scripture: *Isaiah 33:6*
> *And wisdom and knowledge shall be the stability of thy times, and strength of salvation: the fear of the Lord is his treasure.*

DOROTHEA, Dorothy, Dorotea

Cultural Origin: Greek-Latin
Inherent Meaning: *GIFT OF GOD*
Spiritual Connotation: *BLESSED ONE*
Supporting Scripture: *Isaiah 52:7*
> *How beautiful upon the mountains are the feet of him that bringeth good tidings, that publisheth peace...*

DOUGLAS, Douglass, Doug

Cultural Origin: Gaelic
Inherent Meaning: *ADVENTUROUS SPIRIT*
Spiritual Connotation: *GOD'S MESSENGER*
Supporting Scripture: *1 Corinthians 2:7*
> *But we speak the wisdom of God in a mystery, even the hidden wisdom, which God ordained before the world unto our glory.*

DOYLE

Cultural Origin: Gaelic
Inherent Meaning: *COMING FROM AFAR*
Spiritual Connotation: *DIVINE INTELLIGENCE DIRECTS*
Supporting Scripture: *2 Corinthians 3:17*
Now the Lord is that Spirit: and where the Spirit of the Lord is, there is liberty.

DREW

Cultural Origin: Celtic
Inherent Meaning: *WISE ONE*
Spiritual Connotation: *ESTEEMED ONE*
Supporting Scripture: *Romans 12:10*
Be kindly affectioned one to another with brotherly love; in honour preferring one another.

DRUCILLA, Drusilla

Cultural Origin: Latin
Inherent Meaning: *STRONG ONE*
Spiritual Connotation: *STRONG IN SPIRIT*
Supporting Scripture: *John 15:7*
If ye abide in me, and my words abide in you, ye shall ask what ye will, and it shall be done unto you.

DRYDEN

Cultural Origin: Anglo-Saxon
Inherent Meaning: *FRIENDLY SPIRIT*
Spiritual Connotation: *CHEERFUL HEART*
Supporting Scripture: *Proverbs 3:5,6*
Trust in the Lord with all thine heart; and lean not unto thine own understanding. In all thy ways acknowledge him, and he shall direct thy paths.

DUANA

Cultural Origin: Gaelic
Inherent Meaning: *CHEERFUL SONG*
Spiritual Connotation: *HARMONIOUS SPIRIT*
Supporting Scripture: *Psalm 92:4*
> *For thou, Lord, hast made me glad through thy work: I will triumph in the works of thy hands.*

DUANE, see Dwayne

DUDLEY

Cultural Origin: Anglo-Saxon
Inherent Meaning: *GOOD-HEARTED*
Spiritual Connotation: *STEADFAST IN CHRIST*
Supporting Scripture: *John 8:32*
> *And ye shall know the truth, and the truth shall make you free.*

DULCINEA, Dulciana, Dulcie

Cultural Origin: Latin
Inherent Meaning: *SWEET ONE*
Spiritual Connotation: *DELIGHTS IN GOD'S GRACE*
Supporting Scripture: *Psalm 37:5*
> *Commit thy way unto the Lord; trust also in him; and he shall bring it to pass.*

DUNCAN

Cultural Origin: Gaelic
Inherent Meaning: *STEADFAST*
Spiritual Connotation: *STRONG IN FAITH*
Supporting Scripture: *Romans 10:8*
> *. . . The word is nigh thee, even in thy mouth, and in thy heart: that is, the word of faith . . .*

DUNSTAN, Dustin

Cultural Origin: Anglo-Saxon
Inherent Meaning: *INDUSTRIOUS*
Spiritual Connotation: *VICTORIOUS SPIRIT*
Supporting Scripture: *John 5:26*
　　For as the Father hath life in himself; so hath he given to the Son to have life in himself.

DURANT, Durand

Cultural Origin: Latin
Inherent Meaning: *ENDURING ONE*
Spiritual Connotation: *EXCELLENT VIRTUE*
Supporting Scripture: *Psalm 34:7*
　　The angel of the Lord encampeth round about them that fear him, and delivereth them.

DURWARD, see Derward

DUSTIN, see DUNSTAN

DWAYNE, Duane

Cultural Origin: Gaelic
Inherent Meaning: *BLESSED ONE*
Spiritual Connotation: *TRANSFORMED HEART*
Supporting Scripture: *Job 22:28*
　　Thou shalt also decree a thing, and it shall be established unto thee: and the light shall shine upon thy ways.

DWIGHT

Cultural Origin: Teutonic
Inherent Meaning: *FAIR*
Spiritual Connotation: *DILIGENT LEADER*
Supporting Scripture: *Psalm 91:1*
   *He that dwelleth in the secret place of the most High shall
   abide under the shadow of the Almighty.*

DYLAN

Cultural Origin: Gaelic
Inherent Meaning: *WAYFARER FROM THE SEA*
Spiritual Connotation: *RESOLUTE COURAGE*
Supporting Scripture: *Deuteronomy 20:4*
   *For the Lord your God is he that goeth with you, to fight
   for you against your enemies, to save you.*

E

EARL, Errol

Cultural Origin: Anglo-Saxon
Inherent Meaning: *NOBLE*
Spiritual Connotation: *DEVOUT*
Supporting Scripture: *Genesis 1:26*
And God said, Let us make man in our image, after our likeness: and let them have dominion...

EARLENE, Earline, Erline

Cultural Origin: Anglo-Saxon
Inherent Meaning: *NOBLE WOMAN*
Spiritual Connotation: *SPIRITUAL INSIGHT*
Supporting Scripture: *2 Corinthians 6:2*
...behold, now is the accepted time; behold, now is the day of salvation.

EARTHA, Ertha

Cultural Origin: Anglo-Saxon
Inherent Meaning: *STRENGTH OF CHARACTER*
Spiritual Connotation: *DIVINE SPARK*
Supporting Scripture: *Romans 8:37*
Nay, in all these things we are more than conquerors through him that loved us.

EDA

Cultural Origin: Anglo-Saxon
Inherent Meaning: *LOYAL, STEADFAST*
Spiritual Connotation: *PROSPEROUS*
Supporting Scripture: *Psalm 77:14*
Thou art the God that doest wonders: thou hast declared thy strength among the people.

EDGAR

Cultural Origin: Anglo-Saxon
Inherent Meaning: *LOYAL, BRAVE*
Spiritual Connotation: *FAITH IN VICTORIOUS
SPIRIT WITHIN*
Supporting Scripture: *1 Corinthians 12:4,5,6*
*Now there are diversities of gifts, but the same Spirit. And
there are differences of administrations, but the same
Lord. And there are diversities of operations, but it is the
same God which worketh all in all.*

EDITH, Edythe

Cultural Origin: Teutonic
Inherent Meaning: *RICH GIFTS OF HAPPINESS*
Spiritual Connotation: *PROSPERITY AND JOY*
Supporting Scripture: *Matthew 28:20*
*. . . lo, I am with you alway, even unto the end of the
world.*

EDMOND, Edmund

Cultural Origin: Anglo-Saxon
Inherent Meaning: *BLESSED PEACE*
Spiritual Connotation: *PROSPEROUS PROTECTOR*
Supporting Scripture: *John 14:27*
*Peace I leave with you, my peace I give unto you: not as
the world giveth, give I unto you. Let not your heart be
troubled, neither let it be afraid.*

EDNA, Edena

Cultural Origin: Hebrew
Inherent Meaning: *VIGOROUS ONE*
Spiritual Connotation: *FILLED WITH LIFE*
Supporting Scripture: *Psalm 13:6*
*I will sing unto the Lord, because he hath dealt bountiful-
ly with me.*

EDREA

Cultural Origin: Anglo-Saxon
Inherent Meaning: *PROSPEROUS, POWERFUL*
Spiritual Connotation: *TRIUMPHANT SPIRIT*
Supporting Scripture: *John 15:7*
> *If ye abide in me, and my words abide in you, ye shall ask what ye will, and it shall be done unto you.*

EDSEL

Cultural Origin: Anglo-Saxon
Inherent Meaning: *PROSPEROUS ONE*
Spiritual Connotation: *ONE WITH POWER*
Supporting Scripture: *Zechariah 7:9*
> *. . . Execute true judgment, and shew mercy and compassions every man to his brother.*

EDWARD

Cultural Origin: Teutonic
Inherent Meaning: *APPOINTED TO SERVE*
Spiritual Connotation: *GUARDIAN OF HAPPINESS*
Supporting Scripture: *John 14:13*
> *And whatsoever ye shall ask in my name, that will I do, that the Father may be glorified in the Son.*

EDWIN

Cultural Origin: Anglo-Saxon
Inherent Meaning: *HAPPY CONQUEROR*
Spiritual Connotation: *VICTORIOUS ONE*
Supporting Scripture: *John 17:10*
> *And all mine are thine, and thine are mine; and I am glorified in them.*

EDWINA

Cultural Origin: Anglo-Saxon
Inherent Meaning: *PROSPEROUS FRIEND*
Spiritual Connotation: *ABUNDANTLY BLESSED*
Supporting Scripture: *John 15:4*
> *Abide in me, and I in you. As the branch cannot bear fruit of itself, except it abide in the vine; no more can ye, except ye abide in me.*

EFFIE, Euphemia

Cultural Origin: Greek
Inherent Meaning: *WELL SPOKEN OF*
Spiritual Connotation: *BELOVED, HONORED*
Supporting Scripture: *Matthew 5:16*
> *Let your light so shine before men, that they may see your good works, and glorify your Father which is in heaven.*

EGAN

Cultural Origin: Gaelic
Inherent Meaning: *ARDENT, FIERY ONE*
Spiritual Connotation: *FILLED WITH ZEAL*
Supporting Scripture: *1 Corinthians 2:16*
> *For who hath known the mind of the Lord, that he may instruct him? But we have the mind of Christ.*

EGBERT

Cultural Origin: Teutonic
Inherent Meaning: *BRIGHT, FAMOUS*
Spiritual Connotation: *DISTINGUISHED, HONORED*
Supporting Scripture: *Psalm 91:11*
> *For he shall give his angels charge over thee, to keep thee in all thy ways.*

EILEEN, Eilene

Cultural Origin: Gaelic
Inherent Meaning: *LIGHT, BRIGHT*
Spiritual Connotation: *GLORIOUS ONE*
Supporting Scripture: *Psalm 23:6*
   Surely goodness and mercy shall follow me all the days of my life: and I will dwell in the house of the Lord for ever.

EINER

Cultural Origin: Old Norse
Inherent Meaning: *WARRIOR, LEADER*
Spiritual Connotation: *TRUSTWORTHY*
Supporting Scripture: *Isaiah 41:13*
   For I the Lord thy God will hold thy right hand, saying unto thee, Fear not; I will help thee.

ELAINE

Cultural Origin: Teutonic
Inherent Meaning: *BRILLIANT ONE*
Spiritual Connotation: *ADMIRABLE ONE*
Supporting Scripture: *Psalm 84:11*
   . . . the Lord will give grace and glory: no good thing will he withhold from them that walk uprightly.

ELDEN

Cultural Origin: Anglo-Saxon
Inherent Meaning: *GIFT OF WISDOM*
Spiritual Connotation: *KNOWLEDGE AND GOOD JUDGMENT*
Supporting Scripture: *Hebrews 13:20,21*
   Now the God of peace. . . make you perfect in every good work to do his will, working in you that which is well-pleasing in his sight. . .

ELDON

Cultural Origin: Anglo-Saxon
Inherent Meaning: *FROM THE HOLY HILL*
Spiritual Connotation: *ENLIGHTENED ONE*
Supporting Scripture: *Isaiah 30:29*
> *Ye shall have a song, as in the night when a holy solemnity is kept; and gladness of heart...*

ELEANOR, Eleanore, Elinor

Cultural Origin: Latin
Inherent Meaning: *BRIGHT AS THE SUN*
Spiritual Connotation: *KINDHEARTED, WARM*
Supporting Scripture: *John 14:11*
> *Believe me that I am in the Father, and the Father in me: or else believe me for the very works' sake.*

ELENA

Cultural Origin: Greek
Inherent Meaning: *RADIANT ONE*
Spiritual Connotation: *ILLUMINATED ONE*
Supporting Scripture: *Psalm 16:11*
> *Thou wilt shew me the path of life: in thy presence is fulness of joy; at thy right hand there are pleasures for evermore.*

ELFRIDA, see Alfreda

ELI, Ely

Cultural Origin: Hebrew
Inherent Meaning: *THE HIGHEST*
Spiritual Connotation: *EMINENT ONE*
Supporting Scripture: *Psalm 50:14,15*
> *Offer unto God thanksgiving; and pay thy vows unto the most High: and call upon me in the day of trouble: I will deliver thee, and thou shalt glorify me.*

ELIAS, Ellis

Cultural Origin: Hebrew
Inherent Meaning: *GOD IS THE LORD*
Spiritual Connotation: *EXALTED ONE*
Supporting Scripture: *Luke 12:11,12*
> *. . . take ye no thought how or what thing ye shall answer, or what ye shall say: for the Holy Ghost shall teach you in the same hour what ye ought to say.*

ELIJAH

Cultural Origin: Hebrew
Inherent Meaning: *JEHOVAH IS GOD*
Spiritual Connotation: *SPIRITUAL CHAMPION*
Supporting Scripture: *Proverbs 3:6*
> *In all thy ways acknowledge him, and he shall direct thy paths.*

ELISA, Elise, see Elizabeth

ELIZABETH, Elisabeth, Beth, Betty

Cultural Origin: Hebrew
Inherent Meaning: *OATH OF GOD*
Spiritual Connotation: *CONSECRATED ONE*
Supporting Scripture: *Romans 6:23*
> *. . . the gift of God is eternal life through Jesus Christ our Lord.*

ELLA

Cultural Origin: Teutonic
Inherent Meaning: *FAIR, BEAUTIFUL*
Spiritual Connotation: *SUSTAINING FRIEND*
Supporting Scripture: *Psalm 91:11*
> *For he shall give his angels charge over thee, to keep thee in all thy ways.*

ELLARD

Cultural Origin: Anglo-Saxon
Inherent Meaning: *BRAVE, NOBLE*
Spiritual Connotation: *FEARLESS ONE*
Supporting Scripture: *Colossians 3:2,3*
> *Set your affection on things above, not on things on the earth. . . your life is hid with Christ in God.*

ELLEN

Cultural Origin: Teutonic
Inherent Meaning: *BRIGHT ONE*
Spiritual Connotation: *SHINING LIGHT*
Supporting Scripture: *Psalm 139:9,10*
> *If I take the wings of the morning, and dwell in the uttermost parts of the sea; even there shall thy hand lead me, and thy right hand shall hold me.*

ELLERY

Cultural Origin: Anglo-Saxon
Inherent Meaning: *INDEPENDENT*
Spiritual Connotation: *CREATIVE WORKER*
Supporting Scripture: *Psalm 31:23*
> *O love the Lord, all ye his saints: for the Lord preserveth the faithful, and plentifully rewardeth the proud doer.*

ELLIOT

Cultural Origin: Hebrew-French
Inherent Meaning: *JEHOVAH IS MY GOD*
Spiritual Connotation: *CONSECRATED*
Supporting Scripture: *Isaiah 51:16*
> *And I have put my words in thy mouth, and I have covered thee in the shadow of mine hand. . .*

ELLIS, see Elias

ELMER

Cultural Origin: Anglo-Saxon
Inherent Meaning: *NOBLE, FAMOUS*
Spiritual Connotation: *HONORED ONE*
Supporting Scripture: *Psalm 36:7*
> *How excellent is thy lovingkindness, O God! therefore the children of men put their trust under the shadow of thy wings.*

ELMO

Cultural Origin: Latin
Inherent Meaning: *VIGILANT*
Spiritual Connotation: *WISE PROTECTOR*
Supporting Scripture: *John 14:1*
> *Let not your heart be troubled: ye believe in God, believe also in me.*

ELOISE

Cultural Origin: Teutonic
Inherent Meaning: *HOLY ONE*
Spiritual Connotation: *EXALTED ONE*
Supporting Scripture: *Psalm 121:5*
> *The Lord is thy keeper: the Lord is thy shade upon thy right hand.*

ELROY

Cultural Origin: Latin
Inherent Meaning: *MAJESTIC*
Spiritual Connotation: *NOBLE ONE*
Supporting Scripture: *Proverbs 17:24*
> *Wisdom is before him that hath understanding.*

ELSIE

Cultural Origin: Anglo-Saxon
Inherent Meaning: *NOBLE*
Spiritual Connotation: *PRICELESS FRIEND*
Supporting Scripture: *Psalm 89:1*
> *I will sing of the mercies of the Lord for ever: with my mouth will I make known thy faithfulness to all generations.*

ELSWORTH

Cultural Origin: Anglo-Saxon
Inherent Meaning: *NOBLE ONE*
Spiritual Connotation: *DIVINELY PERCEPTIVE*
Supporting Scripture: *Psalm 40:4*
> *Blessed is that man that maketh the Lord his trust, and respecteth not the proud, nor such as turn aside to lies.*

ELVA

Cultural Origin: Anglo-Saxon
Inherent Meaning: *DELICATE, SENSITIVE*
Spiritual Connotation: *ENLIGHTENED ONE*
Supporting Scripture: *Psalm 54:2*
> *Hear my prayer, O God; give ear to the words of my mouth.*

ELVINA

Cultural Origin: Anglo-Saxon
Inherent Meaning: *SUPPORTING FRIEND*
Spiritual Connotation: *PERCEPTIVE UNDERSTANDING*
Supporting Scripture: *Psalm 36:9*
> *For with thee is the fountain of life: in thy light shall we see light.*

ELVIRA

Cultural Origin: Latin
Inherent Meaning: *FAIR ONE*
Spiritual Connotation: *NOBLE SPIRIT*
Supporting Scripture: *James 3:17*
> *But the wisdom that is from above is first pure, then peaceable, gentle, and easy to be entreated, full of mercy and good fruits, without partiality, and without hypocrisy.*

ELVIS

Cultural Origin: Old Norse
Inherent Meaning: *ALL WISE*
Spiritual Connotation: *BELOVED ONE*
Supporting Scripture: *Isaiah 58:8*
> *Then shall thy light break forth as the morning, and thine health shall spring forth speedily; and thy righteousness shall go before thee; the glory of the Lord shall be thy rearward.*

ELWOOD

Cultural Origin: Anglo-Saxon
Inherent Meaning: *FROM THE FOREST*
Spiritual Connotation: *TRUTHFUL ONE*
Supporting Scripture: *Luke 12:31*
> *But rather seek ye the kingdom of God; and all these things shall be added unto you.*

ELYSIA

Cultural Origin: Latin
Inherent Meaning: *SWEETLY BLISSFUL*
Spiritual Connotation: *BLESSEDNESS*
Supporting Scripture: *Matthew 17:20*
> *. . . If ye have faith as a grain of mustard seed, ye shall say unto this mountain, Remove hence to yonder place; and it shall remove; and nothing shall be impossible unto you.*

EMANUEL, Emmanuel, Immanuel

Cultural Origin: Hebrew
Inherent Meaning: *GOD WITH US*
Spiritual Connotation: *FOLLOWER OF CHRIST*
Supporting Scripture: *Romans 6:23*
    . . . the gift of God is eternal life through Jesus Christ our Lord.

EMANUELA

Cultural Origin: Hebrew
Inherent Meaning: *GOD WITH US*
Spiritual Connotation: *FOLLOWER OF CHRIST*
Supporting Scripture: *Romans 6:23*
    . . . the gift of God is eternal life through Jesus Christ our Lord.

EMERY, Emory

Cultural Origin: Teutonic
Inherent Meaning: *MIGHTY*
Spiritual Connotation: *AUTHORITY UNDER GOD*
Supporting Scripture: *Matthew 12:34,35*
    . . . for out of the abundance of the heart the mouth speaketh. A good man out of the good treasure of the heart bringeth forth good things.

EMIL

Cultural Origin: Teutonic-Gothic
Inherent Meaning: *INDUSTRIOUS ONE*
Spiritual Connotation: *DILIGENT WORKER*
Supporting Scripture: *Jeremiah 29:12,13*
    Then shall ye call upon me, and ye shall go and pray unto me, and I will hearken unto you. And ye shall seek me, and find me, when ye shall search for me with all your heart.

EMILY, Emile

Cultural Origin: Teutonic-Gothic
Inherent Meaning: *INDUSTRIOUS ONE*
Spiritual Connotation: *DILIGENT WORKER*
Supporting Scripture: *Matthew 5:16*
   Let your light so shine before men, that they may see your
   good works, and glorify your Father which is in heaven.

EMMA

Cultural Origin: Teutonic
Inherent Meaning: *UNIVERSAL ONE*
Spiritual Connotation: *WISDOM AND UNDERSTANDING*
Supporting Scripture: *Mark 11:24*
   Therefore I say unto you, What things soever ye desire,
   when ye pray, believe that ye receive them, and ye shall
   have them.

EMMET

Cultural Origin: Anglo-Saxon
Inherent Meaning: *EARNEST ONE*
Spiritual Connotation: *GENUINE DEVOTION*
Supporting Scripture: *Philippians 4:4*
   Rejoice in the Lord alway: and again I say, Rejoice.

ENID

Cultural Origin: Celtic
Inherent Meaning: *PURITY*
Spiritual Connotation: *PURE ONE*
Supporting Scripture: *Psalm 30:12*
   To the end that my glory may sing praise to thee, and not
   be silent. O Lord my God, I will give thanks unto thee for
   ever.

ENNIS

Cultural Origin: Gaelic
Inherent Meaning: *TRUE CHOICE*
Spiritual Connotation: *STRONG, ENDURING*
Supporting Scripture: *Psalm 51:12*
   *Restore unto me the joy of thy salvation; and uphold me
   with thy free spirit.*

ENOCH

Cultural Origin: Hebrew
Inherent Meaning: *CONSECRATED*
Spiritual Connotation: *DEDICATED TO CHRIST*
Supporting Scripture: *Exodus 32:29*
   *. . . Consecrate yourselves today to the Lord, even every
   man . . . that he may bestow upon you a blessing this day.*

ENOS

Cultural Origin: Hebrew
Inherent Meaning: *MORTAL*
Spiritual Connotation: *CREATED TO GLORIFY GOD*
Supporting Scripture: *Isaiah 43:7*
   *. . . for I have created him for my glory, I have formed
   him; yea, I have made him.*

ENRICA

Cultural Origin: Latin-French
Inherent Meaning: *HOME RULER*
Spiritual Connotation: *BELOVED ONE*
Supporting Scripture: *Psalm 33:4*
   *For the word of the Lord is right; and all his works are
   done in truth.*

EPHRAIM

Cultural Origin: Hebrew
Inherent Meaning: *FRUITFUL*
Spiritual Connotation: *PROSPEROUS ONE*
Supporting Scripture: *John 6:35*
> *. . . he that cometh to me shall never hunger; and he that believeth on me shall never thirst.*

ERASMUS

Cultural Origin: Greek
Inherent Meaning: *WORTHY TO BE LOVED*
Spiritual Connotation: *TRUSTWORTHY*
Supporting Scripture: *Luke 6:38*
> *Give, and it shall be given unto you; good measure, pressed down, and shaken together, and running over. . . For with the same measure that ye mete withal it shall be measured to you again.*

ERIC, Erik, Erick

Cultural Origin: Old Norse
Inherent Meaning: *BRAVE, POWERFUL*
Spiritual Connotation: *HONORED ONE*
Supporting Scripture: *John 13:34*
> *A new commandment I give unto you, That ye love one another; as I have loved you, that ye also love one another.*

ERICA, Ericka

Cultural Origin: Teutonic
Inherent Meaning: *BRAVE, NOBLE*
Spiritual Connotation: *VICTORIOUS ONE*
Supporting Scripture: *Isaiah 60:1*
> *Arise, shine; for thy light is come, and the glory of the Lord is risen upon thee.*

ERIN

Cultural Origin: Gaelic
Inherent Meaning: *FAIR, PURE*
Spiritual Connotation: *BENEVOLENT ONE*
Supporting Scripture: *Psalm 121:8*
> *The Lord shall preserve thy going out and thy coming in from this time forth, and even for evermore.*

ERNEST

Cultural Origin: Anglo-Saxon
Inherent Meaning: *EARNEST ONE*
Spiritual Connotation: *DISCERNING SPIRIT*
Supporting Scripture: *John 8:31,32*
> *. . . If ye continue in my word, then are ye in my disciples indeed; and ye shall know the truth, and the truth shall make you free.*

ERNESTINE, Ernestina, Ernesta

Cultural Origin: Anglo-Saxon
Inherent Meaning: *STRONG, BRAVE*
Spiritual Connotation: *SERIOUS, ZEALOUS*
Supporting Scripture: *John 14:12*
> *Verily, verily, I say unto you, He that believeth on me, the works that I do shall he do also; and greater works than these shall he do. . .*

ERROL, see Earl

ERSKINE

Cultural Origin: Gaelic
Inherent Meaning: *LOFTY ONE*
Spiritual Connotation: *DISCERNING JUDGMENT*
Supporting Scripture: *1 Thessalonians 5:13-15*
> *And to esteem them very highly in love for their work's sake. . . but ever follow that which is good, both among yourselves and to all men.*

ERWIN, see Irving

ESMERALDA

Cultural Origin: Spanish-Latin
Inherent Meaning: *VICTORY*
Spiritual Connotation: *TRIUMPHANT SPIRIT*
Supporting Scripture: *Luke 12:32*
> *Fear not . . . for it is your Father's good pleasure to give you the kingdom.*

ESMOND

Cultural Origin: Anglo-Saxon
Inherent Meaning: *GRACIOUS PROTECTOR*
Spiritual Connotation: *FILLED WITH WISDOM*
Supporting Scripture: *2 Corinthians 3:17*
> *Now the Lord is that Spirit: and where the Spirit of the Lord is, there is liberty.*

ESTELLE

Cultural Origin: Latin
Inherent Meaning: *A STAR*
Spiritual Connotation: *INFINITE SPIRITUAL POTENTIAL*
Supporting Scripture: *Matthew 9:29*
> *. . . According to your faith be it unto you.*

ESTHER

Cultural Origin: Hebrew-Persian
Inherent Meaning: *A STAR*
Spiritual Connotation: *SHINING ONE, VICTORIOUS*
Supporting Scripture: *Luke 8:48*
> *. . . thy faith hath made thee whole; go in peace.*

ETHAN, Eythan

Cultural Origin: Hebrew
Inherent Meaning: *FIRMNESS, STRENGTH*
Spiritual Connotation: *STEADFAST IN TRUTH*
Supporting Scripture: *Romans 8:28*
> *And we know that all things work together for good to them that love God, to them who are the called according to his purpose.*

ETHEL, Ethyl, Ethelda, Etheline

Cultural Origin: Anglo-Saxon
Inherent Meaning: *ONE OF HIGH REGARD*
Spiritual Connotation: *NOBLE ONE*
Supporting Scripture: *Matthew 7:7*
> *Ask, and it shall be given you; seek, and ye shall find; knock, and it shall be opened unto you.*

ETTA, see Henrietta

EUDORA

Cultural Origin: Greek
Inherent Meaning: *FAVORED ONE*
Spiritual Connotation: *NOBLE*
Supporting Scripture: *2 Peter 3:14*
> *Wherefore, beloved, seeing that ye look for such things, be diligent that ye may be found of him in peace, without spot, and blameless.*

EUGENE, Gene

Cultural Origin: Greek
Inherent Meaning: *GENEROUS, NOBLE*
Spiritual Connotation: *GRACIOUS ONE*
Supporting Scripture: *Isaiah 58:8*
> *Then shall thy light break forth as the morning, and thine health shall spring forth speedily: and thy righteousness shall go before thee...*

EUGENIA

Cultural Origin: Greek
Inherent Meaning: *GENEROUS, NOBLE*
Spiritual Connotation: *GRACIOUS ONE*
Supporting Scripture: *Proverbs 11:16*
> *A gracious woman retaineth honour: and strong men retain riches.*

EUNICE

Cultural Origin: Greek
Inherent Meaning: *HAPPY, JOYOUS*
Spiritual Connotation: *VICTORIOUS ONE*
Supporting Scripture: *Psalm 40:5*
> *Many, O Lord my God, are thy wonderful works which thou hast done, and thy thoughts which are to us-ward: they cannot be reckoned up in order unto thee...*

EUSTACE

Cultural Origin: Latin
Inherent Meaning: *STABLE, TRANQUIL*
Spiritual Connotation: *RESOURCEFUL*
Supporting Scripture: *Isaiah 40:31*
> *But they that wait upon the Lord shall renew their strength; they shall mount up with wings as eagles; they shall run, and not be weary; and they shall walk, and not faint.*

EVA, Eve

Cultural Origin: Hebrew
Inherent Meaning: *MOTHER OF ALL LIVING*
Spiritual Connotation: *FULL OF LIFE*
Supporting Scripture: *Psalm 16:11*
> *Thou wilt show me the path of life: in thy presence is fulness of joy; at thy right hand there are pleasures for evermore.*

EVAN

Cultural Origin: Gaelic
Inherent Meaning: *NOBLE WARRIOR*
Spiritual Connotation: *NOBLE PROTECTOR*
Supporting Scripture: *Philippians 4:13*
> *I can do all things through Christ which strengtheneth me.*

EVANGELINE

Cultural Origin: Greek
Inherent Meaning: *BRINGER OF GOOD NEWS*
Spiritual Connotation: *HAPPY MESSENGER*
Supporting Scripture: *Psalm 37:6*
> *And he shall bring forth thy righteousness as the light, and thy judgment as the noonday.*

EVE, see Eva

EVELYN

Cultural Origin: Latin
Inherent Meaning: *LIGHT*
Spiritual Connotation: *RADIANT ONE*
Supporting Scripture: *Romans 8:28*
> *And we know that all things work together for good to them that love God, to them who are the called according to his purpose.*

EVERARD

Cultural Origin: Teutonic
Inherent Meaning: *STRONG*
Spiritual Connotation: *INVINCIBLE SPIRIT*
Supporting Scripture: *Psalm 95:3,4*
> *For the Lord is a great God, and a great King above all gods. In his hand are the deep places of the earth: the strength of the hills is his also.*

EVERETT

Cultural Origin: Teutonic
Inherent Meaning: *STRONG*
Spiritual Connotation: *INVINCIBLE SPIRIT*
Supporting Scripture: *Psalm 96:1,2*

> *O sing unto the Lord a new song: sing unto the Lord, all the earth. Sing unto the Lord, bless his name; shew forth his salvation from day to day.*

EWALD

Cultural Origin: Anglo-Saxon
Inherent Meaning: *STRONG AND JUST*
Spiritual Connotation: *PERCEPTIVE, WISE*
Supporting Scripture: *Job 34:2-4*

> *Hear my words, O ye wise men; and give ear unto me, ye that have knowledge. For the ear trieth words, as the mouth tasteth meat. Let us choose to us judgment: let us know among ourselves what is good.*

EWING

Cultural Origin: Anglo-Saxon
Inherent Meaning: *FRIEND OF JUSTICE*
Spiritual Connotation: *BENEVOLENT PROTECTOR*
Supporting Scripture: *Psalm 28:7*

> *The Lord is my strength and my shield; my heart trusted in him, and I am helped: therefore my heart greatly rejoiceth; and with my song will I praise him.*

EZEKIEL

Cultural Origin: Hebrew
Inherent Meaning: *WHOM GOD MAKES STRONG*
Spiritual Connotation: *GOD IS MY STRENGTH*
Supporting Scripture: *1 Corinthians 2:12*

> *Now we have received, not the spirit of the world, but the spirit which is of God; that we might know the things that are freely given to us of God.*

EZRA

Cultural Origin: Hebrew
Inherent Meaning: *SEEKER OF TRUTH*
Spiritual Connotation: *ESTABLISHING SPIRITUAL CONSCIOUSNESS*
Supporting Scripture: *Luke 12:12*
> *For the Holy Ghost shall teach you in the same hour what ye ought to say.*

F

FABIAN

Cultural Origin: Latin
Inherent Meaning: *BEAN GROWER*
Spiritual Connotation: *NOURISHING SPIRIT*
Supporting Scripture: *Psalm 16:8*
> *I have set the Lord always before me: because he is at my right hand, I shall not be moved.*

FAITH

Cultural Origin: Latin
Inherent Meaning: *A FIRM BELIEVER*
Spiritual Connotation: *BELIEF IN GOD*
Supporting Scripture: *Mark 9:23*
> *. . . If thou canst believe, all things are possible to him that believeth.*

FANCHETTE

Cultural Origin: Teutonic
Inherent Meaning: *FREE*
Spiritual Connotation: *QUICKENED SPIRIT*
Supporting Scripture: *Proverbs 17:22*
> *A merry heart doeth good like a medicine: but a broken spirit drieth the bones.*

FARLEY

Cultural Origin: Anglo-Saxon
Inherent Meaning: *FROM THE SHEEP MEADOW*
Spiritual Connotation: *STRAIGHTFORWARD SOUL*
Supporting Scripture: *Exodus 14:14*
> *The Lord shall fight for you, and ye shall hold your peace.*

FAY

Cultural Origin: Latin
Inherent Meaning: *RAVEN, SPRITE*
Spiritual Connotation: *MESSENGER OF LOVE*
Supporting Scripture: *Isaiah 65:24*
> *And it shall come to pass, that before they call, I will answer; and while they are yet speaking, I will hear.*

FELICA, Felicia

Cultural Origin: Latin
Inherent Meaning: *HAPPY, FORTUNATE*
Spiritual Connotation: *JOYFUL LIFE*
Supporting Scripture: *John 10:10*
> *. . . I am come that they might have life, and that they might have it more abundantly.*

FELICITY, Falice

Cultural Origin: Latin
Inherent Meaning: *HAPPY, JOYOUS ONE*
Spiritual Connotation: *JOYFUL*
Supporting Scripture: *Psalm 35:9*
> *And my soul shall be joyful in the Lord: it shall rejoice in his salvation.*

FELIX

Cultural Origin: Latin
Inherent Meaning: *HAPPY, FORTUNATE ONE*
Spiritual Connotation: *BLESSED ONE*
Supporting Scripture: *Isaiah 40:31*
> *But they that wait upon the Lord shall renew their strength; they shall mount up with wings as eagles; they shall run, and not be weary; and they shall walk, and not faint.*

FENTON

Cultural Origin: Anglo-Saxon
Inherent Meaning: *FROM THE MARSH ESTATE*
Spiritual Connotation: *SPIRIT OF LIFE*
Supporting Scripture: *Galatians 6:8*
> *...but he that soweth to the Spirit shall of the Spirit reap life everlasting.*

FERDINAND

Cultural Origin: Gothic
Inherent Meaning: *LIFE-ADVENTURING*
Spiritual Connotation: *SEEKER OF TRUTH*
Supporting Scripture: *Psalm 33:3,4*
> *Sing unto him a new song; play skilfully with a loud noise. For the word of the Lord is right; and all his works are done in truth.*

FERGUS

Cultural Origin: Gaelic
Inherent Meaning: *VERY CHOICE ONE*
Spiritual Connotation: *ESTEEMED*
Supporting Scripture: *Psalm 18:2*
> *The Lord is my rock, and my fortress, and my deliverer; my God, my strength, in whom I will trust...*

FERN

Cultural Origin: Anglo-Saxon
Inherent Meaning: *SINCERITY*
Spiritual Connotation: *HEARTFELT, HONEST*
Supporting Scripture: *1 John 4:11*
> *Beloved, if God so loved us, we ought also to love one another.*

FESTES

Cultural Origin: Latin
Inherent Meaning: *JOYFUL*
Spiritual Connotation: *DIVINE LIGHT SHINING*
Supporting Scripture: *Colossians 4:5,6*
> *Walk in wisdom toward them that are without, redeeming the time. Let your speech be alway with grace, seasoned with salt, that he may know how ye ought to answer...*

FIDEL

Cultural Origin: Latin
Inherent Meaning: *FAITHFUL, SINCERE*
Spiritual Connotation: *COMPASSIONATE ONE*
Supporting Scripture: *Romans 8:38,39*
> *For I am persuaded... Nor height, nor depth, nor any other creature, shall be able to separate us from the love of God...*

FINDLAY

Cultural Origin: Gaelic
Inherent Meaning: *VALOROUS ONE*
Spiritual Connotation: *VICTORIOUS LIFE*
Supporting Scripture: *Proverbs 12:28*
> *In the way of righteousness is life; and in the pathway thereof there is no death.*

FIONA

Cultural Origin: Gaelic
Inherent Meaning: *FAIR ONE*
Spiritual Connotation: *PERSEVERING SPIRIT*
Supporting Scripture: *John 10:10*
> *...I am come that they might have life, and that they might have it more abundantly.*

FITZGERALD

Cultural Origin: Anglo-Saxon
Inherent Meaning: *MIGHTY ONE*
Spiritual Connotation: *PROTECTOR*
Supporting Scripture: *Colossians 1:27*
> To whom God would make known what is the riches of
> the glory of this mystery. . . which is Christ in you, the
> hope of glory.

FLETCHER

Cultural Origin: Anglo-Saxon
Inherent Meaning: *ARROW-FEATHERER, CRAFTSMAN*
Spiritual Connotation: *INGENIOUS SPIRIT*
Supporting Scripture: *John 14:12*
> Verily, verily, I say unto you, He that believeth on me, the
> works that I do shall he do also; and greater works than
> these shall he do. . .

FLORA, Florabel

Cultural Origin: Latin
Inherent Meaning: *FLOWER*
Spiritual Connotation: *LIGHT FILLED*
Supporting Scripture: *Luke 2:40*
> And the child grew, and waxed strong in spirit, filled with
> wisdom: and the grace of God was upon him.

FLORENCE, Flossie

Cultural Origin: Latin
Inherent Meaning: *BLOOMING, FLOURISHING,
                   PROSPEROUS*
Spiritual Connotation: *DELIGHTFUL ONE*
Supporting Scripture: *Psalm 91:1*
> He that dwelleth in the secret place of the most High shall
> abide under the shadow of the Almighty.

FLOYD

Cultural Origin: Celtic
Inherent Meaning: *WHITE HAIRED*
Spiritual Connotation: *WISE ONE*
Supporting Scripture: *1 Samuel 10:6*
>   *And the Spirit of the Lord will come upon thee, and thou
>   shalt prophesy with them, and shalt be turned into
>   another man.*

FLYNN

Cultural Origin: Gaelic
Inherent Meaning: *GOODLY HERITAGE*
Spiritual Connotation: *ADVENTUROUS SOUL*
Supporting Scripture: *1 Kings 8:56*
>   *Blessed be the Lord. . . according to all that he promised:
>   there hath not failed one word of all his good promise. . .*

FORBES

Cultural Origin: Gaelic
Inherent Meaning: *MAN OF PROSPERITY*
Spiritual Connotation: *ONE WHO LISTENS TO AND
                        TRUSTS GOD*
Supporting Scripture: *Psalm 138:8*
>   *The Lord will perfect that which concerneth me: thy mer-
>   cy, O Lord, endureth for ever: forsake not the works of
>   thine own hands.*

FORREST

Cultural Origin: Latin
Inherent Meaning: *DWELLER IN THE FOREST*
Spiritual Connotation: *CALM SPIRIT*
Supporting Scripture: *Proverbs 16:20*
>   *He that handleth a matter wisely shall find good: and
>   whoso trusteth in the Lord, happy is he.*

FRANCES, Francine

Cultural Origin: Teutonic
Inherent Meaning: *FREE ONE*
Spiritual Connotation: *TRIUMPHANT ONE*
Supporting Scripture: *Isaiah 65:24*
  . . . before they call, I will answer; and while they are yet speaking, I will hear.

FRANCIS, Franchot

Cultural Origin: Latin
Inherent Meaning: *FREE ONE*
Spiritual Connotation: *VICTORIOUS ONE*
Supporting Scripture: *John 5:24*
  . . . He that heareth my word, and believeth on him that sent me, hath everlasting life. . .

FRANK

Cultural Origin: Latin
Inherent Meaning: *FREE MAN*
Spiritual Connotation: *TRIUMPHANT ONE*
Supporting Scripture: *Matthew 5:14*
  Ye are the light of the world. A city that is set on an hill cannot be hid.

FRANKLIN

Cultural Origin: Anglo-Saxon
Inherent Meaning: *FREE HOLDER OF LAND*
Spiritual Connotation: *FREE SPIRIT*
Supporting Scripture: *Nehemiah 8:10*
  . . . for the joy of the Lord is your strength.

FRASER, Frazer

Cultural Origin: Anglo-Saxon
Inherent Meaning: *FAIR*
Spiritual Connotation: *FILLED WITH LIFE*
Supporting Scripture: *2 Peter 1:4*
> *Whereby are given unto us exceeding great and precious promises: that by these ye might be partakers of the divine nature...*

FREDERICA

Cultural Origin: Teutonic
Inherent Meaning: *PEACEFUL RULER*
Spiritual Connotation: *PERCEPTIVE SPIRIT*
Supporting Scripture: *Psalm 112:4*
> *Unto the upright there ariseth light in the darkness: he is gracious, and full of compassion, and righteous.*

FREDERICK, Frederic, Fred

Cultural Origin: Teutonic
Inherent Meaning: *PEACEFUL RULER*
Spiritual Connotation: *PERCEPTIVE SPIRIT*
Supporting Scripture: *Proverbs 20:12*
> *The hearing ear, and the seeing eye, the Lord hath made even both of them.*

FRIEDA

Cultural Origin: Teutonic
Inherent Meaning: *PEACEFUL*
Spiritual Connotation: *CARING ONE*
Supporting Scripture: *Revelation 2:7*
> *He that hath an ear, let him hear what the Spirit saith.... To him that overcometh will I give to eat of the tree of life...*

FULLER

Cultural Origin: Anglo-Saxon
Inherent Meaning: *WORKER WITH CLOTH*
Spiritual Connotation: *DILIGENT, INGENIOUS SPIRIT*
Supporting Scripture: *Psalm 103:1-4*

> *Bless the Lord, O my soul: and all that is within me, bless his holy name. . . . Who redeemeth thy life from destruction; who crowneth thee with lovingkindness and tender mercies.*

FULTON

Cultural Origin: Anglo-Saxon
Inherent Meaning: *DWELLER*
Spiritual Connotation: *SPIRIT-FILLED LIFE*
Supporting Scripture: *Galatians 5:22,23*

> *But the fruit of the Spirit is love, joy, peace, longsuffering, gentleness, goodness, faith. . . against such there is no law.*

G

GABRIEL

Cultural Origin: Hebrew
Inherent Meaning: *GOD IS MY STRENGTH*
Spiritual Connotation: *SPIRITUAL CONSCIOUSNESS*
Supporting Scripture: *Joshua 1:9*
> *. . . Be strong and of a good courage; be not afraid,
> neither be thou dismayed: for the Lord thy God is with
> thee whithersoever thou goest.*

GABRIELLE

Cultural Origin: Hebrew
Inherent Meaning: *GOD IS MY STRENGTH*
Spiritual Connotation: *SPIRITUAL CONSCIOUSNESS*
Supporting Scripture: *Joshua 1:9*
> *. . . Be strong and of a good courage; be not afraid,
> neither be thou dismayed: for the Lord thy God is with
> thee whithersoever thou goest.*

GAIL, Gale, Gayle

Cultural Origin: Anglo-Saxon
Inherent Meaning: *GAY, LIVELY ONE*
Spiritual Connotation: *A MERRY HEART*
Supporting Scripture: *Psalm 45:7*
> *Thou lovest righteousness, and hatest wickedness:
> therefore God, thy God, hath anointed thee with the oil of
> gladness above thy fellows.*

GALATIA

Cultural Origin: Greek
Inherent Meaning: *PURE*
Spiritual Connotation: *PURE TRUTH*
Supporting Scripture: *Psalm 27:1*
> *The Lord is my light and my salvation; whom shall I fear?
> the Lord is the strength of my life; of whom shall I be
> afraid?*

GALEN, Gaylen

Cultural Origin: Greek
Inherent Meaning: *HEALER*
Spiritual Connotation: *ESTABLISHED IN TRUTH*
Supporting Scripture: *Psalm 37:5*
> *Commit thy way unto the Lord; trust also in him; and he shall bring it to pass.*

GALLAGHER

Cultural Origin: Gaelic
Inherent Meaning: *EAGER HELPER*
Spiritual Connotation: *ENLIGHTENED ONE*
Supporting Scripture: *2 Timothy 1:7*
> *For God hath not given us the spirit of fear; but of power, and of love, and of a sound mind.*

GALVIN

Cultural Origin: Gaelic
Inherent Meaning: *BRIGHT, SHINING ONE*
Spiritual Connotation: *BLESSED ONE*
Supporting Scripture: *Isaiah 49:4*
> *. . . surely my judgment is with the Lord, and my work with my God.*

GAMALIEL

Cultural Origin: Hebrew
Inherent Meaning: *RECOMPENSE OF GOD*
Spiritual Connotation: *TESTER OF TRUTH*
Supporting Scripture: *Proverbs 9:10*
> *The fear of the Lord is the beginning of wisdom: and the knowledge of the holy is understanding.*

GARNET, Garnette

Cultural Origin: Anglo-Saxon
Inherent Meaning: *A GEM*
Spiritual Connotation: *PRECIOUS ONE*
Supporting Scripture: *Deuteronomy 11:1*
   *Therefore thou shalt love the Lord thy God, and keep his
   charge, and his statutes, and his judgments, and his com-
   mandments, alway.*

GARNETT

Cultural Origin: Latin
Inherent Meaning: *BRAVE, FIRM*
Spiritual Connotation: *STEADFAST, CHAMPION*
Supporting Scripture: *Isaiah 49:8*
   *Thus saith the Lord, In an acceptable time have I heard
   thee, and in a day of salvation have I helped thee: and I
   will preserve thee...*

GARTH, Gar

Cultural Origin: Old Norse
Inherent Meaning: *FROM THE GARDEN*
Spiritual Connotation: *QUIET, BLESSED ONE*
Supporting Scripture: *Job 28:28*
   *...Behold, the fear of the Lord, that is wisdom; and to
   depart from evil is understanding.*

GARRETT

Cultural Origin: Anglo-Saxon
Inherent Meaning: *WARRIOR-BRAVE*
Spiritual Connotation: *BRAVE RULER*
Supporting Scripture: *Galatians 5:1*
   *Stand fast therefore in the liberty wherewith Christ hath
   made us free, and be not entangled again with the yoke of
   bondage.*

GARRICK

Cultural Origin: Anglo-Saxon
Inherent Meaning: *RULER*
Spiritual Connotation: *CHAMPION*
Supporting Scripture: *Psalm 24:3,4*
> *Who shall ascend into the hill of the Lord? or who shall stand in his holy place? He that hath clean hands, and a pure heart...*

GARVEY

Cultural Origin: Gaelic
Inherent Meaning: *RUGGED PLACE*
Spiritual Connotation: *INCREASING FAITHFULNESS*
Supporting Scripture: *Ephesians 5:8,9*
> *...now are ye light in the Lord: walk as children of light: (For the fruit of the Spirit is in all goodness and righteousness and truth.)*

GARVIN

Cultural Origin: Anglo-Saxon
Inherent Meaning: *FRIEND*
Spiritual Connotation: *BLESSED ONE*
Supporting Scripture: *Colossians 3:15,16*
> *And let the peace of God rule in your hearts.... Let the word of Christ dwell in you richly in all wisdom; teaching and admonishing one another...*

GARY

Cultural Origin: Celtic
Inherent Meaning: *MERRY HEART*
Spiritual Connotation: *THANKFUL SPIRIT*
Supporting Scripture: *2 Corinthians 5:17*
> *Therefore if any man be in Christ, he is a new creature: old things are passed away; behold, all things are become new.*

GAVIN

Cultural Origin: Celtic
Inherent Meaning: *FROM THE HAWK FIELD*
Spiritual Connotation: *CONTENTED ONE*
Supporting Scripture: *Psalm 119:34*
> *Give me understanding, and I shall keep thy law; yea, I shall observe it with my whole heart.*

GAYLORD

Cultural Origin: Latin
Inherent Meaning: *LIVELY ONE*
Spiritual Connotation: *ESTEEMED ONE*
Supporting Scripture: *Psalm 84:11*
> *For the Lord God is a sun and shield: the Lord will give grace and glory: no good thing will he withhold from them that walk uprightly.*

GEARY

Cultural Origin: Anglo-Saxon
Inherent Meaning: *CHANGEABLE ONE*
Spiritual Connotation: *COURAGEOUS SPIRIT*
Supporting Scripture: *Psalm 16:8*
> *I have set the Lord always before me: because he is at my right hand, I shall not be moved.*

GENE

Cultural Origin: Latin
Inherent Meaning: *WELL BORN, NOBLE*
Spiritual Connotation: *STRONG IN VICTORY*
Supporting Scripture: *Zechariah 7:9*
> *Thus speaketh the Lord of hosts, saying, Execute true judgment, and shew mercy and compassions every man to his brother.*

GENEVA

Cultural Origin: Latin
Inherent Meaning: *JUNIPER TREE*
Spiritual Connotation: *DELIGHTS IN THE LORD*
Supporting Scripture: *Psalm 111:10*
> *The fear of the lord is the beginning of wisdom: a good understanding have all they that do his commandments: his praise endureth for ever.*

GENEVIEVE

Cultural Origin: Celtic
Inherent Meaning: *WHITE AS SEA FOAM, PURE*
Spiritual Connotation: *VICTORIOUS HEART*
Supporting Scripture: *Colossians 3:12-15*
> *Put on therefore, as the elect of God, holy and beloved, bowels [a heart] of mercies, kindness, humbleness of mind, meekness, long-suffering. . . . And let the peace of God rule in your hearts. . .*

GEOFFREY, Godfrey

Cultural Origin: Teutonic
Inherent Meaning: *JOYFUL PEACE*
Spiritual Connotation: *VICTORIOUS HEART*
Supporting Scripture: *James 3:18*
> *And the fruit of righteousness is sown in peace of them that make peace.*

GEORGE

Cultural Origin: Greek
Inherent Meaning: *LAND WORKER, FARMER*
Spiritual Connotation: *WALKS WITH GOD*
Supporting Scripture: *Isaiah 35:1*
> *The wilderness and the solitary place shall be glad for them; and the desert shall rejoice, and blossom as the rose.*

GEORGIA, Georgina, Georgette, Georgene

Cultural Origin: Latin
Inherent Meaning: *FARMER*
Spiritual Connotation: *WALKS WITH GOD*
Supporting Scripture: *Hebrews 8:10*
> *For this is the covenant that I will make. . . . I will put my laws into their mind, and write them in their hearts. . .*

GERALD

Cultural Origin: Teutonic
Inherent Meaning: *MIGHTY ONE*
Spiritual Connotation: *LOYAL ONE*
Supporting Scripture: *Psalm 25:5*
> *Lead me in thy truth, and teach me: for thou art the God of my salvation; on thee do I wait all the day.*

GERALDINE, Geri, Gerry

Cultural Origin: Teutonic
Inherent Meaning: *POWERFUL ONE*
Spiritual Connotation: *VICTORIOUS SPIRIT*
Supporting Scripture: *Psalm 118:14*
> *The Lord is my strength and song, and is become my salvation.*

GERARD

Cultural Origin: Anglo-Saxon
Inherent Meaning: *STRONG, POWERFUL*
Spiritual Connotation: *DISCERNER OF EXCELLENCE*
Supporting Scripture: *Psalm 138:8*
> *The Lord will perfect that which concerneth me: thy mercy, O Lord, endureth for ever: forsake not the works of thine own hands.*

GERDA

Cultural Origin: Old Norse
Inherent Meaning: *PROTECTOR*
Spiritual Connotation: *CHOSEN OF GOD*
Supporting Scripture: *Ephesians 4:32*
> *And be ye kind one to another, tenderhearted, forgiving one another, even as God for Christ's sake hath forgiven you.*

GERMAIN

Cultural Origin: Latin
Inherent Meaning: *REPRESENTATION OF COUNTRY*
Spiritual Connotation: *BELOVED ONE*
Supporting Scripture: *2 Timothy 2:22*
> *. . . But follow righteousness, faith, charity, peace, with them that call on the Lord out of a pure heart.*

GERTRUDE

Cultural Origin: Teutonic
Inherent Meaning: *BATTLE MAIDEN*
Spiritual Connotation: *VICTORIOUS SPIRIT*
Supporting Scripture: *Psalm 27:1*
> *The Lord is my light and my salvation; whom shall I fear? the Lord is the strength of my life; of whom shall I be afraid?*

GIDEON

Cultural Origin: Hebrew
Inherent Meaning: *DENIAL*
Spiritual Connotation: *SPIRITUAL WITNESS*
Supporting Scripture: *Psalm 104:24*
> *O Lord, how manifold are thy works! in wisdom hast thou made them all: the earth is full of thy riches.*

GIFFORD

Cultural Origin: Anglo-Saxon
Inherent Meaning: *GIFTED*
Spiritual Connotation: *HONORABLE, TRUSTWORTHY*
Supporting Scripture: *1 Corinthians 15:58*
   Therefore, my beloved brethren, be ye stedfast, un-
   moveable, always abounding in the work of the Lord...

GILBERT

Cultural Origin: Anglo-Saxon
Inherent Meaning: *BRIGHT PLEDGE*
Spiritual Connotation: *DEVOTED SPIRIT*
Supporting Scripture: *2 Corinthians 1:20*
   For all the promises of God in him are yea, and in him
   Amen, unto the glory of God...

GILCHRIST

Cultural Origin: Gaelic
Inherent Meaning: *SERVANT OF CHRIST*
Spiritual Connotation: *CONSECRATED ONE*
Supporting Scripture: *Psalm 37:37*
   Mark the perfect man, and behold the upright: for the end
   of that man is peace.

GILDA

Cultural Origin: Anglo-Saxon
Inherent Meaning: *COVERED WITH GOLD*
Spiritual Connotation: *CHOSEN ONE*
Supporting Scripture: *Psalm 91:2*
   I will say of the Lord, He is my refuge and my fortress:
   my God; in him will I trust.

GILES, Gilles, Gyles

Cultural Origin: Latin
Inherent Meaning: *YOUTHFUL*
Spiritual Connotation: *STRENGTH, VITALITY, POWER*
Supporting Scripture: *Psalm 66:1,2*
> *Make a joyful noise unto God, all ye lands: sing forth the honour of his name: make his praise glorious.*

GILLIAN, see Jill

GILMORE

Cultural Origin: Gaelic
Inherent Meaning: *DEVOUT ONE*
Spiritual Connotation: *DEPENDENT SPIRIT*
Supporting Scripture: *Job 10:12*
> *Thou hast granted me life and favour, and thy visitation hath preserved my spirit.*

GILROY

Cultural Origin: Gaelic
Inherent Meaning: *VITAL, VIGOROUS ONE*
Spiritual Connotation: *JOY IN FREEDOM*
Supporting Scripture: *Revelation 2:7*
> *. . . To him that overcometh will I give to eat of the tree of life, which is in the midst of the paradise of God.*

GINA

Cultural Origin: Latin
Inherent Meaning: *QUEEN*
Spiritual Connotation: *FULL OF GRACE*
Supporting Scripture: *Colossians 3:12-14*
> *Put on therefore, as the elect of God, holy and beloved, bowels [a heart] of mercies, kindness, humbleness of mind. . . . And above all these things put on charity [love], which is the bond of perfectness.*

GINGER, see Virginia

GLADYS

Cultural Origin: Celtic
Inherent Meaning: *RULER, PRINCESS*
Spiritual Connotation: *SPIRITUAL UNDERSTANDING*
Supporting Scripture: *1 Peter 2:5*
> *Ye also, as lively stones, are built up a spiritual house, an holy priesthood. . . acceptable to God by Jesus Christ.*

GLENDA, see Glenna

GLENN, Glen

Cultural Origin: Celtic
Inherent Meaning: *DWELLER IN THE GLEN*
Spiritual Connotation: *EXCELLENT WORTH*
Supporting Scripture: *Psalm 84:4,5*
> *Blessed are they that dwell in thy house: they will be still praising thee. Blessed is the man whose strength is in thee. . .*

GLENNA, GLENDA

Cultural Origin: Celtic
Inherent Meaning: *DWELLER IN THE GLEN*
Spiritual Connotation: *EXCELLENT WORTH*
Supporting Scripture: *Psalm 52:8*
> *But I am like a green olive tree in the house of God: I trust in the mercy of God for ever and ever.*

GLORIA

Cultural Origin: Latin
Inherent Meaning: *GLORY*
Spiritual Connotation: *GLORIOUS ONE*
Supporting Scripture: *Psalm 19:8*
> *The statutes of the Lord are right, rejoicing the heart: the commandment of the Lord is pure, enlightening the eyes.*

GLYNIS, see Glenna

GODFREY

Cultural Origin: Teutonic
Inherent Meaning: *MAN OF PEACE*
Spiritual Connotation: *DIVINELY PEACEFUL*
Supporting Scripture: *John 7:38*
> *He that believeth on me, as the scripture hath said, out of his belly shall flow rivers of living water.*

GODWIN

Cultural Origin: Anglo-Saxon
Inherent Meaning: *DIVINE FRIEND*
Spiritual Connotation: *FOLLOWER OF CHRIST*
Supporting Scripture: *2 Timothy 1:7*
> *For God hath not given us the spirit of fear; but of power, and of love, and of a sound mind.*

GORDON

Cultural Origin: Gaelic
Inherent Meaning: *STRONG, KIND*
Spiritual Connotation: *VALIANT ONE*
Supporting Scripture: *Matthew 5:14*
> *Ye are the light of the world . . .*

GORMAN

Cultural Origin: Gaelic
Inherent Meaning: *MANLY*
Spiritual Connotation: *WALKS WITH GOD*
Supporting Scripture: *Psalm 84:11*
> *For the Lord God is a sun and shield: the Lord will give grace and glory: no good thing will he withhold from them that walk uprightly.*

GRACE

Cultural Origin: Latin
Inherent Meaning: *GRACE, KINDLY, PATIENT*
Spiritual Connotation: *FULL OF GRACE*
Supporting Scripture: *John 15:16*
> *Ye have not chosen me, but I have chosen you. . . that ye should go and bring forth fruit, and that your fruit should remain: that whatsoever ye shall ask of the Father in my name, he may give it you.*

GRADY

Cultural Origin: Gaelic
Inherent Meaning: *NOBLE, ILLUSTRIOUS*
Spiritual Connotation: *ILLUSTRIOUS ONE*
Supporting Scripture: *Joshua 1:9*
> *. . . Be strong and of a good courage; be not afraid, neither be thou dismayed: for the Lord thy God is with thee whithersoever thou goest.*

GRAHAM

Cultural Origin: Anglo-Saxon
Inherent Meaning: *FROM THE GRAY LAND*
Spiritual Connotation: *SPIRITUALLY QUICKENED*
Supporting Scripture: *1 Corinthians 13:13*
> *And now abideth faith, hope, charity [love], these three; but the greatest of these is charity.*

GRANGER

Cultural Origin: Anglo-Saxon
Inherent Meaning: *FARMER*
Spiritual Connotation: *GOD'S GRACIOUS GIFT*
Supporting Scripture: *Isaiah 48:17*
>*Thus saith the Lord. . .I am the Lord thy God which teacheth thee to profit, which leadeth thee by the way that thou shouldest go.*

GRANT

Cultural Origin: Latin
Inherent Meaning: *BRAVE, VALOROUS*
Spiritual Connotation: *PROMISED ASSURANCE*
Supporting Scripture: *Psalm 18:2*
>*The Lord is my rock, and my fortress, and my deliverer; my God, my strength, in whom I will trust. . .*

GRANTLAND

Cultural Origin: Anglo-Saxon
Inherent Meaning: *GRAND LAND*
Spiritual Connotation: *STRENGTH IN GOD*
Supporting Scripture: *Proverbs 3:5,6*
>*Trust in the Lord with all thine heart; and lean not unto thine own understanding. In all thy ways acknowledge him, and he shall direct thy paths.*

GRANVILLE

Cultural Origin: Latin-French
Inherent Meaning: *GREAT ONE*
Spiritual Connotation: *CHERISHED ONE*
Supporting Scripture: *Psalm 37:6*
>*And he shall bring forth thy righteousness as the light, and thy judgment as the noonday.*

GRAYSON

Cultural Origin: Anglo-Saxon
Inherent Meaning: *SON OF BAILIFF*
Spiritual Connotation: *DIVINE SPARK*
Supporting Scripture: *Proverbs 13:14,15*
> *The law of the wise is a fountain of life, to depart from the snares of death. Good understanding giveth favour...*

GREGORY, Greg

Cultural Origin: Latin
Inherent Meaning: *WATCHMAN, GUARDIAN*
Spiritual Connotation: *GOD'S TRUSTEE*
Supporting Scripture: *1 Corinthians 16:13,14*
> *Watch ye, stand fast in the faith.... Let all your things be done with charity [love].*

GRETCHEN

Cultural Origin: Latin
Inherent Meaning: *A PEARL*
Spiritual Connotation: *PRICELESS ONE*
Supporting Scripture: *Psalm 48:10*
> *According to thy name, O God, so is thy praise unto the ends of the earth: thy right hand is full of righteousness.*

GRIFFITH

Cultural Origin: Celtic
Inherent Meaning: *GREAT FAIT˙*
Spiritual Connotation: *BLESSED OF GOD*
Supporting Scripture: *Psalm 8:4-6*
> *What is man, that thou art mindful of him?... For thou hast made him a little lower than the angels.... Thou madest him to have dominion over the works of thy hands; thou hast put all things under his feet.*

GRISELDA

Cultural Origin: Teutonic
Inherent Meaning: *HEROINE*
Spiritual Connotation: *VICTORIOUS ONE*
Supporting Scripture: *Psalm 23:1*
   The Lord is my shepherd; I shall not want.

GROVER

Cultural Origin: Anglo-Saxon
Inherent Meaning: *FROM THE GROVE OF TREES*
Spiritual Connotation: *CONSECRATED ONE*
Supporting Scripture: *Psalm 37:37*
   *Mark the perfect man, and behold the upright: for the end
   of that man is peace.*

GUNNAR, Gunther

Cultural Origin: Old Norse
Inherent Meaning: *WARRIOR—KING*
Spiritual Connotation: *VICTORIOUS SPIRIT*
Supporting Scripture: *Psalm 119:34*
   *Give me understanding, and I shall keep thy law; yea, I
   shall observe it with my whole heart.*

GUSTAVE, Gust, Gus

Cultural Origin: Teutonic
Inherent Meaning: *STAFF, SUPPORTING STRENGTH*
Spiritual Connotation: *LOYAL ONE*
Supporting Scripture: *Psalm 24:5*
   *He shall receive the blessing from the Lord, and
   righteousness from the God of his salvation.*

GUTHRIE, Guthrey

Cultural Origin: Gaelic
Inherent Meaning: *WARRIOR*
Spiritual Connotation: *GREAT ONE*
Supporting Scripture: *Colossians 3:16*
> Let the word of Christ dwell in you richly in all
> wisdom . . . singing with grace in your hearts to the Lord.

GUY

Cultural Origin: Teutonic
Inherent Meaning: *DIRECTOR*
Spiritual Connotation: *FILLED WITH WISDOM*
Supporting Scripture: *James 3:18*
> And the fruit of righteousness is sown in peace of them
> that make peace.

GWENDOLYN, Gwen

Cultural Origin: Celtic
Inherent Meaning: *FAIR ONE*
Spiritual Connotation: *FULL OF HONOR*
Supporting Scripture: *Psalm 18:35*
> Thou hast also given me the shield of thy salvation: and
> thy right hand hath holden me up, and thy gentleness hath
> made me great.

GWYNN

Cultural Origin: Celtic
Inherent Meaning: *FAIR ONE*
Spiritual Connotation: *SEEKER OF WISDOM*
Supporting Scripture: *Isaiah 58:14*
> Then shalt thou delight thyself in the Lord; and I will
> cause thee to ride upon the high places of the earth . . . the
> mouth of the Lord hath spoken it.

H

HADLEY, Hadleigh

Cultural Origin: Anglo-Saxon
Inherent Meaning: *FROM THE HEATH MEADOW*
Spiritual Connotation: *STEADFAST SPIRIT*
Supporting Scripture: *Psalm 25:21*
Let integrity and uprightness preserve me; for I wait on thee.

HAIDEE, Heidi

Cultural Origin: Greek
Inherent Meaning: *MODEST, HONORED*
Spiritual Connotation: *BELOVED ONE*
Supporting Scripture: *Psalm 29:11*
The Lord will give strength unto his people; the Lord will bless his people with peace.

HALBERT, Hal

Cultural Origin: Anglo-Saxon
Inherent Meaning: *BRILLIANT HERO*
Spiritual Connotation: *RESOLUTE, STRONG*
Supporting Scripture: *Psalm 37:4*
Delight thyself also in the Lord; and he shall give thee the desires of thine heart.

HALEY

Cultural Origin: Gaelic
Inherent Meaning: *INGENIOUS, SCIENTIFIC*
Spiritual Connotation: *CREATIVE HEART*
Supporting Scripture: *Colossians 3:23,24*
And whatsoever ye do, do it heartily, as to the Lord, and not unto men. . .for ye serve the Lord Christ.

HAMILTON

Cultural Origin: Anglo-Saxon
Inherent Meaning: *HOME LOVER*
Spiritual Connotation: *FIDELITY, TRUSTWORTHINESS*
Supporting Scripture: *Ecclesiastes 11:1*
   *Cast thy bread upon the waters: for thou shalt find it after
   many days.*

HANLEY

Cultural Origin: Anglo-Saxon
Inherent Meaning: *FROM THE HIGH PASTURE*
Spiritual Connotation: *PROTECTOR, SHEPHERD*
Supporting Scripture: *Isaiah 49:10*
   *They shall not hunger nor thirst; neither shall the heat nor
   sun smite them: for he that hath mercy on them shall lead
   them, even by the springs of the water shall he guide
   them.*

HANNAH

Cultural Origin: Hebrew
Inherent Meaning: *GRACIOUS, KIND*
Spiritual Connotation: *COMPASSIONATE ONE*
Supporting Scripture: *Colossians 3:16*
   *Let the word of Christ dwell in you richly in all wisdom;
   teaching and admonishing one another in psalms and
   hymns and spiritual songs, singing with grace in your
   hearts to the Lord.*

HANS

Cultural Origin: Anglo-Saxon
Inherent Meaning: *THE LORD'S GRACE*
Spiritual Connotation: *DISCERNING SPIRIT*
Supporting Scripture: *Isaiah 52:7*
   *How beautiful upon the mountains are the feet of him
   that bringeth good tidings, that publisheth peace. . .*

HARLAN, Harland

Cultural Origin: Anglo-Saxon
Inherent Meaning: *FROM THE LAND*
Spiritual Connotation: *RESOLUTE, BRAVE*
Supporting Scripture: *Proverbs 3:6*
> In all thy ways acknowledge him, and he shall direct thy
> paths.

HARLEY

Cultural Origin: Anglo-Saxon
Inherent Meaning: *GUARDIAN*
Spiritual Connotation: *CHOSEN OF GOD*
Supporting Scripture: *Leviticus 19:34*
> But the stranger that dwelleth with you shall be unto you
> as one born among you, and thou shalt love him as
> thyself.

HAROLD

Cultural Origin: Teutonic
Inherent Meaning: *LEADER*
Spiritual Connotation: *PERCEPTIVE INSIGHT*
Supporting Scripture: *Acts 17:28*
> For in him we live, and move, and have our being; as cer-
> tain also of your own poets have said, For we are also his
> offspring.

HARRIET, Hattie

Cultural Origin: Teutonic
Inherent Meaning: *EVER RICH AND POWERFUL*
Spiritual Connotation: *DISCERNER OF EXCELLENCE*
Supporting Scripture: *Proverbs 25:11*
> A word fitly spoken is like apples of gold in pictures of
> silver.

HARRIS, Harrison

Cultural Origin: Anglo-Saxon
Inherent Meaning: *STRONG, MANLY*
Spiritual Connotation: *COURAGEOUS ONE*
Supporting Scripture: *Proverbs 24:5*
> *A wise man is strong, yea, a man of knowledge increaseth strength.*

HARRY

Cultural Origin: Anglo-Saxon
Inherent Meaning: *ARMY MAN, LEADER*
Spiritual Connotation: *DIGNITY, INTEGRITY*
Supporting Scripture: *Ephesians 6:7,8*
> *With good will doing service, as to the Lord, and not to men: Knowing that whatsoever good thing any man doeth, the same shall he receive of the Lord, whether he be bond or free.*

HARTLEY

Cultural Origin: Anglo-Saxon
Inherent Meaning: *FROM THE GREEN, FERTILE MEADOW*
Spiritual Connotation: *VICTORIOUS ONE*
Supporting Scripture: *Psalm 50:15*
> *And call upon me in the day of trouble: I will deliver thee, and thou shalt glorify me.*

HARVEY

Cultural Origin: Teutonic
Inherent Meaning: *NOBLE*
Spiritual Connotation: *HONORABLE, BRAVE*
Supporting Scripture: *Psalm 100:3*
> *Know ye that the Lord he is God: it is he that hath made us, and not we ourselves; we are his people...*

HAYDEN

Cultural Origin: Anglo-Saxon
Inherent Meaning: *FROM THE HEDGED VALLEY*
Spiritual Connotation: *VICTORIOUS SPIRIT*
Supporting Scripture: *2 Corinthians 6:2*
> *. . . behold, now is the accepted time; behold, now is the day of salvation.*

HAZEL

Cultural Origin: Hebrew
Inherent Meaning: *GOD SEES*
Spiritual Connotation: *WATCHING IN LIGHT*
Supporting Scripture: *1 John 1:7*
> *But if we walk in the light as he is in the light, we have fellowship one with another. . .*

HEATHER

Cultural Origin: Gaelic
Inherent Meaning: *HEATH DWELLER*
Spiritual Connotation: *COVER OF BEAUTY*
Supporting Scripture: *Matthew 6:28,29*
> *. . . Consider the lilies of the field; they toil not, neither do they spin. . . . Solomon in all his glory was not arrayed like one of these.*

HECTOR

Cultural Origin: Greek
Inherent Meaning: *STEADFAST*
Spiritual Connotation: *FAITHFUL, TRUE*
Supporting Scripture: *Luke 6:38*
> *Give, and it shall be given unto you; good measure, pressed down, and shaken together, and running over. . .*

HEDDA, Hedwig, Hedy

Cultural Origin: Teutonic
Inherent Meaning: *REFUGE*
Spiritual Connotation: *UNDER DIVINE PROTECTION*
Supporting Scripture: *Psalm 112:4*
>*Unto the upright there ariseth light in the darkness: he is gracious, and full of compassion, and righteous.*

HEIDI, see Haidee

HELEN, Nellie

Cultural Origin: Greek
Inherent Meaning: *LIGHT*
Spiritual Connotation: *WISDOM, UNDERSTANDING*
Supporting Scripture: *Psalm 37:6*
>*And he shall bring forth thy righteousness as the light, and thy judgment as the noonday.*

HELGA

Cultural Origin: Teutonic
Inherent Meaning: *PIOUS, RELIGIOUS, HOLY*
Spiritual Connotation: *DIVINELY PERCEPTIVE*
Supporting Scripture: *John 16:13*
>*Howbeit when he, the Spirit of truth, is come, he will guide you into all truth....*

HELOISE

Cultural Origin: Greek
Inherent Meaning: *BRIGHT AS THE SUN*
Spiritual Connotation: *ENLIGHTENED ONE*
Supporting Scripture: *Zechariah 8:16*
>*These are the things that ye shall do; Speak ye every man the truth to his neighbour; execute the judgment of truth and peace in your gates.*

HENRIETTA

Cultural Origin: Teutonic
Inherent Meaning: *EVER RICH, MIGHTY*
Spiritual Connotation: *PROSPEROUS PROTECTOR*
Supporting Scripture: *Psalm 18:32*
   *It is God that girdeth me with strength, and maketh my
   way perfect.*

HENRY

Cultural Origin: Teutonic
Inherent Meaning: *POWERFUL, EVER WEALTHY*
Spiritual Connotation: *TRUSTED ONE*
Supporting Scripture: *Psalm 37:23*
   *The steps of a good man are ordered by the Lord: and he
   delighteth in his way.*

HERBERT

Cultural Origin: Anglo-Saxon
Inherent Meaning: *DISTINGUISHED ONE*
Spiritual Connotation: *POWERFUL PROTECTOR*
Supporting Scripture: *Psalm 37:31*
   *The law of his God is in his heart; none of his steps shall
   slide.*

HERMAN

Cultural Origin: Anglo-Saxon
Inherent Meaning: *ARMY MAN*
Spiritual Connotation: *COURAGEOUS SPIRIT*
Supporting Scripture: *Psalm 37:37*
   *Mark the perfect man, and behold the upright: for the end
   of that man is peace.*

HERMOINE

Cultural Origin: Greek
Inherent Meaning: *ONE OF HIGH DEGREE*
Spiritual Connotation: *INTEGRITY, DISCERNMENT*
Supporting Scripture: *Colossians 3:16*
> *Let the word of Christ dwell in you richly in all wisdom; teaching and admonishing one another . . . singing with grace in your hearts to the Lord.*

HERTHA

Cultural Origin: Teutonic
Inherent Meaning: *OF THE FERTILE EARTH*
Spiritual Connotation: *IN GOD'S MOLD*
Supporting Scripture: *Isaiah 30:21*
> *And thine ears shall hear a word behind thee, saying, This is the way, walk ye in it, when ye turn to the right hand, and when ye turn to the left.*

HESPER

Cultural Origin: Greek
Inherent Meaning: *EVENING STAR*
Spiritual Connotation: *GIFT OF GOD*
Supporting Scripture: *Philippians 2:5*
> *Let this mind be in you, which was also in Christ Jesus.*

HESTER

Cultural Origin: Greek
Inherent Meaning: *STAR*
Spiritual Connotation: *GIFT OF GOD*
Supporting Scripture: *Psalm 139:9,10*
> *If I take the wings of the morning, and dwell in the uttermost parts of the sea; even there thy hand shall lead me, and thy right hand shall hold me.*

HILARY

Cultural Origin: Latin
Inherent Meaning: *CHEERFUL*
Spiritual Connotation: *BRIGHT, JOYOUS*
Supporting Scripture: *James 1:17*
> *Every good gift and every perfect gift is from above, and cometh down from the Father of lights, with whom is no variableness, neither shadow of turning.*

HILDA

Cultural Origin: Teutonic
Inherent Meaning: *BATTLE MAID*
Spiritual Connotation: *COURAGEOUS ONE*
Supporting Scripture: *Psalm 73:26*
> *. . . but God is the strength of my heart, and my portion for ever.*

HILDEGARD, Hildegarde

Cultural Origin: Teutonic
Inherent Meaning: PROTECTION
Spiritual Connotation: *VALOROUS ONE*
Supporting Scripture: *2 Corinthians 12:9*
> *. . . My grace is sufficient for thee. . .*

HIRAM

Cultural Origin: Hebrew
Inherent Meaning: *MOST NOBLE ONE*
Spiritual Connotation: *SPIRITUALLY PERCEPTIVE*
Supporting Scripture: *Psalm 84:11*
> *For the Lord God is a sun and shield: the Lord will give grace and glory: no good thing will he withhold from them that walk uprightly.*

HOGAN

Cultural Origin: Gaelic
Inherent Meaning: *YOUTHFUL ONE*
Spiritual Connotation: *ADVENTUROUS SOUL*
Supporting Scripture: *2 Corinthians 9:7*
> *Every man according as he purposeth in his heart, so let him give. . .for God loveth a cheerful giver.*

HOLBROOK

Cultural Origin: Anglo-Saxon
Inherent Meaning: *DWELLER AT THE BROOK*
Spiritual Connotation: *PEACEFUL, HONORABLE*
Supporting Scripture: *Psalm 122:7*
> *Peace be within thy walls, and prosperity within thy palaces.*

HOLLIS

Cultural Origin: Anglo-Saxon
Inherent Meaning: *FROM THE HOLLY TREE*
Spiritual Connotation: *OBEDIENT HEART*
Supporting Scripture: *Isaiah 58:8*
> *Then shall thy light break forth as the morning, and thine health shall spring forth speedily: and thy righteousness shall go before thee; the glory of the Lord shall be thy rearward.*

HOLLY

Cultural Origin: Anglo-Saxon
Inherent Meaning: *FRIENDSHIP AND HAPPINESS*
Spiritual Connotation: *GRACIOUS SPIRIT*
Supporting Scripture: *Philippians 4:7*
> *And the peace of God, which passeth all understanding, shall keep your hearts and minds through Christ Jesus.*

HOMER

Cultural Origin: Greek
Inherent Meaning: *PLEDGE, COVENANT*
Spiritual Connotation: *DOER OF HIS WORD*
Supporting Scripture: *Jeremiah 32:40*
> *And I will make an everlasting covenant with them, that I will not turn away from them, to do them good; but I will put my fear in their hearts, that they shall not depart from me.*

HONORIA

Cultural Origin: Latin
Inherent Meaning: *HONORABLE*
Spiritual Connotation: *HONORED ONE*
Supporting Scripture: *Psalm 100:4*
> *Enter into his gates with thanksgiving, and into his courts with praise: be thankful unto him, and bless his name.*

HOPE

Cultural Origin: Anglo-Saxon
Inherent Meaning: *TRUST IN THE FUTURE*
Spiritual Connotation: *FAITHFUL, UNDERSTANDING HEART*
Supporting Scripture: *Psalm 37:4*
> *Delight thyself also in the Lord; and he shall give thee the desires of thine heart.*

HORACE, Horacio, Horatio

Cultural Origin: Latin
Inherent Meaning: *LIGHT OF THE SUN*
Spiritual Connotation: *VICTORIOUS SPIRIT*
Supporting Scripture: *Mark 11:24*
> *Therefore I say unto you, What things soever ye desire, when ye pray, believe that ye receive them, and ye shall have them.*

HORTENSE

Cultural Origin: Latin
Inherent Meaning: *A GARDENER*
Spiritual Connotation: *PEACEFUL, GRACIOUS*
Supporting Scripture: *Proverbs 3:6*
> *In all thy ways acknowledge him, and he shall direct thy paths.*

HORTON

Cultural Origin: Anglo-Saxon
Inherent Meaning: *FROM THE GRAY ESTATE*
Spiritual Connotation: *FAITHFUL STEWARD*
Supporting Scripture: *2 Samuel 22:33*
> *God is my strength and power: and he maketh my way perfect.*

HOSEA

Cultural Origin: Hebrew
Inherent Meaning: *DELIVERANCE*
Spiritual Connotation: *FREEDOM IN CHRIST*
Supporting Scripture: *2 Corinthians 12:9*
> *. . . My grace is sufficient for thee: for my strength is made perfect in weakness.*

HOWARD

Cultural Origin: Teutonic
Inherent Meaning: *CHIEF GUARDIAN*
Spiritual Connotation: *WISE, DISCERNING ONE*
Supporting Scripture: *Psalm 37:23*
> *The steps of a good man are ordered by the Lord: and he delighteth in his way.*

HOWE

Cultural Origin: Teutonic
Inherent Meaning: *HIGH, EMINENT ONE*
Spiritual Connotation: *HONORED, BELOVED*
Supporting Scripture: *Job 36:4*
    . . . he that is perfect in knowledge is with thee.

HOWELL

Cultural Origin: Celtic
Inherent Meaning: *ALERT, ATTENTIVE*
Spiritual Connotation: *VIGILANT SPIRIT*
Supporting Scripture: *2 Corinthians 5:18*
    And all things are of God, who hath reconciled us to
    himself by Jesus Christ, and hath given to us the ministry
    of reconciliation.

HUBERT

Cultural Origin: Teutonic
Inherent Meaning: *BRIGHT MIND, CLEAR THINKER*
Spiritual Connotation: *PERCEPTIVE INSIGHT*
Supporting Scripture: *Deuteronomy 6:5*
    And thou shalt love the Lord thy God with all thine heart,
    and with all thy soul, and with all thy might.

HUGH, Hugo

Cultural Origin: Teutonic
Inherent Meaning: *THOUGHTFUL, WISE*
Spiritual Connotation: *DISCERNING SPIRIT*
Supporting Scripture: *James 3:17*
    But the wisdom that is from above is first pure, then
    peaceable, gentle, and easy to be entreated, full of mercy
    and good fruits, without partiality, and without
    hypocrisy.

HULDA

Cultural Origin: Hebrew
Inherent Meaning: *QUICK, SPRITELY*
Spiritual Connotation: *GRACIOUS, AND BELOVED*
Supporting Scripture: *Ecclesiastes 2:26*
  *For God giveth to a man that is good in his sight wisdom,
  and knowledge, and joy...*

HUMPHREY

Cultural Origin: Teutonic
Inherent Meaning: *PROTECTOR*
Spiritual Connotation: *PEACEFUL PROTECTOR*
Supporting Scripture: *Ecclesiastes 7:12*
  *For wisdom is a defence, and money is a defence: but the
  excellency of knowledge is, that wisdom giveth life to
  them that have it.*

HURLEY

Cultural Origin: Gaelic
Inherent Meaning: *LOVER OF SEA AND TIDE*
Spiritual Connotation: *PEACEFUL, PERCEPTIVE*
Supporting Scripture: *James 1:17*
  *Every good gift and every perfect gift is from above, and
  cometh down from the Father of lights, with whom is no
  variableness, neither shadow of turning.*

HUXLEY

Cultural Origin: Anglo-Saxon
Inherent Meaning: *FROM HUGH'S MEADOW*
Spiritual Connotation: *TRANQUIL SPIRIT*
Supporting Scripture: *Romans 8:14*
  *For as many as are led by the Spirit of God, they are the
  sons of God.*

HYMAN

Cultural Origin: Hebrew
Inherent Meaning: *FILLED WITH LOVE*
Spiritual Connotation: *LOVING SPIRIT*
Supporting Scripture: *Psalm 36:7*

> *How excellent is thy lovingkindness, O God! therefore the children of men put their trust under the shadow of thy wings.*

I

IAN

Cultural Origin: Gaelic
Inherent Meaning: *GOD IS GRACIOUS*
Spiritual Connotation: *APPOINTED BY GOD*
Supporting Scripture: *Matthew 6:6*
> But thou, when thou prayest, enter into thy closet, and
> when thou hast shut thy door, pray to thy Father which is
> in secret; and thy Father which seeth in secret shall reward
> thee openly.

IDA

Cultural Origin: Teutonic
Inherent Meaning: *HAPPY*
Spiritual Connotation: *JOYFUL SPIRIT*
Supporting Scripture: *Psalm 16:11*
> Thou wilt shew me the path of life: in thy presence is
> fulness of joy; at thy right hand there are pleasures for
> evermore.

IGNATIA

Cultural Origin: Latin
Inherent Meaning: *FIERY, ARDENT ONE*
Spiritual Connotation: *FULL OF HONOR*
Supporting Scripture: *Psalm 51:10*
> Create in me a clean heart, O God; and renew a right
> spirit within me.

IGNATIUS

Cultural Origin: Latin
Inherent Meaning: *FIERY, ARDENT ONE*
Spiritual Connotation: *FULL OF HONOR*
Supporting Scripture: *1 Corinthians 15:58*
> *...be ye stedfast, unmoveable, always abounding in the work of the Lord, forasmuch as ye know that your labour is not in vain in the Lord.*

ILA

Cultural Origin: Latin
Inherent Meaning: *FROM THE ISLAND*
Spiritual Connotation: *COURAGEOUS ONE*
Supporting Scripture: *Matthew 7:7*
> *Ask, and it shall be given you; seek, and ye shall find; knock, and it shall be opened...*

ILEANA

Cultural Origin: Greek
Inherent Meaning: *ROYALTY*
Spiritual Connotation: *ESTEEMED ONE*
Supporting Scripture: *Matthew 25:34*
> *...Come, ye blessed of my Father, inherit the kingdom prepared for you from the foundation of the world.*

ILKA

Cultural Origin: Gaelic
Inherent Meaning: *VIVACIOUS, PERSEVERING*
Spiritual Connotation: *HAPPY SPIRIT*
Supporting Scripture: *Psalm 33:5*
> *He loveth righteousness and judgment: the earth is full of the goodness of the Lord.*

ILONA

Cultural Origin: Greek
Inherent Meaning: *LIGHT*
Spiritual Connotation: *FOLLOWER OF CHRIST*
Supporting Scripture: *Psalm 19:1*
The heavens declare the glory of God; and the firmament sheweth his handiwork.

IMMANUEL, see Emmanuel

IMOGENE

Cultural Origin: Latin
Inherent Meaning: *BELOVED*
Spiritual Connotation: *BLESSED ONE*
Supporting Scripture: *Hebrews 8:10*
. . . I will put my laws into their mind, and write them in their hearts: and I will be to them a God, and they shall be to me a people.

INA

Cultural Origin: Greek
Inherent Meaning: *PURE ONE*
Spiritual Connotation: *DIVINE INSPIRATION*
Supporting Scripture: *Job 22:28*
Thou shalt also decree a thing, and it shall be established unto thee: and the light shall shine upon thy ways.

INEZ

Cultural Origin: Greek
Inherent Meaning: *PURE ONE*
Spiritual Connotation: *A PEARL*
Supporting Scripture: *Isaiah 58:11*
And the Lord shall guide thee continually, and satisfy thy soul. . . and thou shalt be like a watered garden, and like a spring of water, whose waters fail not.

INGEMAR

Cultural Origin: Old Norse
Inherent Meaning: *WARRIOR*
Spiritual Connotation: *ADVENTURING SPIRIT*
Supporting Scripture: *Job 23:14*
> *For he performeth the thing that is appointed for me: and many such things are with him.*

INGER

Cultural Origin: Old Norse
Inherent Meaning: *NOBLE*
Spiritual Connotation: *CONSCIENTIOUS IN WELLDOING*
Supporting Scripture: *Matthew 25:40*
> *Verily I say unto you, Inasmuch as ye have done it unto one of the least of these my brethren, ye have done it unto me.*

INGLEBERT

Cultural Origin: Teutonic
Inherent Meaning: *ANGEL-BRILLIANT*
Spiritual Connotation: *SHINING LIGHT*
Supporting Scripture: *Colossians 1:27*
> *To whom God would make known what is the riches of the glory of this mystery . . . which is Christ in you, the hope of glory.*

INGRAM

Cultural Origin: Old Norse
Inherent Meaning: *KING'S RAVEN (WISDOM)*
Spiritual Connotation: *BRINGER OF GLAD TIDINGS*
Supporting Scripture: *Psalm 121:1*
> *I will lift up mine eyes unto the hills, from whence cometh my help.*

INGRID

Cultural Origin: Old Norse
Inherent Meaning: *HERO'S DAUGHTER*
Spiritual Connotation: *CHERISHED ONE*
Supporting Scripture: *1 Corinthians 2:9*
> *. . . Eye hath not seen, nor ear heard, neither have entered into the heart of man, the things which God hath prepared for them that love him.*

INNIS, Innes

Cultural Origin: Gaelic
Inherent Meaning: *FROM THE RIVER LAND*
Spiritual Connotation: *NOBLE, PEACEFUL*
Supporting Scripture: *Psalm 119:30*
> *I have chosen the way of truth: thy judgments have I laid before me.*

IOLA

Cultural Origin: Greek
Inherent Meaning: *DAWN CLOUD*
Spiritual Connotation: *REVERED ONE, HONORED*
Supporting Scripture: *Revelation 2:7*
> *. . . To him that overcometh will I give to eat of the tree of life, which is in the midst of the paradise of God.*

IONE

Cultural Origin: Greek
Inherent Meaning: *VIOLET-COLORED STONE*
Spiritual Connotation: *INNER BEAUTY*
Supporting Scripture: *Psalm 119:34*
> *Give me understanding, and I shall keep thy law; yea, I shall observe it with my whole heart.*

IRA

Cultural Origin: Hebrew
Inherent Meaning: *WATCHFUL ONE*
Spiritual Connotation: *GOD'S STEWARD*
Supporting Scripture: *Galatians 5:22*
   But the fruit of the Spirit is love, joy, peace, longsuffering, gentleness, goodness, faith.

IRENE

Cultural Origin: Greek
Inherent Meaning: *MESSENGER OF PEACE*
Spiritual Connotation: *VICTORIOUS SPIRIT*
Supporting Scripture: *Job 22:26-28*
   For then shalt thou have thy delight in the Almighty, and shalt lift up thy face unto God. . . Thou shalt also decree a thing, and it shall be established unto thee: and the light shall shine upon thy ways.

IRIS

Cultural Origin: Greek
Inherent Meaning: *THE RAINBOW*
Spiritual Connotation: *GOD'S PROMISE*
Supporting Scripture: *Psalm 104:24*
   O Lord, how manifold are thy works! in wisdom hast thou made them all: the earth is full of thy riches.

IRMA

Cultural Origin: Latin
Inherent Meaning: *EXALTED ONE*
Spiritual Connotation: *EXCELLENT VIRTUE*
Supporting Scripture: *Acts 2:28*
   Thou hast made known to me the ways of life; thou shalt make me full of joy with thy countenance.

IRVING, Irvin, Irvine, Erwin

Cultural Origin: Anglo-Saxon
Inherent Meaning: *SEA FRIEND*
Spiritual Connotation: *DWELLING IN THE SPIRIT*
Supporting Scripture: *Isaiah 26:3*
*Thou wilt keep him in perfect peace, whose mind is stayed
on thee: because he trusteth in thee.*

IRWIN, Erwin

Cultural Origin: Anglo-Saxon
Inherent Meaning: *VICTORIOUS ONE*
Spiritual Connotation: *TRIUMPHANT SPIRIT*
Supporting Scripture: *Zechariah 4:6*
*. . . Not by might, nor by power, but by my spirit, saith
the Lord of hosts.*

ISAAC, Ike

Cultural Origin: Hebrew
Inherent Meaning: *LAUGHTER*
Spiritual Connotation: *CHILD OF PROMISE*
Supporting Scripture: *Psalm 16:8*
*I have set the Lord always before me: because he is at my
right hand, I shall not be moved.*

ISABEL

Cultural Origin: Latin
Inherent Meaning: *CONSECRATED TO GOD*
Spiritual Connotation: *DISCERNING SPIRIT*
Supporting Scripture: *Isaiah 60:1*
*Arise, shine; for thy light is come, and the glory of the
Lord is risen upon thee.*

ISADORA

Cultural Origin: Greek
Inherent Meaning: *GIFT OF LIFE*
Spiritual Connotation: *INSPIRED ONE*
Supporting Scripture: *John 5:30*

*I can of mine own self do nothing: as I hear, I judge: and
my judgment is just; because I seek not mine own will,
but the will of the Father which hath sent me.*

ISAIAH

Cultural Origin: Hebrew
Inherent Meaning: *DELIVERANCE OF JEHOVAH*
Spiritual Connotation: *SPIRITUAL UNDERSTANDING*
Supporting Scripture: *Matthew 17:20*

*. . . If ye have faith as a grain of mustard seed, ye shall say
unto this mountain, Remove hence to yonder place; and it
shall remove; and nothing shall be impossible unto you.*

ISIDORE

Cultural Origin: Greek
Inherent Meaning: *GIFT OF LIFE*
Spiritual Connotation: *INSPIRED ONE*
Supporting Scripture: *1 Timothy 4:14*

Neglect not the gift that is in thee. . .

IVA

Cultural Origin: Gaelic
Inherent Meaning: *GOD IS GRACIOUS*
Spiritual Connotation: *BELOVED ONE*
Supporting Scripture: *Romans 8:28*

*And we know that all things work together for good to
them that love God, to them who are the called according
to his purpose.*

IVAN

Cultural Origin: Russian
Inherent Meaning: *THE LORD'S GRACE*
Spiritual Connotation: *TRIUMPHANT SPIRIT*
Supporting Scripture: *Luke 6:38*

> *Give, and it shall be given unto you; good measure,*
> *pressed down, and shaken together, and running over,*
> *shall men give into your bosom. For with the same*
> *measure that ye mete withal it shall be measured to you*
> *again.*

IVAR, Ivor

Cultural Origin: Old Norse
Inherent Meaning: *NOBLE*
Spiritual Connotation: *HONORABLE, TRUSTWORTHY*
Supporting Scripture: *John 14:27*

> *Peace I leave with you, my peace I give unto you: not as*
> *the world giveth, give I unto you. Let not your heart be*
> *troubled, neither let it be afraid.*

IVY

Cultural Origin: Anglo-Saxon
Inherent Meaning: *FRIENDSHIP, FIDELITY*
Spiritual Connotation: *GOD'S GRACIOUS GIFT*
Supporting Scripture: *Isaiah 26:3*

> *Thou wilt keep him in perfect peace, whose mind is stayed*
> *on thee: because he trusteth in thee.*

J

JACK, see John

JACOB, Jake

Cultural Origin: Hebrew
Inherent Meaning: *SUPPLANTER*
Spiritual Connotation: *BENEVOLENT ONE*
Supporting Scripture: *1 John 2:17*
   . . . but he that doeth the will of God abideth for ever.

JACOBA

Cultural Origin: Hebrew
Inherent Meaning: *SUPPLANTER*
Spiritual Connotation: *BENEVOLENT ONE*
Supporting Scripture: *2 Corinthians 3:17*
   Now the Lord is that Spirit: and where the Spirit of the Lord is, there is liberty.

JACQUELINE, Jacquelyn

Cultural Origin: Latin
Inherent Meaning: *SUPPLANTER*
Spiritual Connotation: *REFRESHING, RENEWING*
Supporting Scripture: *Job 33:4*
   The Spirit of God hath made me, and the breath of the Almighty hath given me life.

JADE

Cultural Origin: Latin
Inherent Meaning: *PRECIOUS GEM*
Spiritual Connotation: *PRICELESS ONE*
Supporting Scripture: *James 1:17*
> *Every good gift and every perfect gift is from above, and cometh down from the Father of lights, with whom is no variableness, neither shadow of turning.*

JAKE, see Jacob

JAMES, Jamie, Jimmy, Jim

Cultural Origin: Latin
Inherent Meaning: *SUPPLANTER*
Spiritual Connotation: *PRUDENT ONE*
Supporting Scripture: *Psalm 23:4*
> *. . . for thou art with me; thy rod and thy staff they comfort me.*

JAN

Cultural Origin: Teutonic
Inherent Meaning: *GOD'S GIFT*
Spiritual Connotation: *CHERISHED ONE*
Supporting Scripture: *Psalm 70:4*
> *Let all those that seek thee rejoice and be glad in thee: and let such as love thy salvation say continually, Let God be magnified.*

JANA, Janna

Cultural Origin: Teutonic
Inherent Meaning: *GIFT OF GOD*
Spiritual Connotation: *CHERISHED ONE*
Supporting Scripture: *Deuteronomy 26:11*
> *And thou shalt rejoice in every good thing which the Lord thy God hath given unto thee, and unto thine house. . .*

JANE, Janet, Janice

Cultural Origin: Hebrew
Inherent Meaning: *GOD IS GRACIOUS*
Spiritual Connotation: *BELOVED ONE*
Supporting Scripture: *Romans 12:2*
> *. . . but be ye transformed by the renewing of your mind, that ye may prove what is that good, and acceptable, and perfect, will of God.*

JANELL, Janel

Cultural Origin: Hebrew
Inherent Meaning: *GOD IS GRACIOUS*
Spiritual Connotation: *BLESSED ONE*
Supporting Scripture: *Psalm 138:8*
> *The Lord will perfect that which concerneth me: thy mercy, O Lord, endureth for ever: forsake not the works of thine own hands.*

JARED, Jarred, Jarrod

Cultural Origin: Hebrew
Inherent Meaning: *NEW LIFE IN CHRIST*
Spiritual Connotation: *RENEWED IN CHRIST*
Supporting Scripture: *Matthew 21:22*
> *And all things, whatsoever ye shall ask in prayer, believing, ye shall receive.*

JARVIS

Cultural Origin: Teutonic
Inherent Meaning: *KEEN, BRIGHT*
Spiritual Connotation: *OPEN TO DIVINE INSPIRATION*
Supporting Scripture: *2 Corinthians 6:2*
> *. . . behold, now is the accepted time; behold, now is the day of salvation.*

JASMINE

Cultural Origin: Persian
Inherent Meaning: *JASMINE FLOWER*
Spiritual Connotation: *MESSENGER OF LOVE*
Supporting Scripture: *Isaiah 55:11*
> So shall my word be that goeth forth out of my mouth: it
> shall not return unto me void, but it shall accomplish that
> which I please, and it shall prosper in the thing whereto I
> sent it.

JASON

Cultural Origin: Greek
Inherent Meaning: *HEALER*
Spiritual Connotation: *QUICKENED IN SPIRIT*
Supporting Scripture: *Luke 6:45*
> A good man out of the good treasure of his heart bringeth
> forth that which is good...

JAY

Cultural Origin: Latin
Inherent Meaning: *VIVACIOUS SPIRIT*
Spiritual Connotation: *ADVENTUROUS ONE*
Supporting Scripture: *Psalm 139:3,4*
> Thou compassest my path... and art acquainted with all
> my ways. For there is not a word in my tongue, but, lo, O
> Lord, thou knowest it altogether.

JAYNE

Cultural Origin: Sanskrit
Inherent Meaning: *VICTORIOUS ONE*
Spiritual Connotation: *CONQUERING SPIRIT*
Supporting Scripture: *Romans 8:15*
> For ye have not received the spirit of bondage again to
> fear; but ye have received the Spirit of adoption, whereby
> we cry, Abba, Father.

JEANNETTE, Jean

Cultural Origin: Latin
Inherent Meaning: *GOD IS GRACIOUS*
Spiritual Connotation: *PRECIOUS ONE*
Supporting Scripture: *2 Chronicles 1:12*
   *Wisdom and knowledge is granted unto thee; and I will
   give thee riches, and wealth, and honour...*

JED, Jedidiah

Cultural Origin: Hebrew
Inherent Meaning: *BELOVED OF THE LORD*
Spiritual Connotation: *SPIRITUAL PERCEPTIVENESS*
Supporting Scripture: *Psalm 145:10*
   *All thy works shall praise thee, O Lord; and thy saints
   shall bless thee.*

JEFFREY, Jeffery

Cultural Origin: Anglo-Saxon
Inherent Meaning: *JOYFUL PEACE*
Spiritual Connotation: *BLESSED ONE*
Supporting Scripture: *Proverbs 3:13*
   *Happy is the man that findeth wisdom, and the man that
   getteth understanding.*

JENNIFER, Jenny

Cultural Origin: Celtic
Inherent Meaning: *FAIR*
Spiritual Connotation: *GIFT OF GOD*
Supporting Scripture: *Psalm 28:7*
   *The Lord is my strength and my shield; my heart trusted
   in him, and I am helped: therefore, my heart greatly re-
   joiceth; and with my song will I praise him.*

JEREMY, Jeremiah

Cultural Origin: Hebrew
Inherent Meaning: *APPOINTED OF JEHOVAH*
Spiritual Connotation: *SPIRITUAL TRUTH*
Supporting Scripture: *Luke 12:31*
> *But rather seek ye the kingdom of God; and all these things shall be added unto you.*

JEROME

Cultural Origin: Latin
Inherent Meaning: *SACRED*
Spiritual Connotation: *FAITHFUL, HONORED*
Supporting Scripture: *1 Peter 1:25*
> *But the word of the Lord endureth for ever. And this is the word which by the gospel is preached unto you.*

JESSE

Cultural Origin: Hebrew
Inherent Meaning: *THE LORD EXISTS*
Spiritual Connotation: *UPRIGHT, UPSTANDING*
Supporting Scripture: *2 Corinthians 3:17*
> *Now the Lord is that Spirit: and where the Spirit of the Lord is, there is liberty.*

JESSIE, Jessica

Cultural Origin: Hebrew
Inherent Meaning: *WEALTHY*
Spiritual Connotation: *BLESSED ONE*
Supporting Scripture: *1 Corinthians 13:13*
> *And now abideth faith, hope, charity, these three; but the greatest of these is charity [love].*

JETHRO

Cultural Origin: Hebrew
Inherent Meaning: *EXCELLENCE, SUPERIORITY*
Spiritual Connotation: *BENEVOLENT SPIRIT*
Supporting Scripture: *Psalm 98:4*
> *Make a joyful noise unto the Lord, all the earth: make a loud noise, and rejoice, and sing praise.*

JEWEL

Cultural Origin: Latin
Inherent Meaning: *A GEM*
Spiritual Connotation: *WISDOM OF LOVE*
Supporting Scripture: *Psalm 16:11*
> *Thou wilt shew me the path of life: in thy presence is fulness of joy; at thy right hand there are pleasures for evermore.*

JILL, Jillian, Gillian

Cultural Origin: Latin
Inherent Meaning: *YOUTHFUL*
Spiritual Connotation: *FULL OF GRACE*
Supporting Scripture: *Luke 17:21*
> *Neither shall they say, Lo here! or, lo there! for, behold, the kingdom of God is within you.*

JOAN, Joanna, Joanne, Johanna

Cultural Origin: Hebrew
Inherent Meaning: *GOD IS GRACIOUS*
Spiritual Connotation: *PRECIOUS ONE*
Supporting Scripture: *Proverbs 4:7*
> *Wisdom is the principal thing; therefore get wisdom: and with all thy getting get understanding.*

JOBINA

Cultural Origin: Hebrew
Inherent Meaning: *CHALLENGED ONE*
Spiritual Connotation: *SEEKER OF TRUTH*
Supporting Scripture: *Matthew 7:8*
> *For every one that asketh receiveth; and he that seeketh findeth; and to him that knocketh it shall be opened.*

JOCELYN

Cultural Origin: Anglo-Saxon
Inherent Meaning: *THE JUST ONE*
Spiritual Connotation: *VIRTUOUS ONE*
Supporting Scripture: *Ezekiel 36:26*
> *A new heart also will I give you, and a new spirit will I put within you...*

JODY, see Judith

JOEL

Cultural Origin: Hebrew
Inherent Meaning: *JEHOVAH IS GOD*
Spiritual Connotation: *GOD'S MESSENGER*
Supporting Scripture: *Romans 12:2*
> *...be ye transformed by the renewing of your mind, that ye may prove what is that good, and acceptable, and perfect, will of God.*

JOHAN

Cultural Origin: Old French
Inherent Meaning: *A DOVE*
Spiritual Connotation: *GENEROSITY OF SPIRIT*
Supporting Scripture: *Galatians 5:22,23*
> *But the fruit of the Spirit is love, joy, peace, longsuffering, gentleness, goodness, faith...against such there is no law.*

JOHN, Jon, Jack, Sean,
Shane, Shawn, Zane

Cultural Origin: Hebrew
Inherent Meaning: *GOD IS GRACIOUS*
Spiritual Connotation: *APPOINTED OF GOD*
Supporting Scripture: *Psalm 118:14*
  *The Lord is my strength and song, and is become my
  salvation.*

JONAH

Cultural Origin: Hebrew
Inherent Meaning: *THE DOVE*
Spiritual Connotation: *DECLARER OF ULTIMATE
                    PEACE AND GOOD*
Supporting Scripture: *Psalm 16:11*
  *Thou wilt shew me the path of life: in thy presence is
  fulness of joy...*

JONAS

Cultural Origin: Hebrew
Inherent Meaning: *THE DOVE*
Spiritual Connotation: *DECLARER OF PEACE
                    AND GOOD*
Supporting Scripture: *Colossians 3:15*
  *And let the peace of God rule in your hearts, to the which
  also ye are called in one body; and be ye thankful.*

JONATHAN

Cultural Origin: Hebrew
Inherent Meaning: *GIFT OF THE LORD*
Spiritual Connotation: *GOD'S PRECIOUS GIFT*
Supporting Scripture: *Psalm 92:4*
  *For thou, Lord, hast made me glad through thy work: I
  will triumph in the works of thy hands.*

JORDAN

Cultural Origin: Hebrew
Inherent Meaning: *DESCENDER*
Spiritual Connotation: *COURAGEOUS IN JUDGMENT*
Supporting Scripture: *Proverbs 21:30*
There is no wisdom nor understanding nor counsel against the Lord.

JOSEPH, Joe

Cultural Origin: Hebrew
Inherent Meaning: *HE SHALL ADD WISDOM*
Spiritual Connotation: *SPIRITUAL UNDERSTANDING*
Supporting Scripture: *Proverbs 28:5*
. . . but they that seek the Lord understand all things.

JOSEPHINE

Cultural Origin: Hebrew
Inherent Meaning: *SHE SHALL INCREASE IN WISDOM*
Spiritual Connotation: *SPIRITUAL UNDERSTANDING*
Supporting Scripture: *Romans 12:2*
. . . but be ye transformed by the renewing of your mind, that ye may prove what is that good, and acceptable, and perfect, will of God.

JOSHUA

Cultural Origin: Hebrew
Inherent Meaning: *GOD OF SALVATION*
Spiritual Connotation: *MESSENGER OF TRUTH*
Supporting Scripture: *James 1:25*
But whoso looketh into the perfect law of liberty, and continueth therein. . . this man shall be blessed in his deed.

JOSIAH

Cultural Origin: Hebrew
Inherent Meaning: *THE FIRE OF THE LORD*
Spiritual Connotation: *INTUITIVE PERCEPTION*
Supporting Scripture: *1 Corinthians 2:7*
> *But we speak the wisdom of God in a mystery, even the hidden wisdom, which God ordained before the world unto our glory.*

JOVITA

Cultural Origin: Latin
Inherent Meaning: *JOYFUL ONE*
Spiritual Connotation: *GOD'S GRACIOUS GIFT*
Supporting Scripture: *Isaiah 55:12*
> *For ye shall go out with joy, and be led forth with peace: the mountains and the hills shall break forth before you into singing...*

JOY

Cultural Origin: Latin
Inherent Meaning: *JOYFUL*
Spiritual Connotation: *GOD'S GRACIOUS GIFT*
Supporting Scripture: *Psalm 119:105*
> *Thy word is a lamp unto my feet, and a light unto my path.*

JOYCE

Cultural Origin: Latin
Inherent Meaning: *VIVACIOUS, JOYFUL*
Spiritual Connotation: *GOD'S GRACIOUS GIFT*
Supporting Scripture: *Psalm 16:11*
> *Thou wilt shew me the path of life: in thy presence is fulness of joy; at thy right hand there are pleasures for evermore.*

JUAN

Cultural Origin: Latin
Inherent Meaning: *GOD'S GRACE*
Spiritual Connotation: *FULL OF GRACE*
Supporting Scripture: *Psalm 97:11*
> *Light is sown for the righteous, and gladness for the upright in heart.*

JUANITA

Cultural Origin: Latin
Inherent Meaning: *LORD'S GRACE*
Spiritual Connotation: *FULL OF GRACE*
Supporting Scripture: *Romans 10:8*
> *. . . The word is nigh thee, even in thy mouth, and in thy heart: that is the word of faith. . .*

JUDD

Cultural Origin: Hebrew
Inherent Meaning: *PRAISED*
Spiritual Connotation: *FULL OF WISDOM*
Supporting Scripture: *John 13:34*
> *A new commandment I give unto you, That ye love one another; as I have loved you, that ye also love one another.*

JUDITH, Judy, Jody

Cultural Origin: Hebrew
Inherent Meaning: *SHE WHO PRAISES*
Spiritual Connotation: *WISDOM AND HONOR*
Supporting Scripture: *Isaiah 58:8*
> *Then shall thy light break forth as the morning, and thine health shall spring forth speedily; and thy righteousness shall go before thee. . .*

JULIA, Juliana, Julie

Cultural Origin: Latin
Inherent Meaning: *YOUTHFUL ONE*
Spiritual Connotation: *ONE GUIDED BY TRUTH*
Supporting Scripture: *Matthew 9:29*
> . . . *According to your faith be it unto you.*

JULIAN, Julius, Jules

Cultural Origin: Latin
Inherent Meaning: *GENTLE*
Spiritual Connotation: *PERCEPTIVE SPIRIT*
Supporting Scripture: *Ephesians 4:23,24*
> *And be renewed in the spirit of your mind; And that ye put on the new man, which after God is created in righteousness and true holiness.*

JULIET

Cultural Origin: Latin
Inherent Meaning: *YOUTHFUL HEART*
Spiritual Connotation: *BUOYANT SPIRIT*
Supporting Scripture: *2 Corinthians 13:11*
> . . . *Be perfect, be of good comfort, be of one mind, live in peace; and the God of love and peace shall be with you.*

JUNE

Cultural Origin: Latin
Inherent Meaning: *YOUTHFUL HEART*
Spiritual Connotation: *JOYOUS ONE*
Supporting Scripture: *Romans 13:10*
> *Love worketh no ill to his neighbour: therefore love is the fulfilling of the law.*

JUSTIN, Justine

Cultural Origin: Latin
Inherent Meaning: *JUST, UPRIGHT*
Spiritual Connotation: *EXCELLENT VIRTUE*
Supporting Scripture: *Psalm 138:8*
> *The Lord will perfect that which concerneth me: thy mercy, O Lord, endureth for ever: forsake not the works of thine own hands.*

JUSTINA

Cultural Origin: Latin
Inherent Meaning: *JUST, UPRIGHT*
Spiritual Connotation: *GRACIOUS SPIRIT*
Supporting Scripture: *Psalm 139:17*
> *How precious also are thy thoughts unto me, O God! how great is the sum of them!*

K

KAMA

Cultural Origin: Sanskrit
Inherent Meaning: *LOVE*
Spiritual Connotation: *HONORED ONE*
Supporting Scripture: *Hosea 12:6*
  *Therefore turn thou to thy God: keep mercy and judg-
  ment, and wait on thy God continually.*

KANE

Cultural Origin: Gaelic
Inherent Meaning: *TRIBUTE, HONOR*
Spiritual Connotation: *ESTEEMED ONE*
Supporting Scripture: *Psalm 31:24*
  *Be of good courage, and he shall strengthen your heart,
  all ye that hope in the Lord.*

KARA

Cultural Origin: Latin
Inherent Meaning: *DEAR, BELOVED ONE*
Spiritual Connotation: *CHERISHED ONE*
Supporting Scripture: *Psalm 36:9*
  *For with thee is the fountain of life: in thy light shall we
  see light.*

KAREN, Karin, Kari

Cultural Origin: Teutonic
Inherent Meaning: *PURE*
Spiritual Connotation: *BELOVED ONE*
Supporting Scripture: *Nehemiah 8:10*
  . . . the joy of the Lord is your strength.

KARL, see Carl

KARLA, see Carla

KATHLEEN

Cultural Origin: Celtic
Inherent Meaning: *PURE ONE*
Spiritual Connotation: *BELOVED*
Supporting Scripture: *Psalm 115:15*
    Ye are blessed of the Lord which made heaven and earth.

KATHRYN, Katherine, Katie, Katrina, Katy

Cultural Origin: Teutonic
Inherent Meaning: *PURE ONE*
Spiritual Connotation: *INTUITIVE, PERCEPTIVE*
Supporting Scripture: *Jeremiah 33:3*
    Call unto me, and I will answer thee, and shew thee great and mighty things, which thou knowest not.

KATURAH

Cultural Origin: Hebrew
Inherent Meaning: *WINSOME*
Spiritual Connotation: *FULL OF GRACE*
Supporting Scripture: *Psalm 119:142*
    Thy righteousness is an everlasting righteousness, and thy law is the truth.

KAY, Kaye

Cultural Origin: Celtic
Inherent Meaning: *REJOICER*
Spiritual Connotation: *A MERRY HEART*
Supporting Scripture: *Proverbs 15:23*
    A man hath joy by the answer of his mouth: and a word spoken in due season, how good is it!

KEANE, Kean

Cultural Origin: Gaelic
Inherent Meaning: *COMMANDER*
Spiritual Connotation: *HONORED, BRAVE*
Supporting Scripture: *Psalm 16:8*
> *I have set the Lord always before me: because he is at my right hand, I shall not be moved.*

KEEGAN

Cultural Origin: Gaelic
Inherent Meaning: *FIERY ONE*
Spiritual Connotation: *COURAGEOUS SPIRIT*
Supporting Scripture: *Psalm 37:37*
> *Mark the perfect man, and behold the upright: for the end of that man is peace.*

KEELY

Cultural Origin: Gaelic
Inherent Meaning: *BEAUTIFUL ONE*
Spiritual Connotation: *BEAUTY OF SPIRIT*
Supporting Scripture: *Proverbs 30:5*
> *Every word of God is pure: he is a shield unto them that put their trust in him.*

KEENAN

Cultural Origin: Gaelic
Inherent Meaning: *LITTLE ANCIENT ONE*
Spiritual Connotation: *HONORED ONE*
Supporting Scripture: *Isaiah 12:2*
> *Behold, God is my salvation; I will trust, and not be afraid: for the Lord Jehovah is my strength and my song; he also is become my salvation.*

KEITH

Cultural Origin: Gaelic
Inherent Meaning: *FROM THE BATTLE PLACE*
Spiritual Connotation: *BRAVE, STRONG*
Supporting Scripture: *Galatians 5:25*
    If we live in the Spirit, let us also walk in the Spirit.

KELLY, Kelley

Cultural Origin: Gaelic
Inherent Meaning: *WARRIOR MAID*
Spiritual Connotation: *LOYAL AND BRAVE*
Supporting Scripture: *Proverbs 2:7*
    He layeth up sound wisdom for the righteous: he is a
    buckler to them that walk uprightly.

KELSEY

Cultural Origin: Old Norse
Inherent Meaning: *DWELLER AT SHIP ISLAND*
Spiritual Connotation: *PEACEFUL SPIRIT*
Supporting Scripture: *Jeremiah 18:6*
    . . . Behold, as the clay is in the potter's hand, so are ye in
    mine hand . . .

KELVIN

Cultural Origin: Gaelic
Inherent Meaning: *FROM THE NARROW RIVER*
Spiritual Connotation: *REASONABLE, RESOLUTE*
Supporting Scripture: *Psalm 119:130*
    The entrance of thy words giveth light; it giveth
    understanding unto the simple.

KENDALL

Cultural Origin: Anglo-Saxon
Inherent Meaning: *FROM THE CLEAR RIVER*
Spiritual Connotation: *STEADFAST, ENDURING*
Supporting Scripture: *Psalm 126:3*
>   *The Lord hath done great things for us; whereof we are glad.*

KENDRA

Cultural Origin: Anglo-Saxon
Inherent Meaning: *UNDERSTANDING ONE*
Spiritual Connotation: *FILLED WITH WISDOM*
Supporting Scripture: *Proverbs 24:3,4*
>   *Through wisdom is an house builded; and by understanding it is established: And by knowledge shall the chambers be filled with all precious and pleasant riches.*

KENDRICK

Cultural Origin: Gaelic
Inherent Meaning: *RULER*
Spiritual Connotation: *STRONG IN SPIRIT*
Supporting Scripture: *Deuteronomy 11:1*
>   *Therefore thou shalt love the Lord thy God, and keep his charge, and his statutes, and his judgments, and his commandments, alway.*

KENNETH, Kenney, Ken

Cultural Origin: Gaelic
Inherent Meaning: *ROYAL OATH*
Spiritual Connotation: *LOYAL, TRUSTWORTHY*
Supporting Scripture: *Jeremiah 15:20*
>   *...I am with thee to save thee and to deliver thee, saith the Lord.*

KENRICK

Cultural Origin: Anglo-Saxon
Inherent Meaning: *BOLD RULER*
Spiritual Connotation: *COURAGEOUS SPIRIT*
Supporting Scripture: *Psalm 119:112*
  I have inclined mine heart to perform thy statutes alway,
  even unto the end.

KENT

Cultural Origin: Anglo-Saxon
Inherent Meaning: *BRIGHT, RADIANT*
Spiritual Connotation: *SHINING ONE*
Supporting Scripture: *Colossians 3:16*
  Let the word of Christ dwell in you richly in all wisdom;
  teaching and admonishing one another in psalms and
  hymns and spiritual songs, singing with grace in your
  hearts to the Lord.

KERMIT

Cultural Origin: Gaelic
Inherent Meaning: *YOUTHFUL ONE, FREE*
Spiritual Connotation: *VIVACIOUS SPIRIT*
Supporting Scripture: *Isaiah 33:5,6*
  The Lord is exalted; for he dwelleth on high. . . . And
  wisdom and knowledge shall be the stability of thy times,
  and strength of salvation: the fear of the Lord is his
  treasure.

KERRY, Kerri

Cultural Origin: Celtic
Inherent Meaning: *YOUTHFUL ONE*
Spiritual Connotation: *HAPPY SPIRIT*
Supporting Scripture: *Colossians 3:23,24*
> *And whatsoever ye do, do it heartily, as to the Lord, and
> not unto men; knowing that of the Lord ye shall receive
> the reward of the inheritance: for ye serve the Lord
> Christ.*

KEVIN

Cultural Origin: Celtic
Inherent Meaning: *COMELY, NOBLE, KIND*
Spiritual Connotation: *BELOVED ONE*
Supporting Scripture: *Psalm 91:15*
> *He shall call upon me, and I will answer him: I will be
> with him in trouble; I will deliver him, and honour him.*

KEZIA

Cultural Origin: Hebrew
Inherent Meaning: *SPICE BARK*
Spiritual Connotation: *PROTECTOR*
Supporting Scripture: *Proverbs 20:12*
> *The hearing ear, and the seeing eye, the Lord hath made
> even both of them.*

KIERAN

Cultural Origin: Gaelic
Inherent Meaning: *LITTLE ONE*
Spiritual Connotation: *BLESSED ONE*
Supporting Scripture: *Proverbs 3:13*
> *Happy is the man that findeth wisdom, and the man that
> getteth understanding.*

KIMBALL

Cultural Origin: Celtic
Inherent Meaning: *RULER*
Spiritual Connotation: *PEACEFUL HEART*
Supporting Scripture: *Psalm 29:2*
> *Give unto the Lord the glory due unto his name; worship the Lord in the beauty of holiness.*

KIMBERLY, Kim

Cultural Origin: Anglo-Saxon
Inherent Meaning: *ROYALTY*
Spiritual Connotation: *GRACIOUS SPIRIT*
Supporting Scripture: *Psalm 119:2*
> *Blessed are they that keep his testimonies, and that seek him with the whole heart.*

KIRBY

Cultural Origin: Old Norse
Inherent Meaning: *FROM THE CHURCH VILLAGE*
Spiritual Connotation: *FOLLOWER OF GOD*
Supporting Scripture: *Psalm 1:3*
> *And he shall be like a tree planted by the rivers of water, that bringeth forth his fruit in his season; his leaf also shall not wither; and whatsoever he doeth shall prosper.*

KIRK

Cultural Origin: Celtic
Inherent Meaning: *DWELLER AT THE CHURCH*
Spiritual Connotation: *WORSHIP IN SPIRIT AND IN TRUTH*
Supporting Scripture: *Psalm 4:7*
> *Thou hast put gladness in my heart, more than in the time that their corn and their wine increased.*

KIRSTIN

Cultural Origin: Latin
Inherent Meaning: *CHRISTIAN*
Spiritual Connotation: *CHRIST SPIRIT*
Supporting Scripture: *Philippians 4:19*
> *But my God shall supply all your need according to his riches in glory by Christ Jesus.*

KNUT, Knute, Canute

Cultural Origin: Old Norse
Inherent Meaning: *FREE MAN*
Spiritual Connotation: *TRIUMPHANT SPIRIT*
Supporting Scripture: *Psalm 18:32,33*
> *It is God that girdeth me with strength, and maketh my way perfect. He maketh my feet like hinds' feet, and setteth me upon my high places.*

KRISTEN, Kristina, Krista, Kris

Cultural Origin: Greek
Inherent Meaning: *FREE SPIRIT, CHRISTIAN*
Spiritual Connotation: *CHRIST SPIRIT*
Supporting Scripture: *Isaiah 30:21*
> *And thine ears shall hear a word behind thee, saying, This is the way, walk ye in it, when ye turn to the right hand, and when ye turn to the left.*

KURT

Cultural Origin: Teutonic
Inherent Meaning: *BOLD COUNSELOR*
Spiritual Connotation: *WISDOM AND JUSTICE*
Supporting Scripture: *1 Corinthians 16:13,14*
> *Watch ye, stand fast in the faith, quit you like men, be strong. Let all your things be done with charity.*

KYLE

Cultural Origin: Gaelic
Inherent Meaning: *FROM THE STRAIT*
Spiritual Connotation: *PERCEPTIVE INSIGHT*
Supporting Scripture: *Proverbs 15:33*
The fear of the Lord is the instruction of wisdom; and before honour is humility.

L

LAIRD

Cultural Origin: Celtic
Inherent Meaning: *LAND PROPRIETOR*
Spiritual Connotation: *PROSPEROUS ONE*
Supporting Scripture: *Proverbs 4:7*
> *Wisdom is the principal thing; therefore get wisdom: and with all thy getting get understanding.*

LALITA, Lolita, Lottie

Cultural Origin: Sanskrit
Inherent Meaning: *PLEASING*
Spiritual Connotation: *GRACIOUS ONE*
Supporting Scripture: *Mark 1:2*
> *As it is written in the prophets, Behold, I send my messenger before thy face, which shall prepare thy way before thee.*

LAMBERT

Cultural Origin: Anglo-Saxon
Inherent Meaning: *INNOCENCE*
Spiritual Connotation: *DIVINE SPARK*
Supporting Scripture: *Psalm 121:8*
> *The Lord shall preserve thy going out and thy coming in from this time forth, and even for evermore.*

LAMONT

Cultural Origin: Old Norse
Inherent Meaning: *LAW MAN*
Spiritual Connotation: *WISE, PRUDENT*
Supporting Scripture: *Haggai 2:5*
> *According to the word that I covenanted with you. . .so my spirit remaineth among you: fear ye not.*

LANA, Lanna, Lani

Cultural Origin: Latin
Inherent Meaning: *BRIGHT AS THE DAWN*
Spiritual Connotation: *ENLIGHTENED ONE*
Supporting Scripture: *Psalm 37:3*
>   *Trust in the Lord, and do good; so shalt thou dwell in the
>   land, and verily thou shalt be fed.*

LANCE

Cultural Origin: Latin
Inherent Meaning: *ATTENDANT*
Spiritual Connotation: *GOD'S HELPER*
Supporting Scripture: *Ezekiel 18:31*
>   *Cast away from you all your transgressions, whereby ye
>   have transgressed; and make you a new heart and a new
>   spirit...*

LARA

Cultural Origin: Latin
Inherent Meaning: *SHINING, FAMOUS ONE*
Spiritual Connotation: *GOD'S GRACIOUS GIFT*
Supporting Scripture: *Romans 8:28*
>   *And we know that all things work together for good to
>   them that love God, to them who are the called according
>   to his purpose.*

LARAINE

Cultural Origin: Latin
Inherent Meaning: *SEAGULL, FREEDOM*
Spiritual Connotation: *FREE SPIRIT*
Supporting Scripture: *Malachi 3:1*
>   *Behold, I will send my messenger, and he shall prepare the
>   way before me: and the Lord, whom ye seek, shall sud-
>   denly come to his temple...*

LARK

Cultural Origin: Anglo-Saxon
Inherent Meaning: *SKYLARK*
Spiritual Connotation: *SPIRITUAL FREEDOM*
Supporting Scripture: *Galatians 5:1*
> *Stand fast therefore in the liberty wherewith Christ hath made us free...*

LARRY, see Lawrence

LATHAM

Cultural Origin: Old Norse
Inherent Meaning: *FROM THE FARMSTEAD*
Spiritual Connotation: *FAITHFUL ONE*
Supporting Scripture: *Micah 3:8*
> *But truly I am full of power by the spirit of the Lord...*

LATHROP

Cultural Origin: Teutonic
Inherent Meaning: *FROM THE FARMSTEAD*
Spiritual Connotation: *PEACEFUL, INDUSTRIOUS*
Supporting Scripture: *Psalm 5:11*
> *But let all those that put their trust in thee rejoice: let them ever shout for joy, because thou defendest them: let them also that love thy name be joyful in thee.*

LAURA, Laurel, Laurette, Loretta,
Lori, Lorna, Lorreta

Cultural Origin: Latin
Inherent Meaning: *HONOR, FAME*
Spiritual Connotation: *VICTORIOUS ONE*
Supporting Scripture: *Ephesians 4:24*
> *And that ye put on the new man, which after God is created in righteousness and true holiness.*

LAURENCE, see Lawrence

LAVEDA

Cultural Origin: Latin
Inherent Meaning: *PURIFIED ONE*
Spiritual Connotation: *BLESSED ONE*
Supporting Scripture: *Psalm 84:11*
> *For the Lord God is a sun and shield: the Lord will give grace and glory: no good thing will he withhold from them that walk uprightly.*

LAVERNE

Cultural Origin: Latin
Inherent Meaning: *FROM THE ALDER TREE*
Spiritual Connotation: *BEAUTIFUL LIFE, BEAUTIFUL SPIRIT*
Supporting Scripture: *Isaiah 9:7*
> *Of the increase of his government and peace there shall be no end...*

LAVINIA, Lavina

Cultural Origin: Latin
Inherent Meaning: *PURE, BEAUTY*
Spiritual Connotation: *PRICELESS ONE*
Supporting Scripture: *Job 22:26*
> *For then shalt thou have thy delight in the Almighty, and shalt lift up thy face unto God.*

LAVONNE

Cultural Origin: Latin
Inherent Meaning: *SPRING LIKE*
Spiritual Connotation: *FRUITFUL SPIRIT*
Supporting Scripture: *Psalm 8:6*
> *Thou madest him to have dominion over the works of thy hands; thou hast put all things under his feet.*

LAWRENCE, Laurence, Larry

Cultural Origin: Latin
Inherent Meaning: *LAUREL-CROWNED ONE*
Spiritual Connotation: *HONORED ONE*
Supporting Scripture: *Psalm 118:24*
>   *This is the day which the Lord hath made; we will rejoice and be glad in it.*

LAWTON

Cultural Origin: Anglo-Saxon
Inherent Meaning: *FROM THE HILL-TOWN ESTATE*
Spiritual Connotation: *INDUSTRIOUS LEADER*
Supporting Scripture: *Matthew 6:33*
>   *But seek ye first the kingdom of God, and his righteousness; and all these things shall be added unto you.*

LEAH, Lea, Leigh

Cultural Origin: Hebrew
Inherent Meaning: *GAZELLE*
Spiritual Connotation: *BEAUTY AND GRACE*
Supporting Scripture: *Psalm 18:32,33*
>   *It is God that girdeth me with strength, and maketh my way perfect. He maketh my feet like hinds' feet, and setteth me upon my high places.*

LEANDER

Cultural Origin: Greek
Inherent Meaning: *LION MAN*
Spiritual Connotation: *STRONG IN SPIRIT*
Supporting Scripture: *John 15:4*
>   *Abide in me, and I in you. As the branch cannot bear fruit of itself, except it abide in the vine; no more can ye, except ye abide in me.*

LEATRICE

Cultural Origin: Anglo-Saxon
Inherent Meaning: *JOY*
Spiritual Connotation: *EXULTANT ONE*
Supporting Scripture: *Psalm 9:1*
> *I will praise thee, O Lord, with my whole heart; I will shew forth all thy marvellous works.*

LEDA, see Letha

LEE, Leigh

Cultural Origin: Teutonic
Inherent Meaning: *FROM THE SHELTERED PLACES*
Spiritual Connotation: *GRACIOUS SPIRIT*
Supporting Scripture: *Romans 8:16*
> *The Spirit itself beareth witness with our spirit, that we are the children of God.*

LEILA, Leala, Lela, Lila

Cultural Origin: Arabic-Greek
Inherent Meaning: *LIGHT*
Spiritual Connotation: *BRINGER OF LIGHT*
Supporting Scripture: *Ecclesiastes 3:11*
> *He hath made every thing beautiful in his time: also he hath set the world in their heart...*

LEILANI

Cultural Origin: Hawaiian
Inherent Meaning: *HEAVENLY FLOWER*
Spiritual Connotation: *PRICELESS ONE*
Supporting Scripture: *Luke 12:32*
> *Fear not...for it is your Father's good pleasure to give you the kingdom.*

LELAND

Cultural Origin: Anglo-Saxon
Inherent Meaning: *FROM THE MEADOWLAND*
Spiritual Connotation: *PROSPEROUS SPIRIT*
Supporting Scripture: *2 Corinthians 13:11*
> . . . *Be perfect, be of good comfort, be of one mind, live in peace; and the God of love and peace shall be with you.*

LEMUEL

Cultural Origin: Hebrew
Inherent Meaning: *CONSECRATED TO GOD*
Spiritual Connotation: *RADIATES GOD'S LIGHT*
Supporting Scripture: *2 Timothy 1:7*
> *For God hath not given us the spirit of fear; but of power, and of love, and of a sound mind.*

LENA

Cultural Origin: Greek
Inherent Meaning: *PEACE, GENTLENESS*
Spiritual Connotation: *BLESSED PEACEMAKER*
Supporting Scripture: *Matthew 7:12*
> *Therefore all things whatsoever ye would that men should do to you, do ye even so to them: for this is the law and the prophets.*

LENICE, Lenis, Lenita, Lenise

Cultural Origin: Latin
Inherent Meaning: *WHITE LILY*
Spiritual Connotation: *DISCERNING SPIRIT*
Supporting Scripture: *Proverbs 16:20*
> *He that handleth a matter wisely shall find good: and whoso trusteth in the Lord, happy is he.*

LENNOX

Cultural Origin: Gaelic
Inherent Meaning: *PLACID STREAM*
Spiritual Connotation: *GOD IS ALL-SUFFICIENT*
Supporting Scripture: *Jeremiah 32:27*
 *Behold, I am the Lord, the God of all flesh: is there any
 thing too hard for me?*

LENORE, Lenora

Cultural Origin: Greek
Inherent Meaning: *BRIGHT LIGHT*
Spiritual Connotation: *ENLIGHTENED SPIRIT*
Supporting Scripture: *Philippians 4:7*
 *And the peace of God, which passeth all understanding,
 shall keep your hearts and minds through Christ Jesus.*

LEO

Cultural Origin: Latin
Inherent Meaning: *LIONHEARTED*
Spiritual Connotation: *BRAVE, COURAGEOUS*
Supporting Scripture: *Psalm 104:24*
 *O Lord, how manifold are thy works! in wisdom hast
 thou made them all: the earth is full of thy riches.*

LEON

Cultural Origin: Latin
Inherent Meaning: *LION-LIKE*
Spiritual Connotation: *BRAVE, COURAGEOUS*
Supporting Scripture: *Romans 6:23*
 *. . . the gift of God is eternal life through Jesus Christ our
 Lord.*

LEONA, Leone

Cultural Origin: Latin
Inherent Meaning: *LION, INITIATIVENESS*
Spiritual Connotation: *COURAGEOUS SPIRIT*
Supporting Scripture: *Psalm 25:5*
Lead me in thy truth, and teach me: for thou art the God of my salvation; on thee do I wait all the day.

LEONARD

Cultural Origin: Latin
Inherent Meaning: *LIONHEARTED, BRAVE*
Spiritual Connotation: *FEARLESS SPIRIT*
Supporting Scripture: *Proverbs 8:14*
Counsel is mine, and sound wisdom: I am understanding; I have strength.

LEOPOLD

Cultural Origin: Teutonic
Inherent Meaning: *BRAVE DEFENDER*
Spiritual Connotation: *BELOVED, HONORED ONE*
Supporting Scripture: *Romans 12:10*
Be kindly affectioned one to another with brotherly love; in honour preferring one another...

LEROY

Cultural Origin: Latin
Inherent Meaning: *KING, ROYAL ONE*
Spiritual Connotation: *ESTEEMED ONE*
Supporting Scripture: *1 Corinthians 2:10*
But God hath revealed them unto us by his Spirit: for the Spirit searcheth all things, yea, the deep things of God.

LESLIE, Lesley

Cultural Origin: Gaelic
Inherent Meaning: *LOW MEADOW DWELLER*
Spiritual Connotation: *YOUTHFUL HEART*
Supporting Scripture: *Isaiah 42:16*
> *. . . I will make darkness light before them, and crooked things straight. These things will I do unto them, and not forsake them.*

LESTER

Cultural Origin: Anglo-Saxon
Inherent Meaning: *LUSTROUS ONE*
Spiritual Connotation: *SHINING SPIRIT*
Supporting Scripture: *2 Corinthians 5:17*
> *Therefore if any man be in Christ, he is a new creature: old things are passed away; behold, all things are become new.*

LETA, see Letitia

LETHA, Leda

Cultural Origin: Greek
Inherent Meaning: *GLADNESS, JOY*
Spiritual Connotation: *JOYOUS SPIRIT*
Supporting Scripture: *Psalm 143:8*
> *Cause me to hear thy lovingkindness in the morning; for in thee do I trust: cause me to know the way wherein I should walk; for I lift up my soul unto thee.*

LETITIA, Leta

Cultural Origin: Latin
Inherent Meaning: *GLADNESS, JOY*
Spiritual Connotation: *JOYFUL SPIRIT*
Supporting Scripture: *Psalm 16:11*
Thou wilt shew me the path of life: in thy presence is fulness of joy; at thy right hand there are pleasures for evermore.

LEVI, Levy

Cultural Origin: Hebrew
Inherent Meaning: *UNITED, JOINED*
Spiritual Connotation: *LOVING, ENLIGHTENED SPIRIT*
Supporting Scripture: *Psalm 18:28*
For thou wilt light my candle: the Lord my God will enlighten my darkness.

LEVINA

Cultural Origin: Anglo-Saxon
Inherent Meaning: *FLASH OF LIGHTNING*
Spiritual Connotation: *VICTORIOUS SPIRIT OF TRUTH*
Supporting Scripture: *Psalm 36:7*
How excellent is thy lovingkindness, O God! therefore the children of men put their trust under the shadow of thy wings.

LEWANNA

Cultural Origin: Hebrew
Inherent Meaning: *THE MOON*
Spiritual Connotation: *APPOINTED OF GOD*
Supporting Scripture: *Proverbs 16:20*
He that handleth a matter wisely shall find good: and whoso trusteth in the Lord, happy is he.

LEWIS

Cultural Origin: Anglo-Saxon
Inherent Meaning: *SAFEGUARD OF THE PEOPLE*
Spiritual Connotation: *GOD'S GUARDIAN*
Supporting Scripture: *Matthew 12:35*
> *A good man out of the good treasure of the heart bringeth forth good things...*

LIDA

Cultural Origin: Slavic
Inherent Meaning: *LOVE*
Spiritual Connotation: *BELOVED ONE*
Supporting Scripture: *Ephesians 4:32*
> *And be ye kind one to another, tenderhearted, forgiving one another, even as God for Christ's sake hath forgiven you.*

LIANA, Lena, Lina

Cultural Origin: Latin
Inherent Meaning: *A CLIMBING VINE*
Spiritual Connotation: *GOD'S GRACIOUS GIFT*
Supporting Scripture: *Isaiah 41:10*
> *Fear thou not; for I am with thee: be not dismayed; for I am thy God: I will strengthen thee...I will uphold thee with the right hand of my righteousness.*

LILA, see Leila

LILLIAN, Lily

Cultural Origin: Latin
Inherent Meaning: *PURITY*
Spiritual Connotation: *SHINING LIGHT*
Supporting Scripture: *Zechariah 2:10*
> *Sing and rejoice...for, lo, I come, and I will dwell in the midst of thee, saith the Lord.*

LINAS, see Linus

LINCOLN

Cultural Origin: Gaelic
Inherent Meaning: *FROM THE COLONY BY THE POOL*
Spiritual Connotation: *DISCERNING SPIRIT*
Supporting Scripture: *1 John 5:4*
> *For whatsoever is born of God overcometh the world: and this is the victory that overcometh the world, even our faith.*

LINDA, Lynda

Cultural Origin: Teutonic
Inherent Meaning: *TRUTH EXISTS FOR THE WISE*
Spiritual Connotation: *EXCELLENT VIRTUE*
Supporting Scripture: *James 5:16*
> *...pray one for another, that ye may be healed. The effectual fervent prayer of a righteous man availeth much.*

LINDELL, Lind

Cultural Origin: Anglo-Saxon
Inherent Meaning: *DWELLER BY THE LINDEN TREE*
Spiritual Connotation: *WATCHFUL SPIRIT*
Supporting Scripture: *Luke 12:32*
> *Fear not...for it is your Father's good pleasure to give you the kingdom.*

LINDSEY

Cultural Origin: Anglo-Saxon
Inherent Meaning: *POOL ISLAND*
Spiritual Connotation: *PEACEFUL ONE*
Supporting Scripture: *Isaiah 58:8*
> *Then shall thy light break forth as the morning, and thine health shall spring forth speedily...*

LINLEY

Cultural Origin: Old Norse
Inherent Meaning: *THE LINNET BIRD*
Spiritual Connotation: *HARMONIOUS SPIRIT*
Supporting Scripture: *Acts 17:28*
> *For in him we live, and move, and have our being; as certain also of your own poets have said, For we are also his offspring.*

LINUS, Linas

Cultural Origin: Greek
Inherent Meaning: *FAIR-HAIRED, SCIENTIFIC*
Spiritual Connotation: *TREASURE OF WISDOM*
AND KNOWLEDGE
Supporting Scripture: *Colossians 2:2,3*
> *That their hearts might be comforted. . .to the acknowledgement of the mystery of God. . .In whom are hid all the treasures of wisdom and knowledge.*

LIONEL

Cultural Origin: Latin
Inherent Meaning: *LITTLE LION*
Spiritual Connotation: *SPIRITUAL INITIATIVENESS*
Supporting Scripture: *Ephesians 3:17-19*
> *That Christ may dwell in your hearts by faith; that ye, being rooted and grounded in love, may be able to comprehend. . .and to know the love of Christ, which passeth knowledge, that ye might be filled with all the fulness of God.*

LLEWELLYN

Cultural Origin: Celtic
Inherent Meaning: *RULER*
Spiritual Connotation: *GENEROUS, PEACEFUL*
Supporting Scripture: *1 John 4:18*
> *There is no fear in love; but perfect love casteth out fear. . .*

LLOYD

Cultural Origin: Celtic
Inherent Meaning: *WISE ONE*
Spiritual Connotation: *OPEN TO DIVINE INSPIRATION*
Supporting Scripture: *Proverbs 12:28*
  *In the way of righteousness is life; and in the pathway
  thereof there is no death.*

LOGAN

Cultural Origin: Gaelic
Inherent Meaning: *LITTLE HOLLOW*
Spiritual Connotation: *FAMED, HONORED*
Supporting Scripture: *Philippians 4:6*
  *Be careful for nothing; but in every thing by prayer and
  supplication with thanksgiving let your requests be made
  known unto God.*

LOIS

Cultural Origin: Greek
Inherent Meaning: *VIRTUOUS, FREE*
Spiritual Connotation: *ESTABLISHED IN FAITH
                    AND TRUTH*
Supporting Scripture: *2 Samuel 22:29*
  *For thou art my lamp, O Lord: and the Lord will lighten
  my darkness.*

LOLA

Cultural Origin: Latin
Inherent Meaning: *COMPASSIONATE ONE*
Spiritual Connotation: *PERCEPTIVE INSIGHT*
Supporting Scripture: *Psalm 16:11*
  *Thou wilt shew me the path of life: in thy presence is
  fulness of joy; at the right hand there are pleasures for
  evermore.*

LOLITA, see Lalita

LORETTA, see Laura

LORI, see Laura

LORIN, Loring, Loren

Cultural Origin: Teutonic
Inherent Meaning: *HONORABLE WARRIOR*
Spiritual Connotation: *GOD'S WARRIOR*
Supporting Scripture: *James 1:25*
> But whoso looketh into the perfect law of liberty, and
> continueth therein, he being not a forgetful hearer, but a
> doer of the work, this man shall be blessed in his deed.

LORNA, see Laura

LORRETA, see Laura

LORRAINE

Cultural Origin: Teutonic
Inherent Meaning: *WARRIOR*
Spiritual Connotation: *LOYAL, COURAGEOUS*
Supporting Scripture: *Isaiah 45:2*
> I will go before thee, and make the crooked places
> straight: I will break in pieces the gates of brass, and cut
> in sunder the bars of iron.

LOUELLA, Luella

Cultural Origin: Anglo-Saxon
Inherent Meaning: *FRIEND*
Spiritual Connotation: *PROTECTRESS*
Supporting Scripture: *Psalm 43:3*
> *O send out thy light and thy truth: let them lead me; let them bring me unto thy holy hill, and to thy tabernacles.*

LOUIS

Cultural Origin: Teutonic
Inherent Meaning: *FAMOUS WARRIOR*
Spiritual Connotation: *DECLARER OF GOD*
Supporting Scripture: *Isaiah 43:19*
> *Behold, I will do a new thing; now it shall spring forth; shall ye not know it? I will even make a way in the wilderness, and rivers in the desert.*

LOUISE

Cultural Origin: Teutonic
Inherent Meaning: *PROTECTRESS*
Spiritual Connotation: *WATCHFUL ONE*
Supporting Scripture: *2 Corinthians 3:17*
> *Now the Lord is that Spirit: and where the Spirit of the Lord is, there is liberty.*

LOWELL

Cultural Origin: Latin
Inherent Meaning: *LOYAL, TRUTHFUL*
Spiritual Connotation: *TRUSTWORTHY*
Supporting Scripture: *Colossians 3:14,15*
> *And above all these things put on charity [love], which is the bond of perfectness. And let the peace of God rule in your hearts. . .*

LOYAL

Cultural Origin: Latin
Inherent Meaning: *TRUE, FAITHFUL, UNSWERVING*
Spiritual Connotation: *FAITHFUL FOLLOWER*
OF CHRIST
Supporting Scripture: *Isaiah 40:31*
> But they that wait upon the Lord shall renew their
> strength; they shall mount up with wings as eagles; they
> shall run, and not be weary; and they shall walk, and not
> faint.

LUANA, Luann

Cultural Origin: Hebrew
Inherent Meaning: *GRACEFUL*
Spiritual Connotation: *GRACIOUS, HARMONIOUS*
Supporting Scripture: *Psalm 55:22*
> Cast thy burden upon the Lord, and he shall sustain thee:
> he shall never suffer the righteous to be moved.

LUCIAN, Lucius

Cultural Origin: Latin
Inherent Meaning: *BORN OF LIGHT*
Spiritual Connotation: *ENLIGHTENED ONE*
Supporting Scripture: *Psalm 139:9,10*
> If I take the wings of the morning, and dwell in the utter-
> most parts of the sea; even there shall thy hand lead me,
> and thy right hand shall hold me.

LUCILE, Lucille, Lucy

Cultural Origin: Latin
Inherent Meaning: *LIGHT BRINGER*
Spiritual Connotation: *CHOSEN OF GOD*
Supporting Scripture: *Romans 8:28*
> And we know that all things work together for good to
> them that love God, to them who are the called according
> to his purpose.

LUCRETIA

Cultural Origin: Latin
Inherent Meaning: *RICHES, REWARDS*
Spiritual Connotation: *PROSPEROUS ONE*
Supporting Scripture: *2 Chronicles 20:20*
> *. . . Believe in the Lord your God, so shall ye be established; believe his prophets, so shall ye prosper.*

LUDWIG

Cultural Origin: Teutonic
Inherent Meaning: *GOOD LEADER*
Spiritual Connotation: *INGENIOUS, DISCERNING*
Supporting Scripture: *Psalm 31:24*
> *Be of good courage, and he shall strengthen your heart, all ye that hope in the Lord.*

LUKE, Lucas

Cultural Origin: Hebrew
Inherent Meaning: *LUMINOUS*
Spiritual Connotation: *BRINGER OF LIGHT*
Supporting Scripture: *Exodus 31:3*
> *And I have filled him with the spirit of God, in wisdom, and in understanding, and in knowledge, and in all manner of workmanship.*

LUPE

Cultural Origin: Spanish-Mexican
Inherent Meaning: *WOLF*
Spiritual Connotation: *COURAGEOUS ONE*
Supporting Scripture: *Psalm 91:11*
> *For he shall give his angels charge over thee, to keep thee in all thy ways.*

LURA, see Lurline

LURLINE, Lura

Cultural Origin: Teutonic
Inherent Meaning: *CHARMER*
Spiritual Connotation: *INGENIOUS, INTUITIVE*
Supporting Scripture: *Psalm 119:105*
   *Thy word is a lamp unto my feet, and a light unto my
   path.*

LUTHER

Cultural Origin: Teutonic
Inherent Meaning: *FAMOUS WARRIOR*
Spiritual Connotation: *HONORED, ESTEEMED*
Supporting Scripture: *Isaiah 41:13*
   *For I the Lord thy God will hold thy right hand, saying
   unto thee, Fear not; I will help thee.*

LUVENA

Cultural Origin: Latin
Inherent Meaning: *LITTLE BELOVED ONE*
Spiritual Connotation: *BLESSED ONE*
Supporting Scripture: *Psalm 32:11*
   *Be glad in the Lord, and rejoice, ye righteous: and shout
   for joy, all ye that are upright in heart.*

LYDIA

Cultural Origin: Greek
Inherent Meaning: *WOMANLY*
Spiritual Connotation: *BEAUTIFUL LIGHT*
Supporting Scripture: *2 Corinthians 4:6*
   *For God, who commanded the light to shine out of
   darkness, hath shined in our hearts, to give the light of the
   knowledge of the glory of God in the face of Jesus Christ.*

LYLE

Cultural Origin: Latin
Inherent Meaning: *FROM THE ISLE*
Spiritual Connotation: *TRIUMPHANT SPIRIT*
Supporting Scripture: *Psalm 32:11*
   Be glad in the Lord, and rejoice, ye righteous: and shout
   for joy, all ye that are upright in heart.

LYNDA, see Linda

LYNDON

Cultural Origin: Anglo-Saxon
Inherent Meaning: *DWELLER ON LINDEN*
                 TREE HILL
Spiritual Connotation: *EXCELLENT WORTH*
Supporting Scripture: *Matthew 6:33*
   But seek ye first the kingdom of God, and his
   righteousness; and all these things shall be added unto
   you.

LYNN, Lynette

Cultural Origin: Gaelic
Inherent Meaning: *CLEAR POOL*
Spiritual Connotation: *GENEROUS SPIRIT*
Supporting Scripture: *Proverbs 9:10*
   The fear of the Lord is the beginning of wisdom: and the
   knowledge of the holy is understanding.

LYSANDRA

Cultural Origin: Greek
Inherent Meaning: *LIBERATOR*
Spiritual Connotation: *SPIRIT OF FREEDOM*
Supporting Scripture: *Galatians 5:1*
   Stand fast therefore in the liberty wherewith Christ hath
   made us free, and be not entangled again with the yoke of
   bondage.

M

MABEL

Cultural Origin: Latin
Inherent Meaning: *BEAUTIFUL, BELOVED*
Spiritual Connotation: *EXCELLENT VIRTUE*
Supporting Scripture: *John 15:5*
  . . . He that abideth in me, and I in him, the same bringeth forth much fruit. . .

MADELINE, Mada, Mala, Marlene

Cultural Origin: Greek
Inherent Meaning: *MAGNIFICENT ONE*
Spiritual Connotation: *ESTEEMED ONE*
Supporting Scripture: *1 Corinthians 14:15*
  . . . I will pray with the spirit, and I will pray with the understanding also: I will sing with the spirit, and I will sing with the understanding also.

MADISON

Cultural Origin: Anglo-Saxon
Inherent Meaning: *VALIANT WARRIOR*
Spiritual Connotation: *TRUSTWORTHY, BRAVE*
Supporting Scripture: *Luke 18:27*
  . . . The things which are impossible with men are possible with God.

MAE, see May

MAGNUS

Cultural Origin: Latin
Inherent Meaning: *GREAT ONE*
Spiritual Connotation: *VICTORIOUS SPIRIT*
Supporting Scripture: *Psalm 19:7*
*The law of the Lord is perfect. . . the testimony of the
Lord is sure, making wise the simple.*

MAHALA, Mahalia, Mahalah

Cultural Origin: Hebrew
Inherent Meaning: *A LOVING HEART*
Spiritual Connotation: *TENDERHEARTED*
Supporting Scripture: *Deuteronomy 18:13*
Thou shalt be perfect with the Lord thy God.

MAIA, see May

MAISIE, see Mary

MALA, see Madeline

MALCOLM

Cultural Origin: Gaelic
Inherent Meaning: *DILIGENT WORKER*
Spiritual Connotation: *TEACHABLE SPIRIT*
Supporting Scripture: *Isaiah 42:16*
*. . . I will lead them in paths that they have not known: I
will make darkness light before them, and crooked things
straight.*

MALIN

Cultural Origin: Anglo-Saxon
Inherent Meaning: *MIGHTY WARRIOR*
Spiritual Connotation: *CHAMPION*
Supporting Scripture: *Matthew 5:6*
   *Blessed are they which do hunger and thirst after
   righteousness: for they shall be filled.*

MALINDA

Cultural Origin: Greek
Inherent Meaning: *MILD, GENTLE ONE*
Spiritual Connotation: *TENDERHEARTED*
Supporting Scripture: *1 Corinthians 3:16*
   *Know ye not that ye are the temple of God, and that the
   Spirit of God dwelleth in you?*

MALLORY

Cultural Origin: Teutonic
Inherent Meaning: *COUNSELOR*
Spiritual Connotation: *WISE, ESTEEMED*
Supporting Scripture: *John 15:10,11*
   *If ye keep my commandments, ye shall abide in my
   love. . . . These things have I spoken unto you, that my joy
   might remain in you, and that your joy might be full.*

MALVA

Cultural Origin: Greek
Inherent Meaning: *GENTLE ONE*
Spiritual Connotation: *GRACIOUS ONE*
Supporting Scripture: *Proverbs 3:5*
   *Trust in the Lord with all thine heart; and lean not unto
   thine own understanding.*

MALVIN

Cultural Origin: Gaelic
Inherent Meaning: *COUNCILOR/FRIEND*
Spiritual Connotation: *STEADFAST, COMPASSIONATE*
Supporting Scripture: *Matthew 6:6*
> *. . . pray to thy Father which is in secret; and thy Father which seeth in secret shall reward thee openly.*

MALVINA, Melvina

Cultural Origin: Gaelic
Inherent Meaning: *REFINED, POLISHED*
Spiritual Connotation: *VICTORIOUS SPIRIT*
Supporting Scripture: *Job 22:26*
> *For then shalt thou have thy delight in the Almighty, and shalt lift up thy face unto God. .*

MANFRED

Cultural Origin: Anglo-Saxon
Inherent Meaning: *FAITHFUL, PEACEFUL MAN*
Spiritual Connotation: *ESTABLISHED IN PEACE*
Supporting Scripture: *Isaiah 55:11*
> *So shall my word be that goeth forth out of my mouth: it shall not return unto me void, but it shall accomplish that which I please, and it shall prosper in the thing whereto I sent it.*

MANLEY

Cultural Origin: Anglo-Saxon
Inherent Meaning: *NOBLE QUALITIES*
Spiritual Connotation: *VICTORIOUS SPIRIT*
Supporting Scripture: *Isaiah 58:8*
> *Then shall thy light break forth as the morning, and thine health shall spring forth speedily: and thy righteousness shall go before thee . . .*

MANUEL

Cultural Origin: Hebrew
Inherent Meaning: *GOD WITH US*
Spiritual Connotation: *CONSECRATED TO GOD*
Supporting Scripture: *Psalm 16:5*
> *The Lord is the portion of mine inheritance and of my cup: thou maintainest my lot.*

MANUELA

Cultural Origin: Hebrew
Inherent Meaning: *GOD WITH US*
Spiritual Connotation: *CONSECRATED TO GOD*
Supporting Scripture: *Psalm 16:5*
> *The Lord is the portion of mine inheritance and of my cup: thou maintainest my lot.*

MARA

Cultural Origin: Hebrew
Inherent Meaning: *COMFORTER*
Spiritual Connotation: *BLESSED ONE*
Supporting Scripture: *Galatians 6:6*
> *Let him that is taught in the word communicate unto him that teacheth in all good things.*

MARC, see Mark

MARCEL

Cultural Origin: Latin
Inherent Meaning: *INDUSTRIOUS WORKER*
Spiritual Connotation: *STRONG IN SPIRIT*
Supporting Scripture: *Proverbs 4:23*
> *Keep thy heart with all diligence; for out of it are the issues of life.*

MARCELLA

Cultural Origin: Latin
Inherent Meaning: *LOFTY ONE*
Spiritual Connotation: *STEADFAST IN SPIRIT*
Supporting Scripture: *Psalm 27:1*
> *The Lord is my light and my salvation; whom shall I fear?*
> *The Lord is the strength of my life; of whom shall I be*
> *afraid?*

MARCIA, Marsha

Cultural Origin: Latin
Inherent Meaning: *FEARLESS, BRAVE*
Spiritual Connotation: *EXCELLENT WORTH*
Supporting Scripture: *1 John 3:2*
> *Beloved, now are we the sons of God, and it doth not yet*
> *appear what we shall be . . .*

MARCUS, see Mark

MARGARET, Marguerite, Margot, Peggy, Rita

Cultural Origin: Greek
Inherent Meaning: *A PEARL*
Spiritual Connotation: *GIFT OF GOD*
Supporting Scripture: *Psalm 18:32*
> *It is God that girdeth me with strength, and maketh my*
> *way perfect.*

MARGE, see Marjorie

MARGOT, see Margaret

MARIA, Marie, Marietta, see Mary

MARIAN, Marianna, Marianne

Cultural Origin: Hebrew
Inherent Meaning: *GRACEFUL*
Spiritual Connotation: *HARMONY AND GRACE*
Supporting Scripture: *Isaiah 60:19*
   *. . . the Lord shall be unto thee an everlasting light, and
   thy God thy glory.*

MARILYN

Cultural Origin: Anglo-Saxon
Inherent Meaning: *POOL OF CRYSTAL-
                   CLEAR WATER*
Spiritual Connotation: *DIVINE PERCEPTION*
Supporting Scripture: *Psalm 69:30*
   *I will praise the name of God with a song, and will
   magnify him with thanksgiving.*

MARIO

Cultural Origin: Latin
Inherent Meaning: *MARTIAL SPIRIT*
Spiritual Connotation: *OBEDIENT SPIRIT*
Supporting Scripture: *John 6:63*
   *It is the spirit that quickeneth. . . the words that I speak
   unto you, they are spirit, and they are life.*

MARION

Cultural Origin: Latin
Inherent Meaning: *TRUSTFUL HEART*
Spiritual Connotation: *LOYAL ONE*
Supporting Scripture: *Deuteronomy 33:27*
   *The eternal God is thy refuge, and underneath are the
   everlasting arms. . .*

MARJORIE, Marge

Cultural Origin: Latin
Inherent Meaning: *A PEARL*
Spiritual Connotation: *PRECIOUS GIFT*
Supporting Scripture: *Psalm 104:24*
> *O Lord, how manifold are thy works! in wisdom hast thou made them all: the earth is full of thy riches.*

MARK, Marc, Marcus

Cultural Origin: Latin
Inherent Meaning: *BRILLIANT, SHINING*
Spiritual Connotation: *GRACE AND MERCY*
Supporting Scripture: *John 4:24*
> *God is a Spirit: and they that worship him must worship him in spirit and in truth.*

MARLA, see Mary

MARLYS, see Mary

MARLENE, see Madeline

MARLON

Cultural Origin: Anglo-Saxon
Inherent Meaning: *FROM THE HILL*
Spiritual Connotation: *VICTORIOUS SPIRIT*
Supporting Scripture: *Psalm 8:6*
> *Thou madest him to have dominion over the works of thy hands; thou has put all things under his feet.*

MARSHA, see Marcia

MARSHALL

Cultural Origin: Teutonic
Inherent Meaning: *COMMANDER*
Spiritual Connotation: *HONORED ONE*
Supporting Scripture: *Psalm 40:4*
   Blessed is that man that maketh the Lord his trust...

MARTHA, Marta, Marty, Mattie

Cultural Origin: Hebrew
Inherent Meaning: *TEACHER, HELPER*
Spiritual Connotation: *HELPFUL SPIRIT*
Supporting Scripture: *Romans 12:2*
   *...be ye transformed by the renewing of your mind, that
   ye may prove what is that good, and acceptable, and
   perfect, will of God.*

MARTIN, Marten

Cultural Origin: Latin
Inherent Meaning: *WARLIKE ONE*
Spiritual Connotation: *SEEKER OF TRUTH*
Supporting Scripture: *John 15:7*
   *If ye abide in me, and my words abide in you, ye shall ask
   what ye will, and it shall be done unto you.*

MARVEL

Cultural Origin: Latin
Inherent Meaning: *A MIRACLE*
Spiritual Connotation: *PRICELESS ONE*
Supporting Scripture: *2 Corinthians 12:9*
   ...My grace is sufficient for thee...

MARVIN

Cultural Origin: Anglo-Saxon
Inherent Meaning: *FAMOUS FRIEND*
Spiritual Connotation: *HONORED, ESTEEMED*
Supporting Scripture: *Psalm 91:2*
> *I will say of the Lord, He is my refuge and my fortress:*
> *my God; in him will I trust.*

MARY, Maisie, Marie, Marietta

Cultural Origin: Hebrew
Inherent Meaning: *SPIRITUAL AWARENESS*
Spiritual Connotation: *BLESSED ONE*
Supporting Scripture: *Psalm 130:5*
> *I wait for the Lord, my soul doth wait, and in his word do*
> *I hope.*

MATHER

Cultural Origin: Anglo-Saxon
Inherent Meaning: *CONQUEROR*
Spiritual Connotation: *INTUITIVE, PERCEPTIVE*
Supporting Scripture: *Luke 6:45*
> *A good man out of the good treasure of his heart bringeth*
> *forth that which is good...*

MATHILDA

Cultural Origin: Teutonic
Inherent Meaning: *NOBLE LADY*
Spiritual Connotation: *BELOVED ONE*
Supporting Scripture: *Luke 12:32*
> *Fear not...for it is your Father's good pleasure to give*
> *you the kingdom.*

MATTHEA

Cultural Origin: Hebrew
Inherent Meaning: *GIFT OF GOD*
Spiritual Connotation: *FULL OF GRACE*
Supporting Scripture: *Psalm 145:10*
> *All thy works shall praise thee, O Lord; and thy saints*
> *shall bless thee.*

MATTHEW

Cultural Origin: Hebrew
Inherent Meaning: *GIFT OF JEHOVAH*
Spiritual Connotation: *ONE HONORING GOD*
Supporting Scripture: *Psalm 104:1*
> *Bless the Lord, O my soul. O Lord my God, thou art very*
> *great; thou art clothed with honour and majesty.*

MATTHIAS

Cultural Origin: Hebrew
Inherent Meaning: *GIFT OF JEHOVAH*
Spiritual Connotation: *ONE HONORING GOD*
Supporting Scripture: *Ephesians 6:10,11*
> *Finally, my brethren, be strong in the Lord, and in the*
> *power of his might. Put on the whole armour of God...*

MAUDE, Maud

Cultural Origin: Anglo-Saxon
Inherent Meaning: *NOBLE LADY*
Spiritual Connotation: *DEARLY BELOVED ONE*
Supporting Scripture: *Isaiah 25:8*
> *He will swallow up death in victory; and the Lord God*
> *will wipe away tears from off all faces...*

MAUREEN

Cultural Origin: Gaelic
Inherent Meaning: *GENTLE SPIRIT*
Spiritual Connotation: *BELOVED ONE*
Supporting Scripture: *Psalm 139:17*
> *How precious also are thy thoughts unto me, O God! how great is the sum of them!*

MAURICE, Morris

Cultural Origin: Gaelic
Inherent Meaning: *GALLANT ONE*
Spiritual Connotation: *NOBLE CONDUCT*
Supporting Scripture: *Proverbs 16:7*
> *When a man's ways please the Lord, he maketh even his enemies to be at peace with him.*

MAVIS

Cultural Origin: Latin
Inherent Meaning: *SONG THRUSH*
Spiritual Connotation: *HARMONY, JOY*
Supporting Scripture: *Psalm 138:2*
> *I will worship toward the holy temple, and praise thy name for thy lovingkindness and for thy truth: for thou hast magnified thy word above all thy name.*

MAXIMILLIAN, Max

Cultural Origin: Latin
Inherent Meaning: *DISTINGUISHED ONE*
Spiritual Connotation: *SECURE IN TRUTH*
Supporting Scripture: *Isaiah 64:8*
> *But now, O Lord, thou art our father; we are the clay, and thou our potter; and we all are the work of thy hand.*

MAXINE

Cultural Origin: Latin
Inherent Meaning: *RENOWNED, EMINENT*
Spiritual Connotation: *SECURE IN TRUTH*
Supporting Scripture: *Philippians 3:15*
> *Let us therefore, as many as be perfect, be thus minded:*
> *and if in any thing ye be otherwise minded, God shall*
> *reveal even this unto you.*

MAXELL

Cultural Origin: Anglo-Saxon
Inherent Meaning: *CAPABLE, INFLUENTIAL*
Spiritual Connotation: *FAITHFUL STEWARD*
Supporting Scripture: *Matthew 6:22*
> *The light of the body is the eye: if therefore thine eye be*
> *single, thy whole body shall be full of light.*

MAY, Mae, Maia

Cultural Origin: Hebrew
Inherent Meaning: *ESTEEMED ONE*
Spiritual Connotation: *HONORED, BLESSED*
Supporting Scripture: *Psalm 92:4*
> *For thou, Lord, hast made me glad through thy work: I*
> *will triumph in the works of thy hands.*

MAYA, Maia

Cultural Origin: Latin
Inherent Meaning: *ESTEEMED ONE*
Spiritual Connotation: *HONORED, BLESSED*
Supporting Scripture: *Psalm 143:8*
> *Cause me to hear thy lovingkindness in the morning; for*
> *in thee do I trust: cause me to know the way wherein I*
> *should walk; for I lift up my soul unto thee.*

MAYER

Cultural Origin: Latin
Inherent Meaning: *RENOWNED, HONORED*
Spiritual Connotation: *EXCELLENT WORTH*
Supporting Scripture: *Romans 12:2*
   . . . be ye transformed by the renewing of your mind, that
   ye may prove what is that good, and acceptable, and
   perfect, will of God.

MAYFIELD

Cultural Origin: Anglo-Saxon
Inherent Meaning: *FROM THE WARRIOR FIELD*
Spiritual Connotation: *VALIANT SPIRIT*
Supporting Scripture: *1 John 4:16*
   . . . God is love; and he that dwelleth in love dwelleth in
   God, and God in him.

MAYHEW

Cultural Origin: Latin
Inherent Meaning: *GIFT OF JEHOVAH*
Spiritual Connotation: *MIGHTY IN SPIRIT*
Supporting Scripture: *2 Corinthians 13:11*
   . . . Be perfect, be of good comfort, be of one mind, live in
   peace; and the God of love and peace shall be with you.

MAYNARD

Cultural Origin: Teutonic
Inherent Meaning: *POWERFUL, BRAVE*
Spiritual Connotation: *NOBLE SPIRIT*
Supporting Scripture: *1 Corinthians 14:15*
   . . . I will pray with the spirit, and I will pray with the
   understanding also: I will sing with the spirit, and I will
   sing with the understanding also.

MAYO

Cultural Origin: Gaelic
Inherent Meaning: *MIRTH, JOY*
Spiritual Connotation: *GIFT OF JOY*
Supporting Scripture: *Psalm 96:1,2*
> *O sing unto the Lord a new song: sing unto the Lord, all the earth. Sing unto the Lord, bless his name; shew forth his salvation from day to day.*

MEARA

Cultural Origin: Gaelic
Inherent Meaning: *MIRTH, JOY*
Spiritual Connotation: *GIFT OF JOY*
Supporting Scripture: *Psalm 119:18*
> *Open thou mine eyes, that I may behold wondrous things out of thy law.*

MEGAN

Cultural Origin: Greek
Inherent Meaning: *MIGHTY ONE*
Spiritual Connotation: *VICTORIOUS SPIRIT*
Supporting Scripture: *Isaiah 2:5*
> *. . . come ye, and let us walk in the light of the Lord.*

MELANIE

Cultural Origin: Greek
Inherent Meaning: *REST, RENEWAL*
Spiritual Connotation: *DIVINE SPARK*
Supporting Scripture: *Ezekiel 37:13,14*
> *And ye shall know that I am the Lord. . . and shall put my spirit in you, and ye shall live, and I shall place you in your own land.*

MELICENT

Cultural Origin: Greek
Inherent Meaning: *SWEET AS HONEY*
Spiritual Connotation: *REFRESHING SPIRIT*
Supporting Scripture: *Psalm 62:1*
Truly my soul waiteth upon God: from him cometh my salvation.

MELINDA

Cultural Origin: Greek
Inherent Meaning: *GENTLE ONE*
Spiritual Connotation: *CHERISHED ONE*
Supporting Scripture: *Isaiah 58:11*
And the Lord shall guide thee continually... and thou shalt be like a watered garden, and like a spring of water, whose waters fail not.

MELISSA

Cultural Origin: Greek
Inherent Meaning: *HONEY BEE*
Spiritual Connotation: *INDUSTRIOUS, CREATIVE*
Supporting Scripture: *James 2:22*
...by works was faith made perfect.

MELITA

Cultural Origin: Greek
Inherent Meaning: *SWEETENED WITH HONEY*
Spiritual Connotation: *FILLED WITH JOY*
Supporting Scripture: *Psalm 145:16*
Thou openest thine hand, and satisfiest the desire of every living thing.

MELODY

Cultural Origin: Anglo-Saxon
Inherent Meaning: *SONG*
Spiritual Connotation: *JOYFUL ONE*
Supporting Scripture: *Genesis 28:15*
> *And, behold, I am with thee, and will keep thee in all places whither thou goest...*

MELVILLE

Cultural Origin: Latin
Inherent Meaning: *INDUSTRIOUS ONE*
Spiritual Connotation: *INGENIOUS SPIRIT*
Supporting Scripture: *John 3:21*
> *But he that doeth truth cometh to the light, that his deeds may be made manifest, that they are wrought in God.*

MELVIN

Cultural Origin: Anglo-Saxon
Inherent Meaning: *RELIABLE FRIEND*
Spiritual Connotation: *EXCELLENT VIRTUE*
Supporting Scripture: *Ephesians 3:19*
> *And to know the love of Christ, which passeth knowledge, that ye might be filled with all the fulness of God.*

MERCEDES

Cultural Origin: Latin
Inherent Meaning: *A GIFT*
Spiritual Connotation: *ESTEEMED ONE*
Supporting Scripture: *Isaiah 52:7*
> *How beautiful upon the mountains are the feet of him that bringeth good tidings, that publisheth peace...*

MEREDITH, Meridith, Merry

Cultural Origin: Celtic
Inherent Meaning: *GUARDIAN OF THE SEA*
Spiritual Connotation: *FAITHFUL FRIEND*
Supporting Scripture: *Proverbs 2:10,11*
When wisdom entereth into thine heart, and knowledge is
pleasant unto thy soul; discretion shall preserve thee,
understanding shall keep thee.

MERLE

Cultural Origin: Latin
Inherent Meaning: *THRUSH BIRD*
Spiritual Connotation: *BLESSED OF GOD*
Supporting Scripture: *Ephesians 4:4-6*
There is one body, and one Spirit. . . one God and Father
of all, who is above all, and through all, and in you all.

MERLIN

Cultural Origin: Anglo-Saxon
Inherent Meaning: *FALCON OR HAWK*
Spiritual Connotation: *COURAGEOUS ONE*
Supporting Scripture: *Matthew 5:14-16*
Ye are the light of the world. . . . Let your light so shine
before men, that they may see your good works, and
glorify your Father which is in heaven.

MERRILL

Cultural Origin: Latin
Inherent Meaning: *FAMOUS ONE*
Spiritual Connotation: *HONORED ONE*
Supporting Scripture: *Ecclesiastes 2:26*
For God giveth to a man that is good in his sight wisdom,
and knowledge, and joy. . .

MERRY, see Meredith

MERTON

Cultural Origin: Anglo-Saxon
Inherent Meaning: *FROM AN ESTATE*
Spiritual Connotation: *PROSPEROUS GUARDIAN*
Supporting Scripture: *Romans 8:16*
   *The Spirit itself beareth witness with our spirit, that we
   are the children of God.*

MERVIN

Cultural Origin: Anglo-Saxon
Inherent Meaning: *FAMOUS FRIEND*
Spiritual Connotation: *HONORED ONE*
Supporting Scripture: *Joshua 1:9*
   *. . . Be strong and of a good courage; be not afraid,
   neither be thou dismayed: for the Lord thy God is with
   thee whithersoever thou goest.*

META

Cultural Origin: Latin
Inherent Meaning: *A PEARL*
Spiritual Connotation: *GIFT OF GOD*
Supporting Scripture: *Isaiah 30:15*
   *For thus saith the Lord God. . . in returning and rest shall
   ye be saved; in quietness and in confidence shall be your
   strength. . .*

MICHAEL, Mike

Cultural Origin: Hebrew
Inherent Meaning: *WHO IS LIKE GOD*
Spiritual Connotation: *ESTEEMED ONE*
Supporting Scripture: *Isaiah 41:10*
   *Fear thou not; for I am with thee; be not dismayed; for I
   am thy God.*

MICHELLE

Cultural Origin: Hebrew
Inherent Meaning: *WHO IS LIKE GOD*
Spiritual Connotation: *GODLINESS*
Supporting Scripture: *1 Timothy 4:8*
    *. . . godliness is profitable unto all things, having promise
of the life that now is, and of that which is to come.*

MIDGE, see Mildred

MIGNON

Cultural Origin: Latin
Inherent Meaning: *GRACEFUL, DAINTY*
Spiritual Connotation: *GENTLE HEART*
Supporting Scripture: *Romans 8:28*
    *. . . all things work together for good to them that love
God, to them who are the called according to his purpose.*

MIGUEL

Cultural Origin: Spanish-American
Inherent Meaning: *CHAMPION*
Spiritual Connotation: *VICTORIOUS SPIRIT*
Supporting Scripture: *Philippians 2:13*
    *For it is God which worketh in you both to will and to do
of his good pleasure.*

MIKE, see Michael

MILDRED, Midge

Cultural Origin: Anglo-Saxon
Inherent Meaning: *GENTLE-HEARTED*
Spiritual Connotation: *GRACIOUS SPIRIT*
Supporting Scripture: *1 John 4:7*
    *Beloved, let us love one another: for love is of God; and
every one that loveth is born of God, and knoweth God.*

MILES, Myles

Cultural Origin: Latin
Inherent Meaning: *CHAMPION*
Spiritual Connotation: *HONORED, ESTEEMED*
Supporting Scripture: *Proverbs 18:16*
 A man's gift maketh room for him, and bringeth him
 before great men.

MILLARD

Cultural Origin: Latin
Inherent Meaning: *WINNING, STRONG*
Spiritual Connotation: *EXCELLENT WORTH*
Supporting Scripture: *1 Chronicles 29:12*
 . . . and in thine hand is power and might; and in thine
 hand it is to make great, and to give strength unto all.

MILLICENT, Melisenda, Millie

Cultural Origin: Teutonic
Inherent Meaning: *INDUSTRIOUS AND TRUE*
Spiritual Connotation: *GRACIOUS SPIRIT*
Supporting Scripture: *Ephesians 3:19*
 And to know the love of Christ, which passeth
 knowledge, that ye might be filled with all the fulness of
 God.

MILO

Cultural Origin: Latin
Inherent Meaning: *MILLER, HELPER*
Spiritual Connotation: *PERSEVERING, HELPFUL SPIRIT*
Supporting Scripture: *Isaiah 30:29*
 Ye shall have a song, as in the night when a holy solemni-
 ty is kept; and gladness of heart, as when one goeth with a
 pipe to come into the mountain of the Lord. . .

MILTON

Cultural Origin: Anglo-Saxon
Inherent Meaning: *INDUSTRIOUS, CREATIVE*
Spiritual Connotation: *BLESSED OF GOD*
Supporting Scripture: *Romans 12:5,6*
> *So we, being many, are one body in Christ, and every one
> members one of another. Having then gifts differing ac-
> cording to the grace that is given to us. . .*

MIMI, see Miriam

MINERVA, Minnie

Cultural Origin: Greek
Inherent Meaning: *PURPOSE, THINKER*
Spiritual Connotation: *DILIGENT, DISCERNING SPIRIT*
Supporting Scripture: *Isaiah 40:31*
> *But they that wait upon the Lord shall renew their
> strength; they shall mount up with wings as eagles; they
> shall run, and not be weary; and they shall walk, and not
> faint.*

MINNA, Mina

Cultural Origin: Teutonic
Inherent Meaning: *LOVE*
Spiritual Connotation: *CHERISHED ONE*
Supporting Scripture: *Isaiah 35:1*
> *The wilderness and the solitary place shall be glad for
> them; and the desert shall rejoice, and blossom as the
> rose.*

MINNIE, see Minerva

MIRANDA

Cultural Origin: Latin
Inherent Meaning: *ADMIRABLE ONE*
Spiritual Connotation: *BELOVED ONE*
Supporting Scripture: *Proverbs 3:6*
> *In all thy ways acknowledge him, and he shall direct thy paths.*

MIRIAM, Mimi, Mitzi

Cultural Origin: Hebrew
Inherent Meaning: *DWELLING IN THE SPIRIT*
Spiritual Connotation: *DISCERNING ONE*
Supporting Scripture: *Matthew 5:14*
> *Ye are the light of the world. A city that is set on an hill cannot be hid.*

MISHON

Cultural Origin: Universal
Inherent Meaning: *DIVINELY INSPIRED*
Spiritual Connotation: *GRACIOUS GIFT*
Supporting Scripture: *Psalm 36:7*
> *How excellent is thy lovingkindness, O God! therefore the children of men put their trust under the shadow of thy wings.*

MITCHELL

Cultural Origin: Anglo-Saxon
Inherent Meaning: *WHO IS LIKE GOD*
Spiritual Connotation: *CONSECRATED TO GOD*
Supporting Scripture: *Psalm 36:9*
> *For with thee is the fountain of life: in thy light shall we see light.*

MOLLY, see Mary

MONA

Cultural Origin: Teutonic
Inherent Meaning: *THE MOON*
Spiritual Connotation: *REFLECTION OF WISDOM*
Supporting Scripture: *Proverbs 2:6,7*
> *For the Lord giveth wisdom: out of his mouth cometh knowledge and understanding. He layeth up sound wisdom for the righteous...*

MONICA

Cultural Origin: Latin
Inherent Meaning: *ADVISOR*
Spiritual Connotation: *CONSECRATED ONE*
Supporting Scripture: *2 Corinthians 1:21,22*
> *Now he which stablisheth us with you in Christ, and hath anointed us, is God; who hath also sealed us, and given the earnest of the Spirit in our hearts.*

MONROE

Cultural Origin: Gaelic
Inherent Meaning: *FROM THE HILL*
Spiritual Connotation: *INTEGRITY, TRUST*
Supporting Scripture: *Mark 9:23*
> *...all things are possible to him that believeth.*

MONTGOMERY, Monty

Cultural Origin: Anglo-Saxon
Inherent Meaning: *WEALTHY ONE*
Spiritual Connotation: *PROSPEROUS SPIRIT*
Supporting Scripture: *Psalm 37:5*
> *Commit thy way unto the Lord; trust also in him; and he shall bring it to pass.*

MORGAN

Cultural Origin: Celtic
Inherent Meaning: *WHITE SEA*
Spiritual Connotation: *WISE ONE*
Supporting Scripture: *Isaiah 12:2*
> *. . . I will trust, and not be afraid: for the Lord Jehovah is my strength and my song; he also is become my salvation.*

MORRIS, see Maurice

MORTIMER

Cultural Origin: Latin
Inherent Meaning: *QUIET WATER*
Spiritual Connotation: *CENTERED IN TRUTH*
Supporting Scripture: *Psalm 122:7*
> *Peace be within thy walls, and prosperity within thy palaces.*

MORTON

Cultural Origin: Anglo-Saxon
Inherent Meaning: *FROM THE MOOR ESTATE*
Spiritual Connotation: *DOMINION, AUTHORITY*
Supporting Scripture: *Mark 9:23*
> *. . . all things are possible to him that believeth.*

MOSELLE

Cultural Origin: Hebrew
Inherent Meaning: *TAKEN FROM THE WATER*
Spiritual Connotation: *DELIVERED OF GOD*
Supporting Scripture: *John 8:32*
> *And ye shall know the truth, and the truth shall make you free.*

MOSES

Cultural Origin: Hebrew
Inherent Meaning: *DRAWN FROM THE WATER,*
                       DRAWING FORTH
Spiritual Connotation: *DELIVERED OF GOD*
Supporting Scripture: *Ecclesiastes 3:11*
> *He hath made every thing beautiful in his time: also he hath set the world in their heart, so that no man can find out the work that God maketh from the beginning to the end.*

MURIEL

Cultural Origin: Greek
Inherent Meaning: *MYRRH*
Spiritual Connotation: *GOD'S GRACIOUS GIFT*
Supporting Scripture: *Isaiah 30:29*
> *Ye shall have a song, as in the night when a holy solemnity is kept; and gladness of heart, as when one goeth with a pipe to come into the mountain of the Lord . . .*

MURRAY

Cultural Origin: Gaelic
Inherent Meaning: *SEA MAN*
Spiritual Connotation: *COMPASSIONATE ONE*
Supporting Scripture: *1 Kings 3:9*
> *Give therefore thy servant an understanding heart . . . that I may discern between good and bad . . .*

MYLES, see Miles

MYRA

Cultural Origin: Gaelic
Inherent Meaning: *ABUNDANCE*
Spiritual Connotation: *POWER FOR GOOD*
Supporting Scripture: *Psalm 32:11*
> *Be glad in the Lord, and rejoice, ye righteous: and shout for joy, all ye that are upright in heart.*

MYRNA

Cultural Origin: Gaelic
Inherent Meaning: *GENTLE ONE*
Spiritual Connotation: *BELOVED ONE*
Supporting Scripture: *Isaiah 55:12*
> *For ye shall go out with joy, and be led forth with peace: the mountains and the hills shall break forth before you into singing, and all the trees of the field shall clap their hands.*

MYRON

Cultural Origin: Greek
Inherent Meaning: *FRAGRANT OINTMENT*
Spiritual Connotation: *SPIRITUAL UNDERSTANDING*
Supporting Scripture: *Philippians 4:7*
> *And the peace of God, which passeth all understanding, shall keep your hearts and minds through Christ Jesus.*

MYRTLE

Cultural Origin: Greek
Inherent Meaning: *A TRIBUTE TO OBSTACLES OVERCOME*
Spiritual Connotation: *VICTORIOUS SPIRIT*
Supporting Scripture: *Psalm 36:9*
> *For with thee is the fountain of life: in thy light shall we see light.*

N

NADINE, Nada

Cultural Origin: Sanskrit
Inherent Meaning: *HOPE*
Spiritual Connotation: *SPIRITUAL POTENTIAL*
Supporting Scripture: *Psalm 18:28*
> *For thou wilt light my candle: the Lord my God will enlighten my darkness.*

NADJA

Cultural Origin: Latin
Inherent Meaning: *GIVING LIGHT*
Spiritual Connotation: *BRINGER OF LIGHT*
Supporting Scripture: *Deuteronomy 16:15*
> *. . . the Lord thy God shall bless thee in all thine increase, and in all the works of thine hands, therefore thou shalt surely rejoice.*

NANCY, Nan, Nanette

Cultural Origin: Latin
Inherent Meaning: *GRACE*
Spiritual Connotation: *GRACIOUS ONE*
Supporting Scripture: *2 Samuel 22:33*
> *God is my strength and power: and he maketh my way perfect.*

NAOMI

Cultural Origin: Hebrew
Inherent Meaning: *RENEWAL, DELIGHT*
Spiritual Connotation: *ENLIGHTENED SPIRIT*
Supporting Scripture: *Psalm 52:8*
> *But I am like a green olive tree in the house of God: I trust in the mercy of God for ever and ever.*

NATALIE

Cultural Origin: Latin
Inherent Meaning: *CHRISTMAS CHILD*
Spiritual Connotation: *GOD'S GIFT OF JOY*
Supporting Scripture: *Psalm 9:2*
   I will be glad and rejoice in thee: I will sing praise to thy name, O thou most High.

NATHAN

Cultural Origin: Hebrew
Inherent Meaning: *GIFT OF GOD*
Spiritual Connotation: *SPIRITUAL PERCEPTION*
Supporting Scripture: *1 Corinthians 15:57*
   But thanks be to God, which giveth us the victory through our Lord Jesus Christ.

NEAL, Neil, Niles

Cultural Origin: Celtic
Inherent Meaning: *RULER, CHAMPION*
Spiritual Connotation: *HONORED, ESTEEMED*
Supporting Scripture: *1 John 4:7*
   Beloved, let us love one another: for love is of God; and every one that loveth is born of God, and knoweth God.

NEDRA

Cultural Origin: Latin
Inherent Meaning: *AWARENESS*
Spiritual Connotation: *PERCEPTIVE SPIRIT*
Supporting Scripture: *Joel 2:21*
   Fear not . . . be glad and rejoice: for the Lord will do great things.

NELDA

Cultural Origin: Anglo-Saxon
Inherent Meaning: *FROM THE HOME OF
THE ELDER TREE*
Spiritual Connotation: *ESTABLISHED IN PEACE*
Supporting Scripture: *Proverbs 15:33*
*The fear of the Lord is the instruction of wisdom; and
before honour is humility.*

NELLIE, see Helen

NELSON

Cultural Origin: Anglo-Saxon
Inherent Meaning: *CHAMPION*
Spiritual Connotation: *VALIANT, HONORED*
Supporting Scripture: *Isaiah 33:15,16*
*He that walketh righteously, and speaketh uprightly. . . he
shall dwell on high. . .*

NEVA

Cultural Origin: Latin
Inherent Meaning: *PURITY*
Spiritual Connotation: *VIRTUOUS SPIRIT*
Supporting Scripture: *Psalm 119:2*
*Blessed are they that keep his testimonies, and that seek
him with the whole heart.*

NEVILLE, Nevile

Cultural Origin: Latin
Inherent Meaning: *FROM THE NEW ESTATE*
Spiritual Connotation: *STRONG IN SPIRIT*
Supporting Scripture: *Zechariah 7:9*
*Thus speaketh the Lord of hosts, saying, Execute true
judgment, and shew mercy and compassion, every man to
his brother.*

NEWELL

Cultural Origin: Anglo-Saxon
Inherent Meaning: *FROM THE NEW HALL*
Spiritual Connotation: *SINCERE, DEVOTED*
Supporting Scripture: *Isaiah 58:14*
> *Then shalt thou delight thyself in the Lord; and I will cause thee to ride upon the high places of the earth...*

NEWTON

Cultural Origin: Latin
Inherent Meaning: *NEW TOWN*
Spiritual Connotation: *HELPFUL COUNSELOR*
Supporting Scripture: *Proverbs 20:5*
> *Counsel in the heart of man is like deep water; but a man of understanding will draw it out.*

NICHOLAS, Nicolas, Nikki

Cultural Origin: Greek
Inherent Meaning: *VICTORIOUS ONE*
Spiritual Connotation: *TRIUMPHANT SPIRIT*
Supporting Scripture: *1 Corinthians 15:57*
> *But thanks be to God, which giveth us the victory through our Lord Jesus Christ.*

NICOLE, Nicky, Nikki

Cultural Origin: Greek
Inherent Meaning: *VICTORIOUS ONE*
Spiritual Connotation: *OVERCOMER*
Supporting Scripture: *Revelation 2:7*
> *...To him that overcometh will I give to eat of the tree of life, which is in the midst of the paradise of God.*

NIGEL

Cultural Origin: Latin
Inherent Meaning: *TRAVELER*
Spiritual Connotation: *ADVENTUROUS SPIRIT*
Supporting Scripture: *2 Corinthians 2:14*
> *Now thanks be unto God, which always causeth us to triumph in Christ, and maketh manifest the savour of his knowledge by us in every place.*

NILES, see Neal

NITA

Cultural Origin: Latin
Inherent Meaning: *LITTLE DARLING*
Spiritual Connotation: *PRECIOUS ONE*
Supporting Scripture: *Ephesians 4:32*
> *And be ye kind one to another, tenderhearted, forgiving one another, even as God for Christ's sake hath forgiven you.*

NOAH

Cultural Origin: Hebrew
Inherent Meaning: *COMFORTER, CONSOLATION, REST*
Spiritual Connotation: *PROVIDER OF REFUGE*
Supporting Scripture: *Nahum 1:7*
> *The Lord is good, a strong hold in the day of trouble; and he knoweth them that trust in him.*

NOEL, Nowell

Cultural Origin: Latin
Inherent Meaning: *CHRISTMAS CHILD*
Spiritual Connotation: *PRECIOUS GIFT*
Supporting Scripture: *Psalm 5:12*
> *For thou, Lord, wilt bless the righteous; with favour wilt thou compass him as with a shield.*

NOLA

Cultural Origin: Latin
Inherent Meaning: *A BELL*
Spiritual Connotation: *HARMONIOUS SPIRIT*
Supporting Scripture: *Proverbs 25:11*
> *A word fitly spoken is like apples of gold in pictures of silver.*

NOLAN

Cultural Origin: Gaelic
Inherent Meaning: *FAMOUS, NOBLE*
Spiritual Connotation: *HONORABLE ONE*
Supporting Scripture: *Micah 6:8*
> *He hath shewed thee, O man, what is good; and what doth the Lord require of thee, but to do justly, and to love mercy, and to walk humbly with thy God?*

NONA

Cultural Origin: Latin-Greek
Inherent Meaning: *PURE HEART*
Spiritual Connotation: *FULL OF GRACE*
Supporting Scripture: *Proverbs 2:6*
> *For the Lord giveth wisdom: out of his mouth cometh knowledge and understanding.*

NORA

Cultural Origin: Latin
Inherent Meaning: *HONOR*
Spiritual Connotation: *HONORED, ESTEEMED*
Supporting Scripture: *Isaiah 30:21*
> *And thine ears shall hear a word behind thee, saying, This is the way, walk ye in it, when ye turn to the right hand, and when ye turn to the left.*

NORBERT

Cultural Origin: Teutonic
Inherent Meaning: *BRILLIANT HERO*
Spiritual Connotation: *EXCELLENT WORTH*
Supporting Scripture: *Psalm 25:10*
> *All the paths of the Lord are mercy and truth unto such as keep his covenant and his testimonies.*

NORMA

Cultural Origin: Latin
Inherent Meaning: *PERFECTION*
Spiritual Connotation: *EXCELLENT WORTH*
Supporting Scripture: *1 Timothy 4:14*
> *Neglect not the gift that is in thee, which was given thee...*

NORMAN

Cultural Origin: Teutonic
Inherent Meaning: *A NORTHMAN*
Spiritual Connotation: *COURAGEOUS SPIRIT*
Supporting Scripture: *Psalm 17:7*
> *Shew thy marvellous lovingkindness, O thou that savest by the right hand them which put their trust in thee...*

NORRIS

Cultural Origin: Latin
Inherent Meaning: *NORTHERNER*
Spiritual Connotation: *WISE ONE*
Supporting Scripture: *Psalm 111:10*
> *The fear of the Lord is the beginning of wisdom: a good understanding have all they that do his commandments: his praise endureth for ever.*

NORTON

Cultural Origin: Anglo-Saxon
Inherent Meaning: *FROM THE NORTH TOWN*
Spiritual Connotation: *INTEGRITY AND HONOR*
Supporting Scripture: *Psalm 42:8*

Yet the Lord will command his lovingkindness in the daytime, and in the night his song shall be with me, and my prayer unto the God of my life.

NORVAL

Cultural Origin: Teutonic
Inherent Meaning: *OF THE NORTH*
Spiritual Connotation: *INTEGRITY AND HONOR*
Supporting Scripture: *Psalm 85:12,13*

Yea, the Lord shall give that which is good; and our land shall yield her increase. Righteousness shall go before him; and shall set us in the way of his steps.

NORWOOD

Cultural Origin: Anglo-Saxon
Inherent Meaning: *NORTH FOREST*
Spiritual Connotation: *NOBLE SPIRIT*
Supporting Scripture: *Philippians 3:14*

I press toward the mark for the prize of the high calling of God in Christ Jesus.

NOWELL, see Noel

NYDIA

Cultural Origin: Latin
Inherent Meaning: *A SWEET SEEDLING*
Spiritual Connotation: *SPIRITUAL POTENTIAL*
Supporting Scripture: *Colossians 3:12*

Put on therefore, as the elect of God, holy and beloved, bowels of mercies, kindness, humbleness of mind, meekness, longsuffering.

O

OCTAVIA

Cultural Origin: Latin
Inherent Meaning: *EIGHTH CHILD*
Spiritual Connotation: *ABIDING PLACE OF GOD*
Supporting Scripture: *Psalm 23:6*
> *Surely goodness and mercy shall follow me all the days of my life: and I will dwell in the house of the Lord for ever.*

OCTAVIUS

Cultural Origin: Latin
Inherent Meaning: *EIGHTH*
Spiritual Connotation: *ABIDING PLACE OF GOD*
Supporting Scripture: *Psalm 18:28*
> *For thou wilt light my candle: the Lord my God will enlighten my darkness.*

ODELIA

Cultural Origin: Anglo-Saxon
Inherent Meaning: *WEALTHY ONE*
Spiritual Connotation: *PROSPEROUS SPIRIT*
Supporting Scripture: *James 3:17*
> *But the wisdom that is from above is first pure, then peaceable, gentle, and easy to be entreated, full of mercy and good fruits, without partiality, and without hypocrisy.*

ODESSA

Cultural Origin: Greek
Inherent Meaning: *A LONG JOURNEY*
Spiritual Connotation: *BRINGER OF LIGHT*
Supporting Scripture: *Psalm 37:6*
> *And he shall bring forth thy righteousness as the light,
> and thy judgment as the noonday.*

OGDEN

Cultural Origin: Anglo-Saxon
Inherent Meaning: *FROM THE OAK VALLEY*
Spiritual Connotation: *DIGNITY, NOBILITY*
Supporting Scripture: *Psalm 92:12*
> *The righteous shall flourish like the palm tree: he shall
> grow like a cedar in Lebanon.*

OLAF, Olin

Cultural Origin: Old Norse
Inherent Meaning: *A TALISMAN*
Spiritual Connotation: *PROTECTOR*
Supporting Scripture: *Psalm 18:1,2*
> *I will love thee, O Lord, my strength. The Lord is my
> rock, and my fortress, and my deliverer; my God my
> strength, in whom I will trust; my buckler, and the horn
> of my salvation, and my high tower.*

OLGA

Cultural Origin: Teutonic
Inherent Meaning: *HOLY ONE*
Spiritual Connotation: *PEACE*
Supporting Scripture: *Proverbs 15:33*
> *The fear of the Lord is the instruction of wisdom; and
> before honour is humility.*

OLIN, see Olaf

OLINDA

Cultural Origin: Latin
Inherent Meaning: *FRAGRANT*
Spiritual Connotation: *BLESSED ONE*
Supporting Scripture: *Isaiah 61:10*

> *I will greatly rejoice in the Lord, my soul shall be joyful in*
> *my God; for he hath clothed me with the garments of*
> *salvation, he hath covered me with the robe of*
> *righteousness...*

OLIVE, Olivia

Cultural Origin: Latin
Inherent Meaning: *PEACE*
Spiritual Connotation: *WALKS WITH GOD*
Supporting Scripture: *Matthew 13:44*

> *Again, the kingdom of heaven is like unto treasure hid in*
> *a field; the which when a man hath found, he hideth, and*
> *for joy thereof goeth and selleth all that he hath, and*
> *buyeth that field.*

OLIVER

Cultural Origin: Old Norse
Inherent Meaning: *KINDLY AFFECTIONATE ONE*
Spiritual Connotation: *BRINGER OF PEACE*
Supporting Scripture: *Psalm 23:1,2*

> *The Lord is my shepherd; I shall not want. He maketh me*
> *to lie down in green pastures: he leadeth me beside the still*
> *waters.*

OMAR

Cultural Origin: Arabic
Inherent Meaning: *MOST HIGH*
Spiritual Connotation: *EXALTED ONE*
Supporting Scripture: *Romans 8:37*

> *Nay, in all these things we are more than conquerors*
> *through him that loved us.*

ONA

Cultural Origin: Latin
Inherent Meaning: *UNITY, ONE*
Spiritual Connotation: *WORSHIP IN SPIRIT*
AND IN TRUTH
Supporting Scripture: *Matthew 13:43*
Then shall the righteous shine forth as the sun in the
kingdom of their Father. Who hath ears to hear, let him
hear.

OPAL

Cultural Origin: Sanskrit
Inherent Meaning: *A JEWEL, HOPE*
Spiritual Connotation: *BEAUTIFUL SPIRIT*
Supporting Scripture: *2 Corinthians 6:4*
But in all things approving ourselves as the ministers of
God...

OPHELIA

Cultural Origin: Greek
Inherent Meaning: *HELPER*
Spiritual Connotation: *CONSECRATED ONE*
Supporting Scripture: *2 Corinthians 3:18*
But we all, with open face beholding as in a glass the glory
of the Lord, are changed into the same image from glory
to glory, even as by the Spirit of the Lord.

ORA

Cultural Origin: Latin
Inherent Meaning: *GOLD*
Spiritual Connotation: *PRECIOUS SHINING ONE*
Supporting Scripture: *1 John 4:7*
Beloved, let us love one another: for love is of God; and
every one that loveth is born of God, and knoweth God.

ORIANA

Cultural Origin: Latin
Inherent Meaning: *THE DAWNING AURA*
Spiritual Connotation: *ENLIGHTENED FOR SERVICE*
Supporting Scripture: *Ephesians 6:7,8*
   *With good will doing service, as to the Lord, and not to
   men: knowing that whatsoever good things any man
   doeth, the same shall he receive of the Lord...*

ORIN

Cultural Origin: Greek
Inherent Meaning: *LIGHT*
Spiritual Connotation: *GOD-REVEALED INSIGHT*
Supporting Scripture: *Psalm 27:1*
   *The Lord is my light and my salvation; whom shall I fear?
   the Lord is the strength of my life; of whom shall I be
   afraid?*

ORLANDO, see Roland

ORMOND

Cultural Origin: Anglo-Saxon
Inherent Meaning: *PROTECTOR*
Spiritual Connotation: *ESTABLISHED IN PEACE*
Supporting Scripture: *Psalm 18:1,2*
   *I will love thee, O Lord, my strength. The Lord is my
   rock, and my fortress, and my deliverer; my God, my
   strength, in whom I will trust; my buckler, and the horn
   of my salvation, and my high tower.*

ORSON

Cultural Origin: Anglo-Saxon
Inherent Meaning: *LITTLE BEAR*
Spiritual Connotation: *LOYAL, STEADFAST*
Supporting Scripture: *1 Corinthians 15:58*
> *be ye stedfast, unmoveable, always abounding in the work of the Lord, forasmuch as ye know that your labour is not in vain in the Lord.*

ORVAL

Cultural Origin: Anglo-Saxon
Inherent Meaning: *SPEAR, MIGHTY*
Spiritual Connotation: *CONQUERING SPIRIT*
Supporting Scripture: *Romans 8:37*
> *Nay, in all these things we are more than conquerors through him that loved us.*

ORVILLE

Cultural Origin: Latin
Inherent Meaning: *FROM THE GOLDEN ESTATE*
Spiritual Connotation: *BLESSED, BENEVOLENT*
Supporting Scripture: *2 Corinthians 9:6*
> *But this I say . . . he which soweth bountifully shall reap also bountifully.*

OSBORN

Cultural Origin: Anglo-Saxon
Inherent Meaning: *DIVINE WARRIOR*
Spiritual Connotation: *VICTORIOUS IN TRUTH*
Supporting Scripture: *Isaiah 61:2,3*
> *To proclaim the acceptable year of the Lord . . . that they might be called trees of righteousness, the planting of the Lord, that he might be glorified.*

OSCAR

Cultural Origin: Old Norse
Inherent Meaning: *DIVINE SPEARMAN*
Spiritual Connotation: *APPOINTED OF GOD*
Supporting Scripture: *Colossians 3:23*
   *And whatsoever ye do, do it heartily, as to the Lord, and
   not unto men.*

OSMOND, Osmund

Cultural Origin: Anglo-Saxon
Inherent Meaning: *DIVINE PROTECTOR*
Spiritual Connotation: *GOD'S WARRIOR*
Supporting Scripture: *Matthew 13:43*
   *Then shall the righteous shine forth as the sun in the
   kingdom of their Father. Who hath ears to hear, let him
   hear.*

OSWALD

Cultural Origin: Anglo-Saxon
Inherent Meaning: *DIVINELY POWERFUL*
Spiritual Connotation: *HONORED, ESTEEMED*
Supporting Scripture: *Psalm 77:11,12*
   *I will remember the works of the Lord: surely I will
   remember thy wonders of old. I will meditate also of all
   thy work, and talk of thy doings.*

OTIS

Cultural Origin: Greek
Inherent Meaning: *ACUTE, KEEN OF HEARING*
Spiritual Connotation: *OPEN TO DIVINE INSPIRATION*
Supporting Scripture: *Psalm 37:3*
   *Trust in the Lord, and do good; so shalt thou dwell in the
   land, and verily thou shalt be fed.*

OTTILIE

Cultural Origin: Teutonic
Inherent Meaning: *HAPPY*
Spiritual Connotation: *JOYOUS SPIRIT*
Supporting Scripture: *Philippians 4:13*
  I can do all things through Christ which strengtheneth me.

OTTO

Cultural Origin: Teutonic
Inherent Meaning: *PROSPEROUS ONE*
Spiritual Connotation: *HONORED, ESTEEMED*
Supporting Scripture: *Matthew 13:43*
  Then shall the righteous shine forth as the sun in the king-
  dom of their Father. Who hath ears to hear, let him
  hear.

OWEN

Cultural Origin: Celtic
Inherent Meaning: *DISTINGUISHED, WELL BORN*
Spiritual Connotation: *MIGHTY IN SPIRIT*
Supporting Scripture: *2 Samuel 23:4*
  And he shall be as the light of the morning, when the sun
  riseth, even a morning without clouds; as the tender grass
  springing out of the earth by clear shining after rain.

P

PAIGE, Page

Cultural Origin: Latin
Inherent Meaning: *YOUTHFUL ATTENDANT*
Spiritual Connotation: *BLESSED HELPER*
Supporting Scripture: *Philippians 2:13*
> *For it is God which worketh in you both to will and to do of his good pleasure.*

PALMER

Cultural Origin: Anglo-Saxon
Inherent Meaning: *PEACEFUL PILGRIM*
Spiritual Connotation: *BRINGER OF PEACE*
Supporting Scripture: *Zechariah 4:6*
> *. . . Not by might, nor by power, but by my spirit, saith the Lord of hosts.*

PAMELA

Cultural Origin: Greek
Inherent Meaning: *A SONG OR MELODY*
Spiritual Connotation: *HARMONY AND JOY*
Supporting Scripture: *Matthew 13:43*
> *Then shall the righteous shine forth as the sun in the kingdom of their Father.*

PANSY

Cultural Origin: Latin
Inherent Meaning: *A THOUGHT*
Spiritual Connotation: *SPIRITUAL PURPOSE*
Supporting Scripture: *Matthew 11:10*
> *. . . Behold, I send my messenger before thy face, which shall prepare thy way before thee.*

PARKER

Cultural Origin: Teutonic
Inherent Meaning: *GUARDIAN*
Spiritual Connotation: *SPIRITUAL LIGHT*
Supporting Scripture: *Psalm 27:1*
The Lord is my light and my salvation; whom shall I fear? the Lord is the strength of my life; of whom shall I be afraid?

PARNELL

Cultural Origin: Latin
Inherent Meaning: *LITTLE PETER*
Spiritual Connotation: *FAITHFULNESS, FIDELITY*
Supporting Scripture: *Psalm 95:4,5*
In his hand are the deep places of the earth: the strength of the hills is his also. The sea is his, and he made it: and his hands formed the dry land.

PARRY, Perry

Cultural Origin: Celtic
Inherent Meaning: *SON OF HARRY*
Spiritual Connotation: *COURAGEOUS SPIRIT*
Supporting Scripture: *Psalm 37:11*
But the meek shall inherit the earth; and shall delight themselves in the abundance of peace.

PATIENCE

Cultural Origin: Latin
Inherent Meaning: *ENDURANCE AND FORTITUDE*
Spiritual Connotation: *FIRMNESS OF SPIRIT*
Supporting Scripture: *Psalm 77:12*
I will meditate also of all thy work, and talk of thy doings.

PATRICIA, Pat

Cultural Origin: Latin
Inherent Meaning: *NOBLE ONE*
Spiritual Connotation: *GRACIOUS SPIRIT*
Supporting Scripture: *Romans 8:37*
> *In all these things we are more than conquerors through him that loved us.*

PATRICK

Cultural Origin: Latin
Inherent Meaning: *NOBLE, ADMINISTRATOR*
Spiritual Connotation: *RULES WITH RIGHTEOUSNESS*
Supporting Scripture: *Romans 12:2*
> *. . . be ye transformed by the renewing of your mind, that ye may prove what is that good, and acceptable, and perfect, will of God.*

PAUL

Cultural Origin: Greek
Inherent Meaning: *SMALL*
Spiritual Connotation: *DYNAMO OF ENERGY AND FAITH*
Supporting Scripture: *1 John 3:1*
> *Behold, what manner of love the Father hath bestowed upon us, that we should be called the sons of God. . .*

PAULA, Pauline

Cultural Origin: Latin
Inherent Meaning: *GENTLE*
Spiritual Connotation: *LOVING SPIRIT*
Supporting Scripture: *Matthew 13:43*
> *Then shall the righteous shine forth as the sun in the kingdom of their Father.*

PAULINE, see Paula

PEARL

Cultural Origin: Latin
Inherent Meaning: *A PEARL—HEALTH AND LONG LIFE*
Spiritual Connotation: *WISDOM AND LOVE*
Supporting Scripture: *Psalm 108:3,4*
> *I will praise thee, O Lord. . . . For thy mercy is great above the heavens: and thy truth reacheth unto the clouds.*

PEDRO

Cultural Origin: Latin
Inherent Meaning: *PETER, THE ROCK*
Spiritual Connotation: *STEADFAST IN CHRIST*
Supporting Scripture: *1 Corinthians 15:58*
> *. . . be ye stedfast, unmoveable, always abounding in the work of the Lord, forasmuch as ye know that your labour is not in vain in the Lord.*

PEGGY, see Margaret

PENELOPE, Penny

Cultural Origin: Greek
Inherent Meaning: *A WEAVER, INDUSTRIOUS*
Spiritual Connotation: *CREATIVE SPIRIT*
Supporting Scripture: *Deuteronomy 28:12*
> *The Lord shall open unto thee his good treasure, the heaven to give the rain unto thy land in his season, and to bless all the work of thine hand. . .*

PERCIVAL, Percy

Cultural Origin: Latin
Inherent Meaning: *COURTEOUS, THOUGHTFUL*
Spiritual Connotation: *GRACIOUS, HELPFUL SPIRIT*
Supporting Scripture: *John 8:36*
> *If the Son therefore shall make you free, ye shall be free
> indeed.*

PERRY, see Parry

PETRA

Cultural Origin: Latin
Inherent Meaning: *STRONG AND EVERLASTING*
Spiritual Connotation: *EXCELLENT WORTH*
Supporting Scripture: *John 14:27*
> *Peace I leave with you, my peace I give unto you: not as
> the world giveth, give I unto you. Let not your heart be
> troubled, neither let it be afraid.*

PETER, Pierre

Cultural Origin: Greek
Inherent Meaning: *A STONE, A ROCK*
Spiritual Connotation: *SPIRITUAL FACULTY OF FAITH*
Supporting Scripture: *Psalm 31:1*
> *In thee, O Lord, do I put my trust; let me never be
> ashamed: deliver me in thy righteousness.*

PHEDRA

Cultural Origin: Greek
Inherent Meaning: *BRIGHT ONE*
Spiritual Connotation: *SHINING LIGHT*
Supporting Scripture: *Psalm 42:8*
> *Yet the Lord will command his lovingkindness in the
> daytime, and in the night his song shall be with me, and
> my prayer unto the God of my life.*

PHELAN

Cultural Origin: Gaelic
Inherent Meaning: *LITTLE WOLF*
Spiritual Connotation: *RESOLUTE SPIRIT*
Supporting Scripture: *James 4:10*
> *Humble yourselves in the sight of the Lord, and he shall lift you up.*

PHELPS

Cultural Origin: Anglo-Saxon
Inherent Meaning: *SON OF PHILLIP*
Spiritual Connotation: *LOVING SPIRIT*
Supporting Scripture: *2 Peter 1:3*
> *According as his divine power hath given unto us all things that pertain unto life and godliness, through the knowledge of him that hath called us to glory and virtue.*

PHILOMENA

Cultural Origin: Greek
Inherent Meaning: *LOVER OF MUSIC*
Spiritual Connotation: *JOYOUS SPIRIT*
Supporting Scripture: *John 15:7*
> *If ye abide in me, and my words abide in you, ye shall ask what ye will, and it shall be done unto you.*

PHILLIP, Philip, Phil

Cultural Origin: Greek
Inherent Meaning: *LOVER OF HORSES*
Spiritual Connotation: *THROUGH LOVE IS MASTERY*
Supporting Scripture: *2 Corinthians 3:18*
> *But we all, with open face beholding as in a glass the glory of the Lord, are changed into the same image from glory to glory, even as by the Spirit of the Lord.*

PHILO

Cultural Origin: Greek
Inherent Meaning: *LOVING, FRIENDLY*
Spiritual Connotation: *MESSENGER OF LOVE*
Supporting Scripture: *1 John 4:7*
> *Beloved, let us love one another: for love is of God; and every one that loveth is born of God, and knoweth God.*

PHINEAS

Cultural Origin: Greek
Inherent Meaning: *OPEN AND TRUSTFUL COUNTENANCE*
Spiritual Connotation: *DWELLING IN THE SPIRIT*
Supporting Scripture: *Psalm 119:2*
> *Blessed are they that keep his testimonies, and that seek him with the whole heart.*

PHOEBE, Phebe

Cultural Origin: Greek
Inherent Meaning: *BRIGHT ONE*
Spiritual Connotation: *CHERISHED ONE*
Supporting Scripture: *Matthew 5:14*
> *Ye are the light of the world. A city that is set on an hill cannot be hid.*

PHYLLIS

Cultural Origin: Greek
Inherent Meaning: *A GREEN BRANCH*
Spiritual Connotation: *YOUTHFUL, BUOYANT*
Supporting Scripture: *Psalm 86:11*
> *Teach me thy way, O Lord; I will walk in thy truth . . .*

PIERCE

Cultural Origin: Anglo-Saxon
Inherent Meaning: *ROCK OR STONE*
Spiritual Connotation: *STRONG IN SPIRIT*
Supporting Scripture: *Psalm 18:32, 33*
> It is God that girdeth me with strength, and maketh my
> way perfect. He maketh my feet like hinds' feet, and set-
> teth me upon my high places.

PIERRE, see Peter

PILAR

Cultural Origin: Latin
Inherent Meaning: *A PILLAR*
Spiritual Connotation: *STRONG IN FAITH*
Supporting Scripture: *Matthew 17:20*
> . . . If ye have faith as a grain of mustard seed, ye shall say
> unto this mountain, Remove hence to yonder place; and it
> shall remove; and nothing shall be impossible unto you.

PIPER

Cultural Origin: Anglo-Saxon
Inherent Meaning: *PIPE PLAYER*
Spiritual Connotation: *JOYOUS SPIRIT*
Supporting Scripture: *Isaiah 61:1*
> The Spirit of the Lord God is upon me; because the Lord
> hath anointed me to preach good tidings. . .

POLLY, Pollyanna

Cultural Origin: Hebrew
Inherent Meaning: *GENTLE*
Spiritual Connotation: *LOVING SPIRIT*
Supporting Scripture: *Psalm 149:1*
> Praise ye the Lord. Sing unto the Lord a new song. . .

PORTER

Cultural Origin: Latin
Inherent Meaning: *GATEKEEPER*
Spiritual Connotation: *WATCHFUL SPIRIT*
Supporting Scripture: *Isaiah 12:2*
   *Behold, God is my salvation; I will trust, and not be
   afraid: for the Lord Jehovah is my strength and my song;
   he also is become my salvation.*

PORTIA

Cultural Origin: Latin
Inherent Meaning: *A GIFT OF GOD*
Spiritual Connotation: *PRICELESS ONE*
Supporting Scripture: *Psalm 37:5,6*
   *Commit thy way unto the Lord; trust also in him; and he
   shall bring it to pass. And he shall bring forth thy
   righteousness as the light, and thy judgment as the noon-
   day.*

PRENTICE

Cultural Origin: Anglo-Saxon
Inherent Meaning: *A LEARNER*
Spiritual Connotation: *SEEKER OF TRUTH*
Supporting Scripture: *Isaiah 30:21*
   *And thine ears shall hear a word behind thee, saying, This
   is the way, walk ye in it, when ye turn to the right hand,
   and when ye turn to the left.*

PRESCOTT

Cultural Origin: Anglo-Saxon
Inherent Meaning: *FROM THE PRIEST'S DWELLING*
Spiritual Connotation: *BLESSED ONE*
Supporting Scripture: *1 John 5:11*
   *And this is the record, that God hath given to us eternal
   life, and this life is in his Son.*

PRESLEY

Cultural Origin: Anglo-Saxon
Inherent Meaning: *DWELLER AT THE
                   PRIEST'S MEADOW*
Spiritual Connotation: *PEACEFUL SPIRIT*
Supporting Scripture: *Psalm 146:5,6*
   *Happy is he that hath the God of Jacob for his help,
   whose hope is in the Lord his God: which made heaven,
   and earth, the sea, and all that therein is: which keepeth
   truth for ever.*

PRESTON

Cultural Origin: Anglo-Saxon
Inherent Meaning: *DWELLER AT THE PRIEST'S PLACE*
Spiritual Connotation: *CONSECRATED TO GOD*
Supporting Scripture: *Psalm 37:5,6*
   *Commit thy way unto the Lord; trust also in him; and he
   shall bring it to pass. And he shall bring forth thy
   righteousness as the light, and thy judgment as the noon-
   day.*

PRISCILLA

Cultural Origin: Latin
Inherent Meaning: *FROM THE PAST, OLD-FASHIONED*
Spiritual Connotation: *ETERNAL VALUE*
Supporting Scripture: *Philippians 4:8*
   *. . . whatsoever things are true, whatsoever things are
   honest. . . whatsoever things are lovely, whatsoever things
   are of good report. . . think on these things.*

PRUDENCE

Cultural Origin: Latin
Inherent Meaning: *WISDOM, DISCRETION,*
KNOWLEDGE
Spiritual Connotation: *GOD AWARENESS*
Supporting Scripture: *Psalm 19:8*
   The statutes of the Lord are right, rejoicing the heart: the
   commandment of the Lord is pure, enlightening the eyes.

Q

QUILLAN

Cultural Origin: Gaelic
Inherent Meaning: *ENDEARING*
Spiritual Connotation: *BELOVED ONE*
Supporting Scripture: *Psalm 91:15*
> He shall call upon me, and I will answer him: I will be
> with him in trouble; I will deliver him, and honour him.

QUIMBY

Cultural Origin: Old Norse
Inherent Meaning: *DWELLER AT THE
                    WOMAN'S ESTATE*
Spiritual Connotation: *VIGILANT SPIRIT*
Supporting Scripture: *Matthew 13:43*
> Then shall the righteous shine forth as the sun in the
> kingdom of their Father. Who hath ears to hear, let him
> hear.

QUINCY

Cultural Origin: Latin
Inherent Meaning: *DWELLER AT THE
                    FIFTH SON'S ESTATE*
Spiritual Connotation: *FREEDOM IN CHRIST*
Supporting Scripture: *Romans 8:2*
> For the law of the Spirit of life in Christ Jesus hath made
> me free from the law of sin and death.

QUINN

Cultural Origin: Gaelic
Inherent Meaning: *WISE, INTELLIGENT*
Spiritual Connotation: *GODLY INSIGHT*
Supporting Scripture: *1 John 3:2*

Beloved, now are we the sons of God, and it doth not yet appear what we shall be: but we know that, when he shall appear, we shall be like him; for we shall see him as he is.

QUINTIN, Quinton

Cultural Origin: Latin
Inherent Meaning: *FIFTH*
Spiritual Connotation: *BRAVE, NOBLE*
Supporting Scripture: *Psalm 91:15*

He shall call upon me, and I will answer him: I will be with him in trouble; I will deliver him, and honour him.

R

RACHAEL, Rachel

Cultural Origin: Hebrew
Inherent Meaning: *INNOCENCE, GENTLENESS*
Spiritual Connotation: *BLESSED ONE*
Supporting Scripture: *Hosea 14:9*
> *Who is wise, and he shall understand these things? pru-*
> *dent, and he shall know them? for the ways of the Lord*
> *are right, and the just shall walk in them...*

RAE

Cultural Origin: Anglo-Saxon
Inherent Meaning: *A DOE DEER*
Spiritual Connotation: *FULL OF GRACE*
Supporting Scripture: *Psalm 50:23*
> *Whoso offereth praise glorifieth me; and to him that*
> *ordereth his conversation aright will I shew the salvation*
> *of God.*

RAINA, Rani, Ranee

Cultural Origin: Sanskrit
Inherent Meaning: *QUEENLY*
Spiritual Connotation: *NOBLE, GRACIOUS*
Supporting Scripture: *Psalm 143:8*
> *Cause me to hear thy lovingkindness in the morning; for*
> *in thee do I trust: cause me to know the way wherein I*
> *should walk; for I lift up my soul unto thee.*

RAFFERTY

Cultural Origin: Gaelic
Inherent Meaning: *PROSPEROUS*
Spiritual Connotation: *LOYAL, STEADFAST*
Supporting Scripture: *Psalm 119:16*
> *I will delight myself in thy statutes: I will not forget thy word.*

RALEIGH

Cultural Origin: Anglo-Saxon
Inherent Meaning: *DWELLER AT THE MEADOW*
Spiritual Connotation: *EXCELLENT WORTH*
Supporting Scripture: *2 Corinthians 9:8*
> *And God is able to make all grace abound toward you; that ye, always having all sufficiency in all things, may abound to every good work.*

RALPH, Raoul

Cultural Origin: Teutonic
Inherent Meaning: *ADVISOR, COUNSELOR*
Spiritual Connotation: *WISE, DISCERNING*
Supporting Scripture: *Psalm 13:5*
> *But I have trusted in thy mercy; my heart shall rejoice in thy salvation.*

RAMON, see Raymond

RAMONA

Cultural Origin: Teutonic
Inherent Meaning: *DELICATE STRENGTH*
Spiritual Connotation: *VIRTUOUS WOMAN*
Supporting Scripture: *Proverbs 31:10*
> *Who can find a virtuous woman? for her price is far above rubies.*

RANDALL, see Randolph

RANDOLPH, Randolf, Randall

Cultural Origin: Anglo-Saxon
Inherent Meaning: *SHIELD*
Spiritual Connotation: *ESTABLISHED IN PEACE*
Supporting Scripture: *Matthew 6:33*
> *But seek ye first the kingdom of God, and his*
> *righteousness: and all these things shall be added unto*
> *you.*

RANKIN

Cultural Origin: Anglo-Saxon
Inherent Meaning: *SHIELD*
Spiritual Connotation: *VALIANT SPIRIT*
Supporting Scripture: *Psalm 27:14*
> *Wait on the Lord: be of good courage, and he shall*
> *strengthen thine heart: wait, I say, on the Lord.*

RAOUL, see Ralph

RAPHAEL

Cultural Origin: Hebrew
Inherent Meaning: *HEALED BY GOD*
Spiritual Connotation: *GOD'S CONSECRATED ONE*
Supporting Scripture: *Hosea 14:9*
> *Who is wise, and he shall understand things? prudent, and*
> *he shall know them? for the ways of the Lord are right,*
> *and the just shall walk in them . . .*

RAPHAELA

Cultural Origin: Hebrew
Inherent Meaning: *HEALED OF GOD*
Spiritual Connotation: *GOD'S CONSECRATED ONE*
Supporting Scripture: *2 Chronicles 1:12*
   *Wisdom and knowledge is granted unto thee; and I will
   give thee riches, and wealth, and honour...*

RAY

Cultural Origin: Latin
Inherent Meaning: *HONORED ONE*
Spiritual Connotation: *ESTEEMED ONE*
Supporting Scripture: *Proverbs 9:10*
   *The fear of the Lord is the beginning of wisdom: and the
   knowledge of the holy is understanding.*

RAYBURN

Cultural Origin: Anglo-Saxon
Inherent Meaning: *FROM THE DEER BROOK*
Spiritual Connotation: *PEACEFUL HEART*
Supporting Scripture: *Isaiah 42:10*
   *Sing unto the Lord a new song, and his praise from the
   end of the earth...*

RAYMOND, Ramon

Cultural Origin: Teutonic
Inherent Meaning: *MIGHTY PROTECTOR*
Spiritual Connotation: *DWELLING IN THE SPIRIT*
Supporting Scripture: *Philippians 1:6*
   *Being confident of this very thing, that he which hath
   begun a good work in you will perform it until the day of
   Jesus Christ.*

RAYNOR

Cultural Origin: Old Norse
Inherent Meaning: *MIGHTY ARMY*
Spiritual Connotation: *WATCHFUL ONE*
Supporting Scripture: *Psalm 18:32*
>   *It is God that girdeth me with strength, and maketh my
>   way perfect.*

REBECCA, Rebekah

Cultural Origin: Hebrew
Inherent Meaning: *SOUL'S NATURAL DELIGHT
                    IN BEAUTY*
Spiritual Connotation: *ESTABLISHED IN HARMONY*
Supporting Scripture: *Psalm 23:1*
>   *The Lord is my shepherd; I shall not want.*

REED, see Reid

REGAN

Cultural Origin: Gaelic
Inherent Meaning: *LITTLE KING*
Spiritual Connotation: *SPIRITUAL AUTHORITY*
Supporting Scripture: *Proverbs 24:5*
>   *A wise man is strong; yea, a man of knowledge increaseth
>   strength.*

REGINA

Cultural Origin: Latin
Inherent Meaning: *A QUEEN*
Spiritual Connotation: *GRACIOUS SPIRIT*
Supporting Scripture: *Psalm 19:14*
>   *Let the words of my mouth, and the meditation of my
>   heart, be acceptable in thy sight, O Lord, my strength,
>   and my redeemer.*

REGINALD, Reggie, Reynold

Cultural Origin: Anglo-Saxon
Inherent Meaning: *POWERFUL JUDGMENT, SINCERITY*
Spiritual Connotation: *SPIRITUAL DISCERNMENT*
Supporting Scripture: *Micah 6:8*
> *. . . and what doth the Lord require of thee, but to do just-*
> *ly, and to love mercy, and to walk humbly with thy God?*

REID, Reed, Read

Cultural Origin: Anglo-Saxon
Inherent Meaning: *FAIR COUNTENANCE*
Spiritual Connotation: *DIVINE SPARK*
Supporting Scripture: *Psalm 118:14*
> *The Lord is my strength and song, and is become my*
> *salvation.*

RENATA

Cultural Origin: Latin
Inherent Meaning: *RENEWAL OF FAITH*
Spiritual Connotation: *QUICKENED SPIRIT*
Supporting Scripture: *Psalm 37:5*
> *Commit thy way unto the Lord; trust also in him; and he*
> *shall bring it to pass.*

RENEE

Cultural Origin: Latin
Inherent Meaning: *RENEWED*
Spiritual Connotation: *JOYFUL SPIRIT*
Supporting Scripture: *Psalm 111:10*
> *The fear of the Lord is the beginning of wisdom: a good*
> *understanding have all they that do his commandments:*
> *his praise endureth for ever.*

REUBEN, Ruben

Cultural Origin: Hebrew
Inherent Meaning: *BEHOLD A SON*
Spiritual Connotation: *WONDROUS RECOGNITION*
Supporting Scripture: *Psalm 119:16*
I will delight myself in thy statutes: I will not forget thy word.

REVA

Cultural Origin: Latin
Inherent Meaning: *TO GAIN STRENGTH*
Spiritual Connotation: *NOBLE HEART*
Supporting Scripture: *Matthew 5:9*
Blessed are the peacemakers: for they shall be called the children of God.

REX

Cultural Origin: Latin
Inherent Meaning: *KING*
Spiritual Connotation: *LEADERSHIP*
Supporting Scripture: *Psalm 37:5*
Commit thy way unto the Lord; trust also in him; and he shall bring it to pass.

REXFORD

Cultural Origin: Anglo-Saxon
Inherent Meaning: *DWELLER ON THE KING'S FORD*
Spiritual Connotation: *HONORABLE ONE*
Supporting Scripture: *Deuteronomy 5:33*
Ye shall walk in all the ways which the Lord your God hath commanded you, that ye may live, and that it may be well with you, and that ye may prolong your days in the land which ye shall possess.

REYNARD

Cultural Origin: Teutonic
Inherent Meaning: *MIGHTY, BRAVE*
Spiritual Connotation: *HONORED ONE*
Supporting Scripture: *Isaiah 30:18*
   And therefore will the Lord wait, that he may be gracious
   unto you. . .for the Lord is a God of judgment: blessed
   are all they that wait for him.

REYNOLD, see Reginald

RHEA

Cultural Origin: Greek
Inherent Meaning: *A STREAM*
Spiritual Connotation: *SENT FORTH REFRESHING*
Supporting Scripture: *Isaiah 35:6,7*
   . . .for in the wilderness shall waters break out, and
   streams in the desert. And the parched ground shall
   become a pool, and the thirsty land springs of water. . .

RHODA

Cultural Origin: Greek
Inherent Meaning: *A ROSE, LOVE*
Spiritual Connotation: *GOD'S UNFOLDED*
Supporting Scripture: *Isaiah 35:1,2*
   . . .and the desert shall rejoice, and blossom as the rose. It
   shall blossom abundantly, and rejoice even with joy and
   singing. . .

RHONDA

Cultural Origin: Anglo-Saxon
Inherent Meaning: *STRENGTH OF CHARACTER*
Spiritual Connotation: *VIRTUOUS SPIRIT*
Supporting Scripture: *Jeremiah 15:16*
> *Thy words were found, and I did eat them; and thy word
> was unto me the joy and rejoicing of mine heart: for I am
> called by thy name, O Lord God of hosts.*

RICHARD, Rick, Rich, Dick

Cultural Origin: Teutonic
Inherent Meaning: *POWERFUL, GENEROUS,
                    BENEVOLENT*
Spiritual Connotation: *COMPASSIONATE SPIRIT*
Supporting Scripture: *Psalm 111:10*
> *The fear of the Lord is the beginning of wisdom: a good
> understanding have all they that do his commandments:
> his praise endureth for ever.*

RICHARDA

Cultural Origin: Anglo-Saxon
Inherent Meaning: *POWERFUL RULER*
Spiritual Connotation: *DWELLING IN THE SPIRIT*
Supporting Scripture: *Ephesians 2:10*
> *For we are his workmanship, created in Christ Jesus unto
> good works, which God hath before ordained that we
> should walk in them.*

RILEY

Cultural Origin: Gaelic
Inherent Meaning: *VALIANT*
Spiritual Connotation: *HONORED, BRAVE*
Supporting Scripture: *Psalm 36:7*
> *How excellent is thy lovingkindness, O God! therefore the
> children of men put their trust under the shadow of thy
> wings.*

RIORDAN

Cultural Origin: Gaelic
Inherent Meaning: *SINGER, POET*
Spiritual Connotation: *FULL OF GRACE*
Supporting Scripture: *Isaiah 50:4*
> *The Lord God hath given me the tongue of the learned,*
> *that I should know how to speak a word in season to him*
> *that is weary. . .*

RITA, see Margaret

ROANNA, Rohana

Cultural Origin: Hebrew
Inherent Meaning: *REMINDER OF SWEET INCENSE*
Spiritual Connotation: *SPIRITUAL UNDERSTANDING*
Supporting Scripture: *Psalm 51:6*
> *Behold, thou desirest truth in the inward parts: and in the*
> *hidden part thou shalt make me to know wisdom.*

ROARKE

Cultural Origin: Gaelic
Inherent Meaning: *FAMOUS RULER*
Spiritual Connotation: *COURAGEOUS SPIRIT*
Supporting Scripture: *Psalm 31:24*
> *Be of good courage, and he shall strengthen your heart,*
> *all ye that hope in the Lord.*

ROBERT, Bert, Bob, Bobbie, Robb, Rupert

Cultural Origin: Teutonic
Inherent Meaning: *BRIGHT IN COUNSEL*
Spiritual Connotation: *EXCELLENT WORTH*
Supporting Scripture: *1 John 4:13*
> *Hereby know we that we dwell in him, and he in us,*
> *because he hath given us of his Spirit.*

ROBERTA

Cultural Origin: Teutonic
Inherent Meaning: *BRIGHT IN COUNSEL*
Spiritual Connotation: *EXCELLENT WORTH*
Supporting Scripture: *Ephesians 2:10*
> *For we are his workmanship, created in Christ Jesus unto good works, which God hath before ordained that we should walk in them.*

ROBIN, Robyn

Cultural Origin: Teutonic
Inherent Meaning: *SHINING FAME*
Spiritual Connotation: *VICTORIOUS SPIRIT*
Supporting Scripture: *Psalm 18:32,33*
> *It is God that girdeth me with strength, and maketh my way perfect. He maketh my feet like hinds' feet, and setteth me upon my high places.*

ROCHELLE, Rochella, Rochette

Cultural Origin: Latin
Inherent Meaning: *FROM THE LITTLE ROCK*
Spiritual Connotation: *DIVINE SPARK*
Supporting Scripture: *Psalm 18:30*
> *As for God, his way is perfect: the word of the Lord is tried: he is a buckler to all those that trust in him.*

RODERICK

Cultural Origin: Teutonic
Inherent Meaning: *FAMOUS RULER*
Spiritual Connotation: *HONORED, ESTEEMED*
Supporting Scripture: *Psalm 143:8*
> *Cause me to hear thy lovingkindness in the morning; for in thee do I trust: cause me to know the way wherein I should walk; for I lift up my soul unto thee.*

RODNEY

Cultural Origin: Teutonic
Inherent Meaning: *FAMOUS IN COUNSEL*
Spiritual Connotation: *DIVINELY PERCEPTIVE*
Supporting Scripture: *Psalm 40:3*
> *And he hath put a new song in my mouth, even praise un-
> to our God: many shall see it, and fear, and shall trust in
> the Lord.*

ROGER, Rodger

Cultural Origin: Teutonic
Inherent Meaning: *STRONG OF COUNSEL*
Spiritual Connotation: *FAITHFUL STEWARD*
Supporting Scripture: *Isaiah 48:17*
> *Thus saith the Lord, thy Redeemer. . . I am the Lord thy
> God which teacheth thee to profit, which leadeth thee by
> the way that thou shouldest go.*

ROLAND, Rolland, Rowland, Orlando

Cultural Origin: Teutonic
Inherent Meaning: *COUNSELOR*
Spiritual Connotation: *FULL OF WISDOM*
Supporting Scripture: *Psalm 106:3*
> *Blessed are they that keep judgment, and he that doeth
> righteousness at all times.*

ROLANDA

Cultural Origin: Teutonic
Inherent Meaning: *FROM THE FAMOUS LAND*
Spiritual Connotation: *PEACEFUL SPIRIT*
Supporting Scripture: *Psalm 86:11*
> *Teach me thy way, O Lord; I will walk in thy truth: unite
> my heart to fear thy name.*

ROLF, Rolph, see Rudolph

ROLLO, see Rudolph

ROMAN

Cultural Origin: Latin
Inherent Meaning: *BRAVE AND NOBLE*
Spiritual Connotation: *PROTECTOR OF TRUTH*
Supporting Scripture: *Ephesians 6:10,11*
*Finally, my brethren, be strong in the Lord, and in the
power of his might. Put on the whole armour of God...*

RONALD

Cultural Origin: Old Norse
Inherent Meaning: *MIGHTY POWER*
Spiritual Connotation: *LEADERSHIP, AUTHORITY*
Supporting Scripture: *Micah 6:8*
*He hath shewed thee, O man, what is good; and what
doth the Lord require of thee, but to do justly, and to love
mercy, and to walk humbly with thy God?*

RONNI

Cultural Origin: Anglo-Saxon
Inherent Meaning: *MIGHTY POWER*
Spiritual Connotation: *STRONG AND WOMANLY*
Supporting Scripture: *Isaiah 62:3*
*Thou shalt also be a crown of glory in the hand of the
Lord, and a royal diadem in the hand of thy God.*

RORY

Cultural Origin: Gaelic
Inherent Meaning: *KING*
Spiritual Connotation: *WORTHY OF HONOR*
Supporting Scripture: *Psalm 97:11*
*Light is sown for the righteous, and gladness for the
upright in heart.*

ROSALIE, Roslyn, see Rose

ROSALIND, Rosalinda

Cultural Origin: Teutonic
Inherent Meaning: *BEAUTIFUL ROSE*
Spiritual Connotation: *GRACIOUS ONE*
Supporting Scripture: *Psalm 49:3*
> *My mouth shall speak of wisdom; and the meditation of my heart shall be of understanding.*

ROSAMOND

Cultural Origin: Latin
Inherent Meaning: *PROTECTION*
Spiritual Connotation: *BLESSED ONE*
Supporting Scripture: *Psalm 97:11*
> *Light is sown for the righteous, and gladness for the upright in heart.*

ROSCOE

Cultural Origin: Old Norse
Inherent Meaning: *FROM THE DEER FOREST*
Spiritual Connotation: *CALM, PEACEFUL SPIRIT*
Supporting Scripture: *Proverbs 2:11*
> *Discretion shall preserve thee, understanding shall keep thee.*

ROSE, Rosetta, Rosette, Rosalie, Roslyn

Cultural Origin: Greek
Inherent Meaning: *SYMBOL OF LOVE*
Spiritual Connotation: *GOD'S GRACIOUS GIFT*
Supporting Scripture: *Isaiah 62:3*
> *Thou shalt also be a crown of glory in the hand of the Lord, and a royal diadem in the hand of thy God.*

ROSEMARY

Cultural Origin: Anglo-Saxon
Inherent Meaning: *DEW OF THE SEA*
Spiritual Connotation: *CROWNED ONE*
Supporting Scripture: *Psalm 121:1,2*
I will lift up mine eyes unto the hills, from whence cometh my help. My help cometh from the Lord, which made heaven and earth.

ROSINE, Rosina

Cultural Origin: Latin
Inherent Meaning: *CHERISHED ONE*
Spiritual Connotation: *DWELLER IN THE SPIRIT*
Supporting Scripture: *Isaiah 41:13*
For I the Lord thy God will hold thy right hand, saying unto thee, Fear not; I will help thee.

ROSS

Cultural Origin: Gaelic
Inherent Meaning: *KNIGHT, CHEVALIER*
Spiritual Connotation: *VICTORIOUS SPIRIT*
Supporting Scripture: *1 Corinthians 15:57*
But thanks be to God, which giveth us the victory through our Lord Jesus Christ.

ROWENA

Cultural Origin: Celtic
Inherent Meaning: *PEACE*
Spiritual Connotation: *APPOINTED OF GOD*
Supporting Scripture: *Proverbs 24:3*
Through wisdom is an house builded; and by understanding it is established.

ROXANNE, Roxane, Roxann

Cultural Origin: Persian
Inherent Meaning: *DAWN OF DAY*
Spiritual Connotation: *HEAVENLY LIGHT*
Supporting Scripture: *Psalm 32:8*
> *I will instruct thee and teach thee in the way which thou shalt go: I will guide thee with mine eye.*

ROY

Cultural Origin: Celtic
Inherent Meaning: *A KING*
Spiritual Connotation: *EXCELLENT WORTH*
Supporting Scripture: *Psalm 119:34*
> *Give me understanding, and I shall keep thy law; yea, I shall observe it with my whole heart.*

ROYCE

Cultural Origin: Anglo-Saxon
Inherent Meaning: *ROYALTY*
Spiritual Connotation: *MIGHTY AND POWERFUL*
Supporting Scripture: *Matthew 5:9*
> *Blessed are the peacemakers: for they shall be called the children of God.*

RUBEN, see Reuben

RUBY

Cultural Origin: Latin
Inherent Meaning: *JEWEL, CONTENTED MIND*
Spiritual Connotation: *FULL OF GRACE*
Supporting Scripture: *Psalm 26:3*
> *For thy lovingkindness is before mine eyes: and I have walked in thy truth.*

RUDOLPH, Rolf, Rolph, Rollo

Cultural Origin: Teutonic
Inherent Meaning: *GREAT AND DARING*
Spiritual Connotation: *RESOURCEFUL, COURAGEOUS*
Supporting Scripture: *Psalm 7:10*
   My defence is of God, which saveth the upright in heart.

RUFUS

Cultural Origin: Latin
Inherent Meaning: *FAIR COUNTENANCE*
Spiritual Connotation: *EXCELLENT VIRTUE*
Supporting Scripture: *Zechariah 7:9*
   . . . Execute true judgment, and shew mercy and compassions every man to his brother.

RUPERT, see Robert

RUSSELL

Cultural Origin: Latin
Inherent Meaning: *FAIR COUNTENANCE*
Spiritual Connotation: *WISDOM AND POWER*
Supporting Scripture: *Psalm 143:8*
   Cause me to hear thy lovingkindness in the morning; for in thee do I trust: cause me to know the way wherein I should walk; for I lift up my soul unto thee.

RUTH

Cultural Origin: Hebrew
Inherent Meaning: *COMPASSIONATE, BEAUTIFUL*
Spiritual Connotation: *PURE ONE*
Supporting Scripture: *Psalm 119:73*
   Thy hands have made me and fashioned me: give me understanding, that I may learn thy commandments.

RUTHERFORD

Cultural Origin: Anglo-Saxon
Inherent Meaning: *FROM THE CATTLE-FORD*
Spiritual Connotation: *VIGILANT SPIRIT*
Supporting Scripture: *Psalm 31:3*
> *Thou art my rock and my fortress; therefore for thy
> name's sake lead me, and guide me.*

RUTLEDGE

Cultural Origin: Anglo-Saxon
Inherent Meaning: *CLEAR, SWEET WATER*
Spiritual Connotation: *LOYAL, STEADFAST*
Supporting Scripture: *Psalm 43:3*
> *O send out thy light and thy truth: let them lead me; let
> them bring me unto thy holy hill, and to thy tabernacles.*

RYAN

Cultural Origin: Gaelic
Inherent Meaning: *LITTLE KING*
Spiritual Connotation: *YOUTHFUL HEART*
Supporting Scripture: *Psalm 84:11*
> *For the Lord God is a sun and a shield: the Lord will give
> grace and glory: no good thing will he withhold from
> them that walk uprightly.*

S

SABIN

Cultural Origin: Latin
Inherent Meaning: *PLANTER OF VINES*
Spiritual Connotation: *SPIRITUAL DISCERNMENT*
Supporting Scripture: *Isaiah 45:2*
> *I will go before thee, and make the crooked places straight: I will break in pieces the gates of brass, and cut in sunder the bars of iron.*

SABRINA, Sabina, Zabrina

Cultural Origin: Latin
Inherent Meaning: *VIBRANT*
Spiritual Connotation: *QUICKENED, VITAL*
Supporting Scripture: *Psalm 18:28*
> *For thou wilt light my candle: the Lord my God will enlighten my darkness.*

SADIE, see Sarah

SALLIE, Sally

Cultural Origin: Anglo-Saxon
Inherent Meaning: *PRINCESS, NOBLE LADY*
Spiritual Connotation: *BELOVED ONE*
Supporting Scripture: *1 Peter 2:9*
> *But ye are a chosen generation . . . that ye should shew forth the praises of him who hath called you . . . into his marvellous light.*

SAMANTHA

Cultural Origin: Aramaic
Inherent Meaning: *LISTENER*
Spiritual Connotation: *ATTENTIVE TO GOD'S VOICE*
Supporting Scripture: *Job 22:28*
> Thou shalt also decree a thing, and it shall be established
> unto thee: and the light shall shine upon thy ways.

SAMONA, see Simona

SAMSON, Sampson, Sam

Cultural Origin: Hebrew
Inherent Meaning: *TO HEAR*
Spiritual Connotation: *STRENGTH OF SPIRIT*
Supporting Scripture: *Psalm 138:3*
> In the day when I cried thou answeredst me, and
> strengthenedst me with strength in my soul.

SAMUEL, Sam

Cultural Origin: Hebrew
Inherent Meaning: *HIS NAME IS GOD*
Spiritual Connotation: *INSTRUCTED OF GOD*
Supporting Scripture: *Hebrew 11:3*
> Through faith we understand that the worlds were framed
> by the word of God, so that things which are seen were
> not made of things which do appear.

SANBRON

Cultural Origin: Anglo-Saxon
Inherent Meaning: *DWELLER AT THE SANDY BROOK*
Spiritual Connotation: *HONORABLE ONE*
Supporting Scripture: *1 Corinthians 8:6*
> But to us there is but one God, the Father, of whom are
> all things, and we in him; and one Lord Jesus Christ, by
> whom are all things, and we by him.

SANCHO

Cultural Origin: Latin-Spanish
Inherent Meaning: *SANCTIFIED*
Spiritual Connotation: *APPOINTED OF GOD*
Supporting Scripture: *Nehemiah 9:6*
> *Thou, even thou, art Lord alone; thou hast made heaven, the heaven of heavens, with all their host, the earth, and all things that are therein, the seas, and all that is therein, and thou preservest them all...*

SANDERS

Cultural Origin: Anglo-Saxon
Inherent Meaning: *SON OF ALEXANDER*
Spiritual Connotation: *BELOVED ONE*
Supporting Scripture: *Psalm 119:18*
> *Open thou mine eyes, that I may behold wondrous things out of thy law.*

SANDRA, Sandi, Sandy

Cultural Origin: Anglo-Saxon
Inherent Meaning: *HELPER*
Spiritual Connotation: *QUICKENED BY THE SPIRIT*
Supporting Scripture: *1 John 4:16*
> *And we have known and believed the love that God hath to us. God is love; and he that dwelleth in love dwelleth in God, and God in him.*

SAPPHIRA, Sapphire

Cultural Origin: Greek
Inherent Meaning: *A GEM*
Spiritual Connotation: *PRECIOUS ONE*
Supporting Scripture: *Romans 13:10*
> *Love worketh no ill to his neighbour: therefore love is the fulfilling of the law.*

SARAH, Sara, Sadie

Cultural Origin: Hebrew
Inherent Meaning: *PRINCESS, NOBLE LADY*
Spiritual Connotation: *BELOVED ONE*
Supporting Scripture: *Isaiah 30:29*
> *Ye shall have a song, as in the night when a holy solemnity is kept; and gladness of heart, as when one goeth with a pipe to come into the mountain of the Lord, to the mighty One of Israel.*

SARAPHINA, Seraphina

Cultural Origin: Hebrew
Inherent Meaning: *ARDENT ONE*
Spiritual Connotation: *CONSECRATED*
Supporting Scripture: *Psalm 42:8*
> *Yet the Lord will command his lovingkindness in the daytime, and in the night his song shall be with me, and my prayer unto the God of my life.*

SAUL

Cultural Origin: Hebrew
Inherent Meaning: *CALLED OF GOD*
Spiritual Connotation: *GOD'S WARRIOR*
Supporting Scripture: *John 15:5*
> *...He that abideth in me, and I in him, the same bringeth forth much fruit: for without me ye can do nothing.*

SAVILLE, Seville, Sevilla

Cultural Origin: Latin
Inherent Meaning: *FAIR*
Spiritual Connotation: *CREATIVE SPIRIT*
Supporting Scripture: *Psalm 143:8*
> *Cause me to hear thy lovingkindness in the morning; for in thee do I trust: cause me to know the way wherein I should walk; for I lift up my soul unto thee.*

SCOTT

Cultural Origin: Anglo-Saxon
Inherent Meaning: *FROM SCOTLAND*
Spiritual Connotation: *EXCELLENT VIRTUE*
Supporting Scripture: *1 Corinthians 3:16*
   *Know ye not that ye are the temple of God, and that the
   Spirit of God dwelleth in you?*

SEAN, see John

SEBASTIAN

Cultural Origin: Greek
Inherent Meaning: *VENERATED, HONORABLE*
Spiritual Connotation: *ESTEEMED ONE*
Supporting Scripture: *Philippians 2:13*
   *For it is God which worketh in you both to will and to do
   of his good pleasure.*

SELBY

Cultural Origin: Anglo-Saxon
Inherent Meaning: *FROM THE MANOR HOUSE*
Spiritual Connotation: *DIVINELY PROTECTED*
Supporting Scripture: *Acts 17:28*
   *For in him we live and move, and have our being; as cer-
   tain also of your own poets have said, For we are also his
   offspring.*

SELENA

Cultural Origin: Greek
Inherent Meaning: *FAIR AS THE MOON*
Spiritual Connotation: *FULL OF WISDOM*
Supporting Scripture: *Matthew 10:20*
   *For it is not ye that speak, but the Spirit of your Father
   which speaketh in you.*

SELMA

Cultural Origin: Celtic
Inherent Meaning: *DIVINELY PROTECTED*
Spiritual Connotation: *ENLIGHTENED SPIRIT*
Supporting Scripture: *Luke 12:31*
> *But rather seek ye the kingdom of God; and all these things shall be added unto you.*

SERENA

Cultural Origin: Latin
Inherent Meaning: *FAIR, BRIGHT, SECURE*
Spiritual Connotation: *CONTENTED SPIRIT*
Supporting Scripture: *1 Corinthians 2:12*
> *Now we have received, not the spirit of the world, but the spirit which is of God; that we might know the things that are freely given to us of God.*

SETH

Cultural Origin: Hebrew
Inherent Meaning: *APPOINTED OF GOD*
Spiritual Connotation: *ESTABLISHED IN GRACE*
Supporting Scripture: *2 Corinthians 3:17*
> *Now the Lord is that Spirit: and where the Spirit of the Lord is, there is liberty.*

SEYMOUR

Cultural Origin: Latin
Inherent Meaning: *FROM THE TOWN OF ST. MAUR*
Spiritual Connotation: *SPEAKER OF TRUTH*
Supporting Scripture: *1 John 3:24*
> *And he that keepeth his commandments dwelleth in him, and he in him. And hereby we know that he abideth in us, by the Spirit which he hath given us.*

SHANE, see John

SHANNON

Cultural Origin: Hebrew
Inherent Meaning: *GOD'S GIFT*
Spiritual Connotation: *INSPIRED OF GOD*
Supporting Scripture: *Matthew 10:20*
> *For it is not ye that speak, but the Spirit of your Father which speaketh in you.*

SHARON

Cultural Origin: Hebrew
Inherent Meaning: *FLORAL PLAIN*
Spiritual Connotation: *VISION OF BEAUTY*
Supporting Scripture: *Song of Solomon 2:1,2*
> *I am the rose of Sharon, and the lily of the valleys. As the lily among thorns, so is my love among the daughters.*

SHAWN, see John

SHEILA

Cultural Origin: Gaelic
Inherent Meaning: *INNER BEAUTY*
Spiritual Connotation: *SPIRITUAL INSIGHT*
Supporting Scripture: *Psalm 111:10*
> *The fear of the Lord is the beginning of wisdom: a good understanding have all they that do his commandments: his praise endureth for ever.*

SHELBY

Cultural Origin: Anglo-Saxon
Inherent Meaning: *FROM THE LEDGE ESTATE*
Spiritual Connotation: *FAITHFUL STEWARD*
Supporting Scripture: *Zechariah 4:6*
> *...Not by might, nor by power, but by my spirit, saith the Lord of hosts.*

SHELDON

Cultural Origin: Anglo-Saxon
Inherent Meaning: *FROM THE LEDGE HILL*
Spiritual Connotation: *MAN OF VIRTUE*
Supporting Scripture: *Ezekiel 36:27*
> *And I will put my spirit within you, and cause you to walk in my statutes, and ye shall keep my judgments, and do them.*

SHELLEY, Shelly

Cultural Origin: Anglo-Saxon
Inherent Meaning: *DWELLER ON THE LEDGE MEADOW*
Spiritual Connotation: *WALKS WITH GOD*
Supporting Scripture: *Luke 12:11,12*
> *...take ye no thought how or what thing ye shall answer, or what ye shall say: for the Holy Ghost shall teach you in the same hour what ye ought to say.*

SHELTON

Cultural Origin: Anglo-Saxon
Inherent Meaning: *DWELLER ON THE EDGE OF TOWN*
Spiritual Connotation: *CREATIVE HEART*
Supporting Scripture: *1 Corinthians 2:12*
> *Now we have received, not the spirit of the world, but the spirit which is of God; that we might know the things that are freely given to us of God.*

SHERIDAN

Cultural Origin: Gaelic
Inherent Meaning: *MAN OF SHERIDAN DOWNY*
Spiritual Connotation: *FREE IN SPIRIT*
Supporting Scripture: *Job 33:4*
> *The Spirit of God hath made me, and the breath of the Almighty hath given me life.*

SHERMAN

Cultural Origin: Anglo-Saxon
Inherent Meaning: *WOODCUTTER*
Spiritual Connotation: *ABIDING PLACE OF GOD*
Supporting Scripture: *James 1:17*
> *Every good gift and every perfect gift is from above, and cometh down from the Father of lights, with whom is no variableness, neither shadow of turning.*

SHERRE, Sherry, Sheri, see Charlotte

SHERWIN

Cultural Origin: Anglo-Saxon
Inherent Meaning: *SWIFT RUNNER*
Spiritual Connotation: *STEADY, SURE JUDGMENT*
Supporting Scripture: *Ezekiel 36:27*
> *And I will put my spirit within you, and cause you to walk in my statutes, and ye shall keep my judgments, and do them.*

SHERYL, see Charlotte

SHIRLEY

Cultural Origin: Anglo-Saxon
Inherent Meaning: *FROM THE BRIGHT MEADOW*
Spiritual Connotation: *HAPPINESS OF HEART*
Supporting Scripture: *1 John 4:12*
> *. . . If we love one another, God dwelleth in us, and his love is perfected in us.*

SIBYL

Cultural Origin: Greek
Inherent Meaning: *WISE WOMAN*
Spiritual Connotation: *BELOVED ONE*
Supporting Scripture: *Colossians 3:14*
> *And above all these things put on charity, which is the bond of perfectness.*

SIDNEY, Sydney

Cultural Origin: Anglo-Saxon
Inherent Meaning: *FROM ST. DENIS*
Spiritual Connotation: *TENDERHEARTED*
Supporting Scripture: *Psalm 32:11*
> *Be glad in the Lord, and rejoice, ye righteous: and shout for joy, all ye that are upright in heart.*

SIEGFRIED

Cultural Origin: Teutonic
Inherent Meaning: *VICTORIOUS*
Spiritual Connotation: *ENLIGHTENED ONE*
Supporting Scripture: *Psalm 92:4*
> *For thou, Lord, hast made me glad through thy work: I will triumph in the works of thy hands.*

SIGRID

Cultural Origin: Old Norse
Inherent Meaning: *VICTORIOUS COUNSELOR*
Spiritual Connotation: *ENLIGHTENED ONE*
Supporting Scripture: *Proverbs 4:18*
> *But the path of the just is as the shining light, that shineth more and more unto the perfect day.*

SIGURD

Cultural Origin: Old Norse
Inherent Meaning: *VICTORIOUS GUARDIAN*
Spiritual Connotation: *BLESSED SPIRIT*
Supporting Scripture: *Psalm 16:8*
> *I have set the Lord always before me: because he is at my right hand, I shall not be moved.*

SILAS

Cultural Origin: Hebrew
Inherent Meaning: *COMPANION OF ST. PAUL*
Spiritual Connotation: *STEADFAST IN TRUST*
Supporting Scripture: *Proverbs 29:25*
> *The fear of man bringeth a snare: but whoso putteth his trust in the Lord shall be safe.*

SILVANUS

Cultural Origin: Latin
Inherent Meaning: *FOREST DWELLER*
Spiritual Connotation: *GODLY ENLIGHTENMENT*
Supporting Scripture: *2 Samuel 22:31*
> *As for God, his way is perfect; the word of the Lord is tried: he is a buckler to all them that trust in him.*

SILVESTER, Sylvester

Cultural Origin: Latin
Inherent Meaning: *FROM THE FOREST*
Spiritual Connotation: *STRONG IN SPIRIT*
Supporting Scripture: *1 Kings 8:61*
> Let your heart therefore be perfect with the Lord our
> God, to walk in his statutes, and to keep his command-
> ments, as at this day.

SILVIA, Sylvia

Cultural Origin: Latin
Inherent Meaning: *OF THE FOREST*
Spiritual Connotation: *DWELLING IN SPIRIT*
Supporting Scripture: *Psalm 138:8*
> The Lord will perfect that which concerneth me. . .

SIMEON, see Simon

SIMON, Simeon

Cultural Origin: Hebrew
Inherent Meaning: *ONE WHO HEARS*
Spiritual Connotation: *DILIGENT, STEADFAST*
Supporting Scripture: *Psalm 8:6*
> Thou madest him to have dominion over the works of thy
> hands; thou hast put all things under his feet.

SIMONA, Simone, Samona

Cultural Origin: Hebrew
Inherent Meaning: *ONE WHO HEARS*
Spiritual Connotation: *DILIGENT, STEADFAST*
Supporting Scripture: *Psalm 112:4*
> Unto the upright there ariseth light in the darkness: he is
> gracious, and full of compassion, and righteous.

SLOAN

Cultural Origin: Gaelic
Inherent Meaning: *WARRIOR*
Spiritual Connotation: *VICTORIOUS SPIRIT*
Supporting Scripture: *James 3:17*
> *But the wisdom that is from above is first pure, then peaceable, gentle, and easy to be entreated, full of mercy and good fruits, without partiality, and without hypocrisy.*

SOLOMON, Sol

Cultural Origin: Hebrew
Inherent Meaning: *PEACEFUL*
Spiritual Connotation: *WHERE GOD DWELLS*
Supporting Scripture: *Job 22:26-28*
> *For then shalt thou have thy delight in the Almighty, and shalt lift up thy face unto God. . . . Thou shalt also decree a thing, and it shall be established unto thee: and the light shall shine upon thy ways.*

SONYA, Sonia, Sonja

Cultural Origin: Greek
Inherent Meaning: *WISDOM*
Spiritual Connotation: *SPIRITUAL DISCERNMENT*
Supporting Scripture: *Jeremiah 33:3*
> *Call unto me, and I will answer thee, and shew thee great and mighty things, which thou knowest not.*

SOPHIA, Sophie, Sofia

Cultural Origin: Greek
Inherent Meaning: *WISDOM*
Spiritual Connotation: *EXCELLENT VIRTUE*
Supporting Scripture: *James 1:5*
> *If any of you lack wisdom, let him ask of God, that giveth to all men liberally, and upbraideth not; and it shall be given him.*

SPENCER

Cultural Origin: Anglo-Saxon
Inherent Meaning: *DISPENSER OF PROVISIONS*
Spiritual Connotation: *FAITHFUL STEWARD*
Supporting Scripture: *Proverbs 3:5,6*
> *Trust in the Lord with all thine heart; and lean not unto thine own understanding. In all thy ways acknowledge him, and he shall direct thy paths.*

SPRING

Cultural Origin: Anglo-Saxon
Inherent Meaning: *SPRINGTIME*
Spiritual Connotation: *RENEWED ONE*
Supporting Scripture: *Psalm 16:11*
> *Thou wilt shew me the path of life: in thy presence is fulness of joy; at thy right hand there are pleasures for evermore.*

STACEY, Stacy

Cultural Origin: Greek
Inherent Meaning: *SPRING, RENEWAL*
Spiritual Connotation: *ABOUNDING WITH LIFE*
Supporting Scripture: *Isaiah 40:31*
> *But they that wait upon the Lord shall renew their strength; they shall mount up with wings as eagles; they shall run, and not be weary; and they shall walk, and not faint.*

STANISLAUS

Cultural Origin: Slavic
Inherent Meaning: *WITHOUT FEAR OR WAVERING*
Spiritual Connotation: *STABLE IN FAITH*
Supporting Scripture: *Proverbs 2:11*
> *Discretion shall preserve thee, understanding shall keep thee.*

STANLEY

Cultural Origin: Anglo-Saxon
Inherent Meaning: *DWELLER AT THE ROCKY MEADOW*
Spiritual Connotation: *SINCERE DEVOTION*
Supporting Scripture: *Acts 2:28*
Thou hast made known to me the ways of life; thou shalt make me full of joy with thy countenance.

STANTON

Cultural Origin: Anglo-Saxon
Inherent Meaning: *FROM THE STONE ESTATE*
Spiritual Connotation: *EXCELLENT WORTH*
Supporting Scripture: *1 John 2:10*
He that loveth his brother abideth in the light, and there is none occasion of stumbling in him.

STELLA

Cultural Origin: Latin
Inherent Meaning: *A STAR*
Spiritual Connotation: *ESTEEMED ONE*
Supporting Scripture: *Psalm 91:11*
For he shall give his angels charge over thee, to keep thee in all thy ways.

STEPHEN, Steven, Steve

Cultural Origin: Greek
Inherent Meaning: *CROWNED ONE*
Spiritual Connotation: *ESTABLISHED IN TRUTH*
Supporting Scripture: *James 1:25*
But whoso looketh into the perfect law of liberty, and continueth therein, he being not a forgetful hearer, but a doer of the work, this man shall be blessed in his deed.

STEPHANIE

Cultural Origin: Greek
Inherent Meaning: *CROWNED ONE*
Spiritual Connotation: *ILLUMINATED ONE*
Supporting Scripture: *1 Corinthians 2:9*
> *...Eye hath not seen, nor ear heard, neither have entered into the heart of man, the things which God hath prepared for them that love him.*

STERLING, Stirling

Cultural Origin: Anglo-Saxon
Inherent Meaning: *PURE, GENUINE*
Spiritual Connotation: *EXCELLENT WORTH*
Supporting Scripture: *1 Corinthians 2:12*
> *Now we have received, not the spirit of the world, but the spirit which is of God; that we might know the things that are freely given to us of God.*

STEVEN, see Stephen

STEWART, Stuart

Cultural Origin: Anglo-Saxon
Inherent Meaning: *STEWARD*
Spiritual Connotation: *HELPFUL SPIRIT*
Supporting Scripture: *Galatians 5:22,23*
> *But the fruit of the Spirit is love, joy, peace...meekness, temperance: against such there is no law.*

STORM

Cultural Origin: Anglo-Saxon
Inherent Meaning: *TURBULENT*
Spiritual Connotation: *COURAGEOUS, BRAVE*
Supporting Scripture: *Psalm 145:18*
> *The Lord is nigh unto all them that call upon him, to all that call upon him in truth.*

SULLIVAN, Sullie, Sully

Cultural Origin: Gaelic
Inherent Meaning: *BLACK-EYED ONE*
Spiritual Connotation: *DEEP WISDOM*
Supporting Scripture: *Proverbs 13:14,15*
> *The law of the wise is a fountain of life.... Good*
> *understanding giveth favour...*

SUSAN, Sue, Suzette

Cultural Origin: Hebrew
Inherent Meaning: *GRACEFUL LILY*
Spiritual Connotation: *PURITY, GRACE*
Supporting Scripture: *Proverbs 4:18*
> *But the path of the just is as the shining light, that shineth*
> *more and more unto the perfect day.*

SUSANNA, Suzanna, Suzanne

Cultural Origin: Hebrew
Inherent Meaning: *LILY*
Spiritual Connotation: *BRILLIANT, PURE*
Supporting Scripture: *Psalm 18:32*
> *It is God that girdeth me with strength, and maketh my*
> *way perfect.*

SYLVESTER, see Silvester

SYLVIA, see Silvia

T

TABER

Cultural Origin: Anglo-Saxon
Inherent Meaning: *DRUM BEATER*
Spiritual Connotation: *A MERRY HEART*
Supporting Scripture: *Proverbs 15:13*
    A merry heart maketh a cheerful countenance...

TABITHA

Cultural Origin: Greek
Inherent Meaning: *GRACE, CHARM*
Spiritual Connotation: *SERENE IN SPIRIT*
Supporting Scripture: *Job 22:21*
    Acquaint now thyself with him, and be at peace: thereby good shall come unto thee.

TAGGERT

Cultural Origin: Gaelic
Inherent Meaning: *SON OF THE PRELATE*
Spiritual Connotation: *BLESSED ONE*
Supporting Scripture: *John 6:63*
    It is the spirit that quickeneth... the words that I speak unto you, they are spirit, and they are life.

TALLULAH

Cultural Origin: Choctaw Indian
Inherent Meaning: *LEAPING WATER*
Spiritual Connotation: *REFRESHING SPIRIT*
Supporting Scripture: *Genesis 1:31*
    And God saw every thing that he had made, and, behold, it was very good.

TAMARA, Tammy

Cultural Origin: Hebrew
Inherent Meaning: *PERFECTION*
Spiritual Connotation: *VICTORIOUS SPIRIT*
Supporting Scripture: *Psalm 119:160*
*Thy word is true from the beginning: and every one of thy
righteous judgments endureth for ever.*

TANA, Tania, Tanya

Cultural Origin: Latin
Inherent Meaning: *A QUEEN*
Spiritual Connotation: *GRACIOUS, HONORED*
Supporting Scripture: *1 Corinthians 3:16*
*Know ye not that ye are the temple of God, and that the
Spirit of God dwelleth in you?*

TARA

Cultural Origin: Gaelic
Inherent Meaning: *ROCKY PINNACLE*
Spiritual Connotation: *EXCELLENT WORTH*
Supporting Scripture: *1 Corinthians 2:12*
*Now we have received, not the spirit of the world, but the
spirit which is of God; that we might know the things that
are freely given to us of God.*

TARRENCE, Terrence

Cultural Origin: Latin
Inherent Meaning: *TENDER*
Spiritual Connotation: *GENTLE, GRACIOUS*
Supporting Scripture: *Job 33:4*
*The Spirit of God hath made me, and the breath of the
Almighty hath given me life.*

TERESA, Teri, Terry, see Theresa

TERRELL

Cultural Origin: Anglo-Saxon
Inherent Meaning: *THUNDER RULER*
Spiritual Connotation: *MIGHTY PROTECTOR*
Supporting Scripture: *Exodus 31:3*
> *And I have filled him with the spirit of God, in wisdom, and in understanding, and in knowledge, and in all manner of workmanship.*

TESSA, Tessie, Tess

Cultural Origin: Greek
Inherent Meaning: *FOURTH CHILD*
Spiritual Connotation: *GRACIOUS SPIRIT*
Supporting Scripture: *1 Timothy 4:4*
> *For every creature of God is good, and nothing to be refused, if it be received with thanksgiving.*

THADDEUS, Thad

Cultural Origin: Aramaic
Inherent Meaning: *LOVE, TENDERNESS*
Spiritual Connotation: *HONORED ONE*
Supporting Scripture: *Psalm 28:7*
> *The Lord is my strength and my shield; my heart trusted in him, and I am helped: therefore my heart greatly rejoiceth; and with my song will I praise him.*

THALIA

Cultural Origin: Greek
Inherent Meaning: *BLOOMING, LUXURIANT*
Spiritual Connotation: *CHERISHED ONE*
Supporting Scripture: *Isaiah 55:12*
> *For ye shall go out with joy, and be led forth with peace: the mountains and the hills shall break forth before you into singing, and all the trees of the field shall clap their hands.*

THANE, Thaine, Thayne

Cultural Origin: Anglo-Saxon
Inherent Meaning: *FOLLOWER*
Spiritual Connotation: *LOYAL, TRUSTWORTHY*
Supporting Scripture: *Psalm 40:8*
> *I delight to do thy will, O my God: yea, thy law is within my heart.*

THAYER

Cultural Origin: Anglo-Saxon
Inherent Meaning: *NATIONAL ARMY*
Spiritual Connotation: *BRAVE DEFENDER*
Supporting Scripture: *Psalm 13:6*
> *I will sing unto the Lord, because he hath dealt bountifully with me.*

THEA

Cultural Origin: Greek
Inherent Meaning: *GODDESS*
Spiritual Connotation: *BELOVED ONE*
Supporting Scripture: *2 Chronicles 20:20*
> *. . . Believe in the Lord your God, so shall ye be established; believe his prophets, so shall ye prosper.*

THEOLA

Cultural Origin: Greek
Inherent Meaning: *DIVINE FLAME*
Spiritual Connotation: *GIVEN OF GOD*
Supporting Scripture: *John 8:32*

And ye shall know the truth, and the truth shall make you free.

THELMA

Cultural Origin: Greek
Inherent Meaning: *LITTLE ONE*
Spiritual Connotation: *PRICELESS ONE*
Supporting Scripture: *2 Timothy 1:7*

For God hath not given us the spirit of fear; but of power, and of love, and of a sound mind.

THEODORA

Cultural Origin: Greek
Inherent Meaning: *GIFT OF GOD*
Spiritual Connotation: *PRECIOUS ONE*
Supporting Scripture: *1 John 4:16*

. . . God is love; and he that dwelleth in love dwelleth in God, and God in him.

THEODORE

Cultural Origin: Greek
Inherent Meaning: *DIVINE GIFT*
Spiritual Connotation: *GIFT OF GOD*
Supporting Scripture: *Ecclesiastes 2:26*

For God giveth to a man that is good in his sight wisdom, and knowledge, and joy . . .

THERESA, Teresa, Terry, Terri, Teri

Cultural Origin: Greek
Inherent Meaning: *HARVESTER, BEAUTIFUL*
Spiritual Connotation: *BOUNTIFUL SPIRIT*
Supporting Scripture: *Psalm 1:3*
And he shall be like a tree planted by the rivers of water,
that bringeth forth his fruit in his season; his leaf also
shall not wither; and whatsoever he doeth shall prosper.

THOMAS

Cultural Origin: Greek
Inherent Meaning: *A TWIN*
Spiritual Connotation: *DIVINELY BLESSED*
Supporting Scripture: *Proverbs 2:11*
Discretion shall preserve thee, understanding shall keep
thee.

THOMASINA, Thomasa, Thomasine

Cultural Origin: Greek
Inherent Meaning: *A TWIN*
Spiritual Connotation: *DIVINELY BLESSED*
Supporting Scripture: *Proverbs 13:14,15*
The law of the wise is a fountain of life....Good
understanding giveth favour...

THOR

Cultural Origin: Old Norse
Inherent Meaning: *THUNDER*
Spiritual Connotation: *GOD'S WARRIOR*
Supporting Scripture: *Proverbs 24:3-4*
Through wisdom is an house builded; and by understand-
ing it is established: and by knowledge shall the chambers
be filled with all precious and pleasant riches.

THORA

Cultural Origin: Old Norse
Inherent Meaning: *THUNDER*
Spiritual Connotation: *GOD'S WARRIOR*
Supporting Scripture: *Jeremiah 32:27*
> *Behold, I am the Lord, the God of all flesh: is there any thing too hard for me?*

TIERNEY

Cultural Origin: Gaelic
Inherent Meaning: *LORDLY ONE*
Spiritual Connotation: *GRACIOUS SPIRIT*
Supporting Scripture: *Ephesians 4:7*
> *But unto every one of us is given grace according to the measure of the gift of Christ.*

TIFFANY

Cultural Origin: Latin
Inherent Meaning: *DIVINE SHOWING*
Spiritual Connotation: *BELOVED ONE*
Supporting Scripture: *Isaiah 48:17*
> *...I am the Lord thy God which teacheth thee to profit, which leadeth thee by the way that thou shouldest go.*

TILDA, Tillie, see Matilda

TILDEN

Cultural Origin: Anglo-Saxon
Inherent Meaning: *FROM THE GOOD BLESSED VALLEY*
Spiritual Connotation: *PEACEFUL SPIRIT*
Supporting Scripture: *Psalm 23:6*
> *Surely goodness and mercy shall follow me all the days of my life: and I will dwell in the house of the Lord for ever.*

TIMOTHY

Cultural Origin: Greek
Inherent Meaning: *VENERATION OF GOD*
Spiritual Connotation: *BLESSED OF GOD*
Supporting Scripture: *Leviticus 19:34*
> *But the stranger that dwelleth with you shall be unto you as one born among you, and thou shalt love him as thyself. . .*

TINA, see Christina

TITUS

Cultural Origin: Greek
Inherent Meaning: *OF THE GIANTS*
Spiritual Connotation: *HONORABLE, GLORIOUS*
Supporting Scripture: *Matthew 12:35*
> *A good man out of the good treasure of the heart bringeth forth good things. . .*

TOBIAS, Toby

Cultural Origin: Hebrew
Inherent Meaning: *THE LORD IS GOOD*
Spiritual Connotation: *GOD'S WORKMANSHIP*
Supporting Scripture: *Matthew 5:16*
> *Let your light so shine before men, that they may see your good works, and glorify your Father which is in heaven.*

TODD

Cultural Origin: Anglo-Saxon
Inherent Meaning: *A FOX*
Spiritual Connotation: *DIVINE INGENUITY*
Supporting Scripture: *John 15:7*
> *If ye abide in me, and my words abide in you, ye shall ask what ye will, and it shall be done unto you.*

TONIA, see Antonia

TONY, see Anthony

TOPAZ

Cultural Origin: Latin
Inherent Meaning: *A GEM*
Spiritual Connotation: *FIDELITY, TRUSTWORTHY*
Supporting Scripture: *Isaiah 62:3*
> *Thou shalt also be a crown of glory in the hand of the Lord, and a royal diadem in the hand of thy God.*

TORRANCE

Cultural Origin: Gaelic
Inherent Meaning: *FROM THE KNOLLS*
Spiritual Connotation: *MAN OF PEACE*
Supporting Scripture: *Psalm 91:15*
> *He shall call upon me, and I will answer him: I will be with him in trouble; I will deliver him, and honour him.*

TOWNSEND

Cultural Origin: Anglo-Saxon
Inherent Meaning: *FROM THE END OF TOWN*
Spiritual Connotation: *INDUSTRIOUS ONE*
Supporting Scripture: *1 Corinthians 12:4,5*
> *Now there are diversities of gifts, but the same Spirit. And there are differences of administrations, but the same Lord.*

TRACY, Tracey

Cultural Origin: Latin
Inherent Meaning: *BOLD, COURAGEOUS*
Spiritual Connotation: *NOBLE SPIRIT*
Supporting Scripture: *Isaiah 52:7*
　　How beautiful upon the mountains are the feet of him
　　that bringeth good tidings, that publisheth peace...

TRAVERS, Travis

Cultural Origin: Latin
Inherent Meaning: *FROM THE CROSSROADS*
Spiritual Connotation: *COURAGEOUS SPIRIT*
Supporting Scripture: *Psalm 29:11*
　　The Lord will give strength unto his people; the Lord will
　　bless his people with peace.

TRENT

Cultural Origin: Latin
Inherent Meaning: *RAPID STREAM*
Spiritual Connotation: *MIGHTY IN SPIRIT*
Supporting Scripture: *Isaiah 65:17*
　　For, behold, I create new heavens and a new earth: and
　　the former shall not be remembered, nor come into mind.

TREVOR

Cultural Origin: Gaelic
Inherent Meaning: *PRUDENT, DISCREET*
Spiritual Connotation: *FULL OF WISDOM*
Supporting Scripture: *Psalm 84:11*
　　For the Lord God is a sun and shield: the Lord will give
　　grace and glory: no good thing will he withhold from
　　them that walk uprightly.

TROY

Cultural Origin: Latin
Inherent Meaning: *AT THE PLACE OF THE
CURLY-HAIRED PEOPLE*
Spiritual Connotation: *STEADFAST, LOYAL*
Supporting Scripture: *2 Corinthians 9:8*
*And God is able to make all grace abound toward you;
that ye, always having all sufficiency in all things, may
abound to every good work.*

TRUMAN

Cultural Origin: Anglo-Saxon
Inherent Meaning: *FAITHFUL ONE*
Spiritual Connotation: *DWELLING IN THE SPIRIT*
Supporting Scripture: *Psalm 91:15*
*He shall call upon me, and I will answer him: I will be
with him in trouble; I will deliver him, and honour him.*

TURNER

Cultural Origin: Anglo-Saxon
Inherent Meaning: *LATHE-WORKER*
Spiritual Connotation: *INFINITE CREATIVITY*
Supporting Scripture: *Proverbs 3:6*
*In all thy ways acknowledge him, and he shall direct thy
paths.*

TYE

Cultural Origin: Anglo-Saxon
Inherent Meaning: *FROM THE ENCLOSURE*
Spiritual Connotation: *RESOLUTE COURAGE*
Supporting Scripture: *Isaiah 45:2*
*I will go before thee, and make the crooked places
straight: I will break in pieces the gates of brass, and cut
in sunder the bars of iron.*

TYLER

Cultural Origin: Anglo-Saxon
Inherent Meaning: *TILE MAKER AND ROOFER*
Spiritual Connotation: *RESOURCEFUL, INDUSTRIOUS*
Supporting Scripture: *Mark 11:24*
> *Therefore I say unto you, What things soever ye desire,*
> *when ye pray, believe that ye receive them, and ye shall*
> *have them.*

TYRONE

Cultural Origin: Greek
Inherent Meaning: *SOVEREIGN, FAMOUS*
Spiritual Connotation: *HONORED, ESTEEMED*
Supporting Scripture: *Psalm 1:3*
> *And he shall be like a tree planted by the rivers of water,*
> *that bringeth forth his fruit in his season; his leaf also*
> *shall not wither; and whatsoever he doeth shall prosper.*

TYSON

Cultural Origin: Latin
Inherent Meaning: *SON*
Spiritual Connotation: *SUSTAINING POWER*
Supporting Scripture: *1 Timothy 4:14*
> *Neglect not the gift that is in thee. . .*

U

UDA, Udelle

Cultural Origin: Teutonic
Inherent Meaning: *PROSPEROUS ONE*
Spiritual Connotation: *FAITHFUL STEWARD*
Supporting Scripture: *Revelation 21:5*
  . . . Behold, I make all things new.

ULRIC

Cultural Origin: Teutonic
Inherent Meaning: *RULER*
Spiritual Connotation: *STRONG IN VIRTUE*
Supporting Scripture: *Colossians 3:10*
  *. . . put on the new man, which is renewed in knowledge
  after the image of him that created him.*

ULRICA

Cultural Origin: Teutonic
Inherent Meaning: *RULER*
Spiritual Connotation: *STRONG IN VIRTUE*
Supporting Scripture: *Psalm 86:4*
  *Rejoice the soul of thy servant: for unto thee, O Lord, do
  I lift up my soul.*

ULYSSES

Cultural Origin: Greek
Inherent Meaning: *ONE WHO DETESTS DECEIT
            OR INJUSTICE*
Spiritual Connotation: *COURAGEOUS SPIRIT*
Supporting Scripture: *Jeremiah 29:12-14*
  *Then shall ye call upon me. . . And I will be found of you,
  saith the Lord. . .*

UNA

Cultural Origin: Latin
Inherent Meaning: *ONE, UNITY*
Spiritual Connotation: *HUMBLE ONE*
Supporting Scripture: *Isaiah 41:13*
> *For I the Lord thy God will hold thy right hand, saying unto thee, Fear not; I will help thee.*

UPTON

Cultural Origin: Anglo-Saxon
Inherent Meaning: *UPPER ESTATE*
Spiritual Connotation: *HONORABLE, JUST*
Supporting Scripture: *Deuteronomy 8:3*
> *. . . man doth not live by bread only, but by every word that proceedeth out of the mouth of the Lord doth man live.*

URIAH

Cultural Origin: Hebrew
Inherent Meaning: *MY LIGHT IS JEHOVAH*
Spiritual Connotation: *EXCELLENT VIRTUE*
Supporting Scripture: *Proverbs 12:28*
> *In the way of righteousness is life; and in the pathway thereof there is no death.*

URIEL

Cultural Origin: Hebrew
Inherent Meaning: *FLAME OF GOD*
Spiritual Connotation: *TRANSFORMED ONE*
Supporting Scripture: *Isaiah 58:8*
> *Then shall thy light break forth as the morning, and thine health shall spring forth speedily: and thy righteousness shall go before thee.*

URSULA

Cultural Origin: Latin
Inherent Meaning: *FEARLESS ONE*
Spiritual Connotation: *STEADFAST, COURAGEOUS*
Supporting Scripture: *Deuteronomy 31:6*

> *Be strong and of a good courage. . .for the Lord thy God,
> he it is that doth go with thee; he will not fail thee, nor
> forsake thee.*

V

VALA

Cultural Origin: Old Norse
Inherent Meaning: *CHOSEN ONE*
Spiritual Connotation: *CONSECRATED ONE*
Supporting Scripture: *Ephesians 1:4*
> *According as he hath chosen us in him before the foundation of the world, that we should be holy and without blame before him in love.*

VALDEMAR

Cultural Origin: Teutonic
Inherent Meaning: *FAMOUS RULER*
Spiritual Connotation: *BENEVOLENT, HONORED*
Supporting Scripture: *Romans 13:8*
> *Owe no man any thing, but to love one another: for he that loveth another hath fulfilled the law.*

VALERIE

Cultural Origin: Latin
Inherent Meaning: *STRENGTH*
Spiritual Connotation: *SPIRITUAL PURPOSE*
Supporting Scripture: *Isaiah 65:18*
> *But be ye glad and rejoice for ever in that which I create...*

VALESKA

Cultural Origin: Slavic
Inherent Meaning: *GLORIOUS RULER*
Spiritual Connotation: *VALIANT, ESTEEMED*
Supporting Scripture: *Psalm 92:4*
> *For thou, Lord, hast made me glad through thy work: I will triumph in the works of thy hands.*

VANCE, Van

Cultural Origin: Anglo-Saxon
Inherent Meaning: *MILLER*
Spiritual Connotation: *BLESSED IN SERVICE*
Supporting Scripture: *Deuteronomy 16:15*
> *. . . the Lord thy God shall bless thee in all thine increase, and in all the works of thine hands, therefore thou shalt surely rejoice.*

VANESSA

Cultural Origin: Latin
Inherent Meaning: *A BUTTERFLY*
Spiritual Connotation: *FREE SPIRIT*
Supporting Scripture: *Psalm 37:4*
> *Delight thyself also in the Lord; and he shall give thee the desires of thine heart.*

VASHTI

Cultural Origin: Persian
Inherent Meaning: *BEAUTIFUL ONE*
Spiritual Connotation: *BELOVED ONE*
Supporting Scripture: *Philippians 4:19*
> *But my God shall supply all your need according to his riches in glory by Christ Jesus.*

VAUGHN

Cultural Origin: Gaelic
Inherent Meaning: *SMALL ONE*
Spiritual Connotation: *COMPASSIONATE ONE*
Supporting Scripture: *1 Corinthians 13:1*
> *Though I speak with the tongues of men and of angels, and have not charity [love], I am become as sounding brass, or a tinkling cymbal.*

VEDA

Cultural Origin: Sanskrit
Inherent Meaning: *KNOWLEDGE, WISDOM*
Spiritual Connotation: *DWELLING IN THE SPIRIT*
Supporting Scripture: *1 Peter 4:10*
> As every man hath received the gift, even so minister the
> same one to another, as good stewards of the manifold
> grace of God.

VELMA

Cultural Origin: Teutonic
Inherent Meaning: *RESOLUTE PROTECTOR*
Spiritual Connotation: *WATCHFUL, CARING ONE*
Supporting Scripture: *1 Timothy 1:5*
> Now the end of the commandment is charity [love] out of
> a pure heart, and of a good conscience, and of faith
> unfeigned.

VERA

Cultural Origin: Latin
Inherent Meaning: *TRUTH*
Spiritual Connotation: *STRONG IN VIRTUE*
Supporting Scripture: *Psalm 32:11*
> Be glad in the Lord, and rejoice, ye righteous: and shout
> for joy, all ye that are upright in heart.

VERNA

Cultural Origin: Latin
Inherent Meaning: *SPRING-LIKE*
Spiritual Connotation: *LIVELY, JOYOUS*
Supporting Scripture: *Deuteronomy 26:11*
> And thou shalt rejoice in every good thing which the Lord
> thy God hath given unto thee. . . .

VERNE, Vern

Cultural Origin: Latin
Inherent Meaning: *SPRING-LIKE*
Spiritual Connotation: *VITAL, RENEWING*
Supporting Scripture: *John 15:16*
> *Ye have not chosen me, but I have chosen you, and ordained you, that ye should go and bring forth fruit, and that your fruit should remain: that whatsoever ye shall ask of the Father in my name, he may give it you.*

VERNON

Cultural Origin: Latin
Inherent Meaning: *SPRING-LIKE, YOUTHFUL*
Spiritual Connotation: *VIGOROUS, VITAL*
Supporting Scripture: *Ecclesiastes 3:22*
> *. . . there is nothing better, than that a man should rejoice in his own works; for that is his portion. . .*

VERONICA, Vonny

Cultural Origin: Latin
Inherent Meaning: *TRUE IMAGE*
Spiritual Connotation: *IN GOD'S REFLECTION*
Supporting Scripture: *Psalm 36:9*
> *For with thee is the fountain of life: in thy light shall we see light.*

VESTA

Cultural Origin: Latin
Inherent Meaning: *SHE WHO DWELLS OR LINGERS*
Spiritual Connotation: *PEACEFUL HEART*
Supporting Scripture: *Psalm 36:9*
> *For with thee is the fountain of life: in thy light shall we see light.*

VICTOR

Cultural Origin: Latin
Inherent Meaning: *CONQUEROR*
Spiritual Connotation: *TRIUMPHANT SPIRIT*
Supporting Scripture: *Mark 11:24*
Therefore I say unto you, What things soever ye desire, when ye pray, believe that ye receive them, and ye shall have them.

VICTORIA, Vicki

Cultural Origin: Latin
Inherent Meaning: *CONQUEROR*
Spiritual Connotation: *TRIUMPHANT SPIRIT*
Supporting Scripture: *Philippians 4:19*
But my God shall supply all your need according to his riches in glory by Christ Jesus.

VINCENT

Cultural Origin: Latin
Inherent Meaning: *CONQUERING ONE*
Spiritual Connotation: *EXCELLENT WORTH*
Supporting Scripture: *Matthew 9:29*
. . .According to your faith be it unto you.

VIOLET, Viola

Cultural Origin: Latin
Inherent Meaning: *MODEST, A FLOWER*
Spiritual Connotation: *GRACIOUS SPIRIT*
Supporting Scripture: *Psalm 139:9,10*
If I take the wings of the morning, and dwell in the uttermost parts of the sea; even there shall thy hand lead me, and thy right hand shall hold me.

VIRGIL, Vergil

Cultural Origin: Latin
Inherent Meaning: *ROD OR STAFF BEARER*
Spiritual Connotation: *LOYAL SPIRIT*
Supporting Scripture: *Isaiah 41:13*
> For I the Lord thy God will hold thy right hand, saying
> unto thee, Fear not; I will help thee.

VIRGINIA, Ginger

Cultural Origin: Latin
Inherent Meaning: *PURE*
Spiritual Connotation: *UNBLEMISHED, REFRESHING*
Supporting Scripture: *2 Corinthians 5:17*
> Therefore if any man be in Christ, he is a new creature:
> old things are passed away; behold, all things are become
> new.

VIVIAN

Cultural Origin: Latin
Inherent Meaning: *LIVELY, MERRY*
Spiritual Connotation: *JOYOUS SPIRIT*
Supporting Scripture: *Psalm 37:4*
> Delight thyself also in the Lord; and he shall give thee the
> desires of thine heart.

VLADIMIR

Cultural Origin: Slavic
Inherent Meaning: *ROYALLY PEACEFUL OR FAMOUS*
Spiritual Connotation: *UPRIGHT SPIRIT*
Supporting Scripture: *Jeremiah 29:13*
> And ye shall seek me, and find me, when ye shall search
> for me with all your heart.

VOLNEY

Cultural Origin: Teutonic
Inherent Meaning: *NATIONAL SPIRIT*
Spiritual Connotation: *LOYAL, FAITHFUL*
Supporting Scripture: *Psalm 84:5*

> *Blessed is the man whose strength is in thee; in whose heart are the ways of them.*

W

WADE

Cultural Origin: Anglo-Saxon
Inherent Meaning: *THE ADVANCER*
Spiritual Connotation: *COURAGEOUS SPIRIT*
Supporting Scripture: *Matthew 10:8*
 . . . freely ye have received, freely give.

WAGNER

Cultural Origin: Teutonic
Inherent Meaning: *FROM THE ADVANCER'S ESTATE*
Spiritual Connotation: *GENEROUS PROTECTOR*
Supporting Scripture: *Isaiah 26:3*
 Thou wilt keep him in perfect peace, whose mind is stayed on thee: because he trusteth in thee.

WAINRIGHT

Cultural Origin: Anglo-Saxon
Inherent Meaning: *WAGON MAKER*
Spiritual Connotation: *INDUSTRIOUS, CREATIVE*
Supporting Scripture: *Joshua 1:9*
 . . . be not afraid, neither be thou dismayed: for the Lord thy God is with thee whithersoever thou goest.

WALCOTT

Cultural Origin: Anglo-Saxon
Inherent Meaning: *DWELLER AT THE
                    WALL-ENCLOSED COTTAGE*
Spiritual Connotation: *LEARNED, WISE*
Supporting Scripture: *Psalm 50:15*
 And call upon me in the day of trouble: I will deliver thee, and thou shalt glorify me.

WALDEMAR

Cultural Origin: Teutonic
Inherent Meaning: *FAMOUS RULER*
Spiritual Connotation: *DISCERNING, WISE*
Supporting Scripture: *Matthew 5:16*
> *Let your light so shine before men, that they may see your good works, and glorify your Father which is in heaven.*

WALDEN

Cultural Origin: Anglo-Saxon
Inherent Meaning: *FROM THE FOREST VALLEY*
Spiritual Connotation: *CALM IN SPIRIT*
Supporting Scripture: *Psalm 73:26*
> *. . . God is the strength of my heart, and my portion for ever.*

WALDO

Cultural Origin: Teutonic
Inherent Meaning: *RULER*
Spiritual Connotation: *HONORABLE, ESTEEMED*
Supporting Scripture: *Philippians 4:6*
> *Be careful for nothing; but in every thing by prayer and supplication with thanksgiving let your requests be made known unto God.*

WALLACE, Wally

Cultural Origin: Gaelic
Inherent Meaning: *FROM WALES*
Spiritual Connotation: *MAN OF PEACE*
Supporting Scripture: *Proverbs 22:29*
> *Seest thou a man diligent in his business? he shall stand before kings; he shall not stand before mean men.*

WALLIS

Cultural Origin: Anglo-Saxon
Inherent Meaning: *ONE FROM WALES*
Spiritual Connotation: *PEACEFUL SPIRIT*
Supporting Scripture: *1 Corinthians 3:16*
   *Know ye not that ye are the temple of God, and that the
   Spirit of God dwelleth in you?*

WALTER

Cultural Origin: Teutonic
Inherent Meaning: *POWERFUL WARRIOR*
Spiritual Connotation: *STRONG PROTECTOR*
Supporting Scripture: *Matthew 6:22*
   *The light of the body is the eye: if therefore thine eye be
   single, thy whole body shall be full of light.*

WALTON

Cultural Origin: Anglo-Saxon
Inherent Meaning: *DWELLER AT THE FOREST-TOWN*
Spiritual Connotation: *FREEDOM OF SPIRIT*
Supporting Scripture: *Deuteronomy 8:18*
   *But thou shalt remember the Lord thy God: for it is he
   that giveth thee power to get wealth . . .*

WANDA, Wendy

Cultural Origin: Teutonic
Inherent Meaning: *WANDERER*
Spiritual Connotation: *SEEKER OF TRUTH*
Supporting Scripture: *Psalm 139:17*
   *How precious also are thy thoughts unto me, O God! how
   great is the sum of them!*

WARD

Cultural Origin: Teutonic
Inherent Meaning: *A KEEPER, DEFENDER*
Spiritual Connotation: *WATCHFUL SPIRIT*
Supporting Scripture: *Job 33:4*
> *The Spirit of God hath made me, and the breath of the
> Almighty hath given me life.*

WARDELL

Cultural Origin: Anglo-Saxon
Inherent Meaning: *FROM THE WATCH-HILL*
Spiritual Connotation: *DEFENDER, PROTECTOR*
Supporting Scripture: *Isaiah 40:29*
> *He giveth power to the faint; and to them that have no
> might he increaseth strength.*

WARNER

Cultural Origin: Teutonic
Inherent Meaning: *DEFENDER*
Spiritual Connotation: *COURAGEOUS SPIRIT*
Supporting Scripture: *Luke 12:32*
> *Fear not. . .for it is your Father's good pleasure to give
> you the kingdom.*

WARREN

Cultural Origin: Teutonic
Inherent Meaning: *PROTECTING FRIEND*
Spiritual Connotation: *WATCHFUL SPIRIT*
Supporting Scripture: *Psalm 112:4*
> *Unto the upright there ariseth light in the darkness: he is
> gracious, and full of compassion, and righteous.*

WARWICK

Cultural Origin: Anglo-Saxon
Inherent Meaning: *DEFENDER*
Spiritual Connotation: *CHAMPION*
Supporting Scripture: *Psalm 23:3*
> *He restoreth my soul: he leadeth me in the paths of righteousness for his name's sake.*

WAYNE

Cultural Origin: Anglo-Saxon
Inherent Meaning: *WAGON MAKER*
Spiritual Connotation: *INDUSTRIOUS, CREATIVE*
Supporting Scripture: *Philippians 2:16*
> *Holding forth the word of life; that I may rejoice in the day of Christ, that I have not run in vain, neither laboured in vain.*

WEBSTER

Cultural Origin: Anglo-Saxon
Inherent Meaning: *A WEAVER*
Spiritual Connotation: *IN GOD'S PATTERN*
Supporting Scripture: *Titus 2:7*
> *In all things shewing thyself a pattern of good works: in doctrine shewing uncorruptness, gravity, sincerity.*

WELBY

Cultural Origin: Anglo-Saxon
Inherent Meaning: *DWELLER AT THE SPRING FARM*
Spiritual Connotation: *STRONG IN SPIRIT*
Supporting Scripture: *Psalm 36:7*
> *How excellent is thy lovingkindness, O God! therefore the children of men put their trust under the shadow of thy wings.*

WELDON

Cultural Origin: Anglo-Saxon
Inherent Meaning: *FROM THE SPRING HILL*
Spiritual Connotation: *DISCERNING SPIRIT*
Supporting Scripture: *Isaiah 42:6*
> *I the Lord have called thee in righteousness, and will hold thine hand, and will keep thee...*

WELLINGTON

Cultural Origin: Anglo-Saxon
Inherent Meaning: *WEALTHY, PROSPEROUS*
Spiritual Connotation: *CONQUERING SPIRIT*
Supporting Scripture: *Acts 2:25*
> *...I foresaw the Lord always before my face, for he is on my right hand, that I should not be moved.*

WENDELL

Cultural Origin: Teutonic
Inherent Meaning: *WANDERER*
Spiritual Connotation: *MESSENGER OF PEACE*
Supporting Scripture: *1 Corinthians 2:9*
> *But as it is written, Eye hath not seen nor ear heard, neither have entered into the heart of man, the things which God hath prepared for them that love him.*

WENDY, see Wanda

WERNER

Cultural Origin: Teutonic
Inherent Meaning: *DEFENDING WARRIOR*
Spiritual Connotation: *PROTECTOR*
Supporting Scripture: *John 14:27*
> *Peace I leave with you, my peace I give unto you:... Let not your heart be troubled, neither let it be afraid.*

WESLEY

Cultural Origin: Anglo-Saxon
Inherent Meaning: *FROM THE WEST MEADOW*
Spiritual Connotation: *DIVINE PERSPECTIVE*
Supporting Scripture: *Proverbs 3:23*
> *Then shalt thou walk in thy way safely, and thy foot shall not stumble.*

WHITNEY

Cultural Origin: Anglo-Saxon
Inherent Meaning: *FROM THE WHITE-HAIRED ONE'S ISLAND*
Spiritual Connotation: *ENLIGHTENED ONE*
Supporting Scripture: *Psalm 91:11*
> *For he shall give his angels charge over thee, to keep thee in all thy ways.*

WILBUR

Cultural Origin: Teutonic
Inherent Meaning: *RESOLUTE, BRILLIANT ONE*
Spiritual Connotation: *WALKING IN LIGHT*
Supporting Scripture: *James 1:25*
> *But whoso looketh into the perfect law of liberty, and continueth therein . . . shall be blessed in his deed.*

WILEY, see William

WILFRED

Cultural Origin: Anglo-Saxon
Inherent Meaning: *PEACEFUL*
Spiritual Connotation: *CALM, CONTENTED*
Supporting Scripture: *1 John 2:10*
> *He that loveth his brother abideth in the light, and there is none occasion of stumbling in him.*

WILHELMINA, Wilma

Cultural Origin: Teutonic
Inherent Meaning: *PROTECTOR*
Spiritual Connotation: *NOBLE SPIRIT*
Supporting Scripture: *Psalm 16:11*
> *Thou wilt shew me the path of life: in thy presence is fulness of joy; at thy right hand there are pleasures for evermore.*

WILLARD

Cultural Origin: Anglo-Saxon
Inherent Meaning: *RESOLUTE AND BRAVE*
Spiritual Connotation: *CHAMPION*
Supporting Scripture: *Romans 8:28*
> *And we know that all things work together for good to them that love God, to them who are the called according to his purpose.*

WILLIAM, Will, Wiley, Wilson, Bill, Billy

Cultural Origin: Teutonic
Inherent Meaning: *RESOLUTE PROTECTOR*
Spiritual Connotation: *NOBLE SPIRIT*
Supporting Scripture: *Deuteronomy 5:33*
> *Ye shall walk in all the ways which the Lord your God hath commanded you, that ye may live, and that it may be well with you, and that ye may prolong your days in the land which ye shall possess.*

WILMA, see Wilhelmina

WILSON, see William

WINFRED

Cultural Origin: Anglo-Saxon
Inherent Meaning: *PEACEFUL FRIEND*
Spiritual Connotation: *SPIRITUAL DISCERNMENT*
Supporting Scripture: *Psalm 4:7*
> *Thou hast put gladness in my heart, more than in the time that their corn and their wine increased.*

WINIFRED, Winnie

Cultural Origin: Teutonic
Inherent Meaning: *PEACEFUL FRIEND*
Spiritual Connotation: *SPIRITUAL DISCERNMENT*
Supporting Scripture: *Psalm 4:7,8*
> *Thou hast put gladness in my heart. . .for thou, Lord, only makest me dwell in safety.*

WINNIE, see Winifred

WINONA

Cultural Origin: Sioux Indian
Inherent Meaning: *FIRST-BORN DAUGHTER*
Spiritual Connotation: *BELOVED ONE*
Supporting Scripture: *Philippians 4:7*
> *And the peace of God, which passeth all understanding, shall keep your hearts and minds through Christ Jesus.*

WINSTON

Cultural Origin: Anglo-Saxon
Inherent Meaning: *FROM THE FRIEND'S ESTATE*
Spiritual Connotation: *TRUSTFUL HEART*
Supporting Scripture: *Proverbs 18:16*
> *A man's gift maketh room for him, and bringeth him before great men.*

WINTHROP

Cultural Origin: Anglo-Saxon
Inherent Meaning: *FROM THE FRIEND'S ESTATE*
Spiritual Connotation: *TRUSTFUL HEART*
Supporting Scripture: *Proverbs 18:16*
> *A man's gift maketh room for him, and bringeth him before great men.*

WINTON

Cultural Origin: Anglo-Saxon
Inherent Meaning: *FROM THE FRIEND'S ESTATE*
Spiritual Connotation: *TRUSTFUL HEART*
Supporting Scripture: *Psalm 42:8*
> *Yet the Lord will command his lovingkindness in the daytime, and in the night his song shall be with me, and my prayer unto the God of my life.*

WOLCOTT

Cultural Origin: Anglo-Saxon
Inherent Meaning: *FROM THE WOLF'S COTTAGE*
Spiritual Connotation: *COURAGEOUS, BRAVE*
Supporting Scripture: *Proverbs 2:6*
> *For the Lord giveth wisdom: out of his mouth cometh knowledge and understanding.*

WOODROW

Cultural Origin: Anglo-Saxon
Inherent Meaning: *DWELLER AT THE HEDGE*
Spiritual Connotation: *EXCELLENT WORTH*
Supporting Scripture: *John 3:33*
> *He that hath received his testimony hath set to his seal that God is true.*

WOODWARD

Cultural Origin: Anglo-Saxon
Inherent Meaning: *FOREST WARDEN*
Spiritual Connotation: *GUARDIAN, PROTECTOR*
Supporting Scripture: *Isaiah 26:3*
> *Thou wilt keep him in perfect peace, whose mind is stayed on thee: because he trusteth in thee.*

WORRELL

Cultural Origin: Anglo-Saxon
Inherent Meaning: *DWELLER AT THE
     TRUE MAN'S MANOR*
Spiritual Connotation: *JUSTICE AND HONOR*
Supporting Scripture: *Mark 9:23*
> *. . . If thou canst believe, all things are possible to him that believeth.*

WORTH

Cultural Origin: Anglo-Saxon
Inherent Meaning: *FARMSTEAD*
Spiritual Connotation: *DILIGENT, TRUSTWORTHY*
Supporting Scripture: *Psalm 1:3*
> *And he shall be like a tree planted by the rivers of water, that bringeth forth his fruit in his season; his leaf also shall not wither; and whatsoever he doeth shall prosper.*

WYNN

Cultural Origin: Celtic
Inherent Meaning: *FAIR ONE*
Spiritual Connotation: *GRACIOUS, MANLY*
Supporting Scripture: *Proverbs 4:18*
> *But the path of the just is as the shining light, that shineth more and more unto the perfect day.*

WYNNE, Wynette

Cultural Origin: Celtic
Inherent Meaning: *FAIR ONE*
Spiritual Connotation: *FULL OF GRACE*
Supporting Scripture: *Romans 8:14*
> For as many as are led by the Spirit of God, they are the
> sons of God.

X

XAVIER

Cultural Origin: Arabic
Inherent Meaning: *CHRISTIAN HOSPITALITY*
Spiritual Connotation: *BLESSED ONE*
Supporting Scripture: *Proverbs 2:10,11*
> *When wisdom entereth into thine heart, and knowledge is pleasant unto thy soul; discretion shall preserve thee, understanding shall keep thee.*

XENIA, Xena, Zenia

Cultural Origin: Greek
Inherent Meaning: *HOSPITABLE ONE*
Spiritual Connotation: *BLESSED ONE*
Supporting Scripture: *Psalm 119:133-135*
> *Order my steps in thy word. . . Make thy face to shine upon thy servant; and teach me thy statutes.*

Y

YOLANDA

Cultural Origin: Greek
Inherent Meaning: *VIOLET FLOWER*
Spiritual Connotation: *PURE IN GRACE*
Supporting Scripture: *Psalm 36:9*
> *For with thee is the fountain of life: in thy light shall we see light.*

YORK

Cultural Origin: Celtic
Inherent Meaning: *FROM THE YEW-TREE ESTATE*
Spiritual Connotation: *VIGILANT SPIRIT*
Supporting Scripture: *Proverbs 3:23*
> *Then shalt thou walk in thy way safely, and thy foot shall not stumble.*

YVES

Cultural Origin: Anglo-Saxon
Inherent Meaning: *LITTLE ARCHER*
Spiritual Connotation: *VIGILANT SPIRIT*
Supporting Scripture: *Psalm 37:5*
> *Commit thy way unto the Lord; trust also in him; and he shall bring it to pass.*

YVETTE, see Yvonne

YVONNE, Yvette

Cultural Origin: Latin
Inherent Meaning: *GOD'S GRACE*
Spiritual Connotation: *VICTORIOUS SPIRIT*
Supporting Scripture: *Leviticus 25:18*
> *Wherefore ye shall do my statutes, and keep my judgments, and do them; and ye shall dwell in the land in safety.*

Z

ZABRINA, see Sabrina

ZACHERY

Cultural Origin: Hebrew
Inherent Meaning: *THE LORD HAS REMEMBERED*
Spiritual Connotation: *SPIRITUALLY AWAKENED*
Supporting Scripture: *Colossians 3:10*
>   *And have put on the new man, which is renewed in knowledge after the image of him that created him.*

ZANE, see John

ZECHARIAH

Cultural Origin: Hebrew
Inherent Meaning: *JEHOVAH HAS REMEMBERED*
Spiritual Connotation: *SPIRITUALLY AWAKENED*
Supporting Scripture: *Psalm 25:14*
>   *The secret of the Lord is with them that fear him; and he will shew them his covenant.*

ZEDEKIAH

Cultural Origin: Hebrew
Inherent Meaning: *RIGHTEOUSNESS OF JEHOVAH*
Spiritual Connotation: *SPIRITUAL AWARENESS*
Supporting Scripture: *Proverbs 3:6*
>   *In all thy ways acknowledge him, and he shall direct thy paths.*

ZELDA

Cultural Origin: Greek
Inherent Meaning: *CHERISHED ONE*
Spiritual Connotation: *BELOVED ONE*
Supporting Scripture: *Ecclesiastes 2:26*
> *For God giveth. . . that is good in his sight wisdom, and knowledge, and joy. . .*

ZENIA, see Xenia

ZINA

Cultural Origin: Hebrew
Inherent Meaning: *BRILLIANT, SPARKLING*
Spiritual Connotation: *RADIANT LOVE, UNDERSTANDING*
Supporting Scripture: *2 Corinthians 4:6*
> *For God, who commanded the light to shine out of darkness, hath shined in our hearts, to give the light of the knowledge of the glory of God. . .*

ZOE, Zoa

Cultural Origin: Greek
Inherent Meaning: *LIFE*
Spiritual Connotation: *DWELLING IN THE SPIRIT*
Supporting Scripture: *Psalm 91:15*
> *He shall call upon me, and I will answer him: I will be with him in trouble; I will deliver him and honour him.*

ZORA

Cultural Origin: Slavic
Inherent Meaning: *DAWN*
Spiritual Connotation: *BRINGER OF LIGHT*
Supporting Scripture: *Isaiah 60:1*
> *Arise, shine; for thy light is come, and the glory of the Lord is risen upon thee.*